Asho Craine Writings 1993-2009

Asho I. Craine

Published in honor of her 95th birthday
January 7, 2010

authorHOUSE®

AuthorHouse™
1663 Liberty Drive
Bloomington, IN 47403
www.authorhouse.com
Phone: 1-800-839-8640

First published by AuthorHouse   12/20/2011

ISBN: 978-1-4685-0872-7 (sc)
ISBN: 978-1-4685-0873-4 (ebk)

Printed in the United States of America

Cover photo: Asho at Sedge Point, Douglas Lake, by Lyle Craine (mid 1980s)
Photo at right appeared in the Ann Arbor News, *ca. 1991.*

Asho Craine: Writings 1993-2009

Table of Contents

ASHO'S STORY

Chapter 1
Parents and Grandparents
My Mother—Marion Crary Ingersoll

My mother was a strong, handsome, and outspoken woman who left a vivid impression on everyone she encountered. A nonconformist, she was adventurous and eager to embrace new ways. Her expansive spirit, enthusiasm, and spontaneity endeared her to her friends and especially to my father.

Yet as a child I found her overwhelming and unpredictable. Somehow the rules kept changing so I never knew where I stood. We had many clashes often ending in tears. Even when I was being most careful, a conversation with her might suddenly switch to an explosive topic. Once I complained about this to Dad when I was a teenager. He reassured me by acknowledging that while my mother had many wonderful qualities she just was not logical. This gave me a new perspective on her as a person. Maybe that is when I started piecing together the scraps of information about her childhood to better understand her contradictions.

Marion A. Crary was born December 17, 1880, in Sheffield, Pennsylvania. The village was in the northwestern part of the state in the upper reaches of the Allegheny River basin. The nearby hills were thickly covered with hemlock trees, which provided tanbark for the local tannery, the main industry in town. My grandfather, Jerry Crary, was born in 1842 on a farm east of Liberty, New York. After being wounded in a leg in the Civil War he came to work as a bookkeeper for Horace, one of his five older brothers, who was part owner of the tannery named Horton, Crary, and Co. In 1870 Jerry married Laura Antoinette Dunham, a schoolteacher who had graduated from the Female Institute at Lewiston, Pennsylvania, three years earlier. They had three sons—Horace, Miner, and Clare—before Marion, the youngest, was born.

When Marion was seven years old a traumatic event occurred as she and her mother were out for a drive. Suddenly a runaway team of horses struck their carriage and passed right over it. Marion's injuries were slight but her mother's left her an invalid off and on for the rest of her life. I have no hint as to my grandmother's personality before the accident but by all accounts and my memory of her in later life she was severe, distant, and demanding. She even criticized the way her daughter laughed saying she opened her mouth too wide.

So my mother grew up in an oppressive household where she had to be very quiet not to disturb her mother and where her father and brothers did their best to keep a lid on her high spirits. Clare was close enough in age to be her occasional playmate. But once out of

9

the house Marion was free and unrestrained. She loved to roam in the woods gathering nuts and wildflowers. She would tell me of her delight in picking trailing arbutus, a spring flower with pretty pink and white blossoms and a delicious fragrance, which grows only in hemlock forests. There were daring adventures, such as walking on the railroad trestle and sneaking into the tent of a traveling revival meeting, which would have shocked her staid Methodist parents. Mother confessed to being rather bossy with her schoolmates, probably getting away with it because their fathers worked for hers. Once she even kicked her teacher.

A significant event in Marion's childhood was the discovery of oil in Cherry Grove not far from Sheffield. Soon her father and uncle tried their luck on the land they had bought to supply tanbark for the tannery. After drilling in several places there was much excitement when they too struck oil. My mother would tell us of being wakened in the night by the sound of horses' hoofs and shouts that a well had blown. After much commotion the men rode off to cap the well while she watched the bright flames shooting up against the dark sky.

Oil changed the lives of the Crary family. By the turn of the century grandfather had become engaged in several enterprises centered in Warren. He served for ten years as president of the Penn Tanning Co. after it bought out Horton, Crary, and Co. in 1893. The new firm owned and operated all the tanneries in four counties. In 1902 the family moved from Sheffield to the substantial new house, really a mansion, they had built in Warren.

Meanwhile when Marion was fourteen she was sent away to Bucknell boarding school. However she did not stay long as she made the mistake of writing home to a friend about a mild escapade with a boy. When her parents got wind of it they snatched her home and hired a tutor. How dreary! Eventually she went off to another boarding school, Miss Capen's in Northampton, Massachusetts. There she made her first lasting friends with whom she moved on to Smith College in the fall of 1900.

Marion loved college, but after her freshman year she was again called home this time to help her mother prepare to make the move to the new house and to learn the art of homemaking. This always seemed cruel to me as mother was an eager learner who would have benefited so much from the intellectual discipline and self-confidence a college education could have given her.

As it turned out she became one of the most loyal alumna of the Smith class of "naughty four," attending many reunions including her sixtieth. It gave her great satisfaction to see my sister, Mario, graduate from her alma mater in 1942. After marriage my mother pursued wide-ranging topics with a small group of women in Brooklyn, New York, who had formed a study club that met for nearly fifty years.

It must have been very difficult for Mother to return home to care for her cantankerous mother and a massive house that reflected the oppressive respectability of her father and three brothers. The fact that she spoke so seldom of those seven years before her marriage suggests that it was a period she would have rather forgotten. At least she did not burden her children with her unhappy memories.

Instead she told us of learning to play the game of golf, newly imported from Scotland, at the golf course which her brothers had helped establish. They were also among the first to sport motor cars in the community. She enjoyed boating and picnicking at the family cottage on Coniwango Creek a few miles out of town. Several beaus courted her before she became engaged to my father.

Mother seldom mentioned her mother and was rather vague about the nature of her invalidism. Although it was attributed to the buggy accident she did not seem to be physically crippled. She was able to attend Church, her Ladies Shakespeare Club, the D.A.R. [Daughters of the American Revolution], and even to travel extensively. I have her small square trunk with a label from Havana still on it. The one vivid memory Mother recounted was of times after some late party such as Christmas when, exhausted as she was, Grandmother would grab a broom and insist on sweeping up. Nobody could get that broom away from her and take her to bed. It sounded rather frightening. All this leads me to believe that she probably had some kind of underlying mental illness. One of Uncle Miner's granddaughters speculates that she was schizophrenic. Uncle Miner himself suffered from bouts of depression. Whatever may have ailed her, my grandmother underwent many "cures" including bloodletting by leeches. It's a wonder she survived the quacks to live to the age of 84.

During my childhood, every year or two, Mother packed us up for the overnight trip to Warren in a Pullman sleeper, often to celebrate a holiday or special event. I remember the little gold boxes of wedding cake at my grandparents' golden wedding anniversary when I was five and the large cake decorated like the American flag to celebrate grandfather's eightieth birthday on Flag Day, June 14, 1922. There was a Christmas when Dad played Santa Claus and another when Uncle Clare took the part. Once we missed connections in Philadelphia and we spent Thanksgiving seeing the Liberty Bell.

Grandpa was always glad to see us. He was a large, heavy-set man who seemed to fit well into his huge house. In spite of being nearly blind, very hard of hearing, and having to walk on crutches, he was remarkably cheerful. At times he was quite jolly. Then he would sing us civil war songs, ask us riddles, or challenge us with mental arithmetic problems. It was hard for me to converse with him because even though I shouted he couldn't hear my child's high-pitched voice, but I felt he was fond of me.

In contrast, my grandmother was very remote. She spent much of her time resting in her room—a place I never entered. I was admonished to be very quiet so as not to disturb her. When she did emerge from her room I found her rather unapproachable. Her bony, sharp face with its sallow complexion had a severe expression, and there was a distinct medicinal odor about her. I was certainly ill at ease with her. Once I had such a horrendous stomach ache that a doctor was called in. He said it was merely caused by gas, but I believe it reflected my mother's tension as well as my own.

These memory fragments and speculations help me appreciate how marriage to my father was truly liberating for mother. My parents had met briefly at Amherst College in 1897 when Marion had come to attend her brother Miner's graduation. His classmate and fraternity brother, Raymond Ingersoll, (nicknamed Bob after the famous agnostic Robert

Ingersoll), was the class poet. When he stood up and read his long philosophical poem about the universality of spirit and the unity of body and soul, Mother fell for him on the spot. Dad saw her then only as a cute young girl of sixteen. However he took another look eight years later at a chance meeting in the lobby of a New York hotel where Marion and Miner happened to be staying for a brief visit to the city. When they extended a warm invitation to visit in Warren, the idealistic young lawyer readily accepted.

The romance developed rapidly and they were soon engaged. About that time word spread that a blossom had opened on Grandmother's rare night blooming cereus, and many friends and neighbors came to admire it. However my father had the distinct impression that the callers were more interested in viewing him than the cactus flower. He was well received by the family even though they deplored the fact that he was a Democrat. Grandfather prided himself on having cast his vote for every Republican nominee for president since Lincoln's second election.

The engagement lasted for three years because my father was burdened with financial obligations to his family. His brother Andrew's health had broken down due to TB and maybe other things so he had to quit his job and go west for a better climate. Then Dad's mother died. Naturally my mother rushed to be at his side, but this was not an auspicious moment to meet his two adoring, unmarried sisters. Lena and Grace, modest, gentle, and petite, must have been bowled over by the tall, stylish stranger who intruded on their grief. Aunt Grace once told me, with indignation, that when mother entered the dining room and saw pickles on the table she loudly exclaimed as she took one "Oh I just love pickles!"

The wedding day finally came on September 29, 1908. Now it's time to tell about my father's origins.

My Father—Raymond Vail Ingersoll

My father was a compassionate man of a philosophical turn of mind and a dedicated social reformer. Mediation was his natural style both in public and private life. He was a good listener with a gentle sense of humor and a kind of detachment which put him above the battle. A rock of stability for my mother and a refuge for me, he had a calming influence on both of us. He had a way of elevating a conversation above the personal and particular. I loved to discuss ideas with him. Dad was my most important teacher and I adored him.

In his last years when he was borough president of Brooklyn in the reform city administration of Fiorello LaGuardia, press interviews often stressed his modesty. Once when I teased him about this, he said that he would let me in on a secret, namely that he really had a good opinion of himself so he could let others take credit for his accomplishments. The important thing was that the job got done. Such high self-esteem must have originated in a loving family.

Raymond Vail Ingersoll was born on April 3, 1875, at Pinewood, his father's sanitarium, near Corning, N.Y. He was next to the youngest of seven children. Kate came first followed in the next seven years by Andrew, Elma, Lena, a boy who died in infancy, and Raymond. Grace was the youngest. The story goes that when Raymond first saw his baby sister in their mother's arm and complained about where he could sit she held out her other arm saying, "right here." My grandfather wanted to name him Pharsiphis after some author he was reading at the time, but my grandmother teased him out of it by referring to "mama's little Farsie boy".

My grandfather, Andrew Jackson Ingersoll, was fifty-seven at the time of my father's birth having been born in 1818 exactly a century before my brother Raymond. In many ways ahead of his time, he became a self-taught physician and faith healer. He grew up in a large religious family near Hammondsport, New York, on a farm overlooking Lake Keuka. In spite of having very little education he undertook study for the ministry, but was so confused by theological controversies that he became a doubter.

In his book, *In Health*, he wrote that on one occasion his unrest and discontent, together with some troubles at home, reduced him to sickness and unfitted him for active work. Believing his sickness was caused by mental and spiritual strife and that there is a natural curative power in the human body, he turned to relaxation. His method was "hanging the head" which was simply dropping the chin on the chest and completely relaxing body and mind. By this means he rapidly regained his strength.

After this he began taking patients as he had earlier discovered that he had the power in his hand to relieve headaches and other complaints. At first he treated only men until he found that by entrusting his sexual powers to God he was free of lust. From then on most of his patients were women suffering from hysteria and other nervous conditions. Among our family files is a "diploma" issued by the Eclectic Medical Society of the Southern Tier, dated June 1879, which states that A.J. Ingersoll has been found to be "duly qualified to practice his specialty in curing diseases." I also have a large, beautifully etched, glass tumbler depicting Columbus discovering America, which was made for my grandfather by a grateful patient who worked in the Corning glass works.

Our grandfather's book describes some of his many successful cases, which he attributed to his teaching that the body is the temple of the soul and that sexual life is divinely given. A noted psychiatrist, Dr. A.A. Brill, to whom my father showed the book, wrote a paper about Dr. Ingersoll as an American precursor of Freud.

In 1865 he married Ellen Vail from Bordentown, NJ and built his sanitarium in a pine forest a few miles outside Corning. Not till after both our parents died and we found a divorce paper dated in the 1840's did we realize that this was our grandfather's second marriage. He must have been at least twenty or possibly twenty-five years older than our grandmother. My father had very little contact with his father until his last year or two of high school when they discovered each other. Then he absorbed his father's teachings and they became very close. Just a few weeks after my father entered Amherst College he received word that his father had fallen on a sharp spike in the woods and died.

My aunts, Lena and Grace, used to tell me stories about their mother, Ellen Vail, or Nellie, as she was often called. In the days of her childhood the Friends were required to wear very plain gray or black clothing. One day when she was quite small Nellie found a bucket of red paint being used to paint the barn. She took the brush and carefully painted her shoes. When her father saw what she had done he told her, "If thee wishes to have red shoes we will have the cobbler make thee a pair when next he comes."

My grandmother used to give the younger children a penny for every ten pins they picked up. Once one of my aunts saw her scattering pins on the floor when she thought she was unobserved.

Writing verses was a popular pastime in my father's family. I have a long poem my grandmother wrote about each of her children containing the following verses about my father.

And still another cometh, so full of manly grace,
So full of fun and frolic yet with such earnest face.
Oh Robbin, precious Robbin, known to none as well as me,
Great rich wells of golden treasure lieth hidden deep in thee.
Cometh now my little treasure, strong of limb and stout of heart,
Boy thou art to be a blessing, of thy father counter part.

In a less sentimental vein my two aunts and Uncle Andy could dash off a ditty for any occasion. Often when I used to visit them we would play a parlor game which required writing a rhyme that answered a question passed by the person on one side of the player and included an unrelated word passed by the person on her other side.

When my father was about eight years old his mother and the children moved into town supposedly to be closer to schools. In reality it was a marital separation because my grandmother believed her husband was unduly fond of his head nurse. This may be why my father thought that jealousy was one of the worst emotions.

School was a new experience for Raymond as he had until then been taught at home. He used to tell me of the time when just as he had gotten up courage to throw a spitball he glanced up through the transom and saw the principal descending the stairs. He was sure that his misdeed had been observed. His fears seemed confirmed when the principal walked into the classroom and spoke to the teacher who then told Raymond to report to the office. He dreaded the unknown punishment that awaited him. To his great relief it was just a matter of his being transferred to the next higher grade.

A year or two after the move to Corning, Elma died of some common infectious disease. The loss was especially hard for Lena who was very close to her sister.

Summers were spent at a cottage on Lake Keuka in the grape-growing region of the Finger Lakes. There Raymond found a good friend, Adolph Giffen. As teenagers their greatest adventure was playing tramp. They would go to the back door of a farmhouse and ask the farmwife if she had any wood to chop or other chores which they could do in exchange for supper and the privilege of sleeping in the barn. Mostly they were kindly received, but once they had a scary encounter with an angry farmer who sicced his dog on them. Altogether they were gone for a week or so and must have walked many miles. I envied them their adventures. Their friendship lasted all their lives. Adolph stayed on in Hammondsport in the wine business, I believe. During prohibition he would send us a keg of fresh grape juice, which my parents would try to make into wine. They never knew what to expect when they opened a bottle. I remember one explosion which splattered red wine drops on the dining room ceiling.

In his last year or two of high school my father used to walk the several miles to Pinewood to spend weekends with his father. That must have been an intellectual awakening for him as they discussed the ideas of John Ruskin whom my grandfather greatly admired. No wonder that Raymond majored in philosophy when he went to college.

My childhood impressions of my father's college were limited to playing with his Phi Beta Kappa key that dangled from his watch chain and learning the song about Lord Jeffery Amherst, a solder of the king. There was another song that went "Left and right 'neath the purple and the white we will march in grand array" which came true for me when I was seven. Then, wearing a purple and white gingham dress and bonnet made especially for the occasion, I proudly marched in the alumni parade for Dad's twenty-fifth reunion. Some years later he remarked that the saddest thing about reunions was meeting classmates for whom college remained the happiest and most fulfilling time of their lives.

At Amherst my father studied the classics and became enamored of the Greeks. He was particularly inspired by Professor C.E. Garman who taught mental and moral philosophy and with whom he corresponded after graduation. Most of all I heard, from Mother, about his being the class poet. His long poem, attempting a grand summary of his philosophy of life, was titled "The Breath of the Spirit" and was introduced by the following prelude.

Call me if you will religion,
Call me life, or call me love;
Name me what to your soul's vision
Towers in worth all else above.
For the forms I take are many;
Different shapes to each I wear;
And few men who see me near them
Know my home is everywhere.

Prior to graduation in 1897 my father applied for a position with the Department of History and Literature at Buchtel College, in Akron, Ohio, for which Professor Garman wrote a glowing letter of recommendation. However nothing came of it and he ended up with a job teaching high school English in Duluth, Minnesota. A rough frontier town of lumberjacks and miners, it was an intellectual desert. Fortunately he found a local dentist, Dr. Warner Woodberry, who shared some of his interests. They became close friends.

During the first summer Dad traveled about the countryside as a salesman for a textbook and educational materials company. At one crossroads town when he inquired where to find the president of the school board he was directed to the owner of the local saloon who invited Dad to spread out his catalogues on the bar while the few customers crowded around. In the section on globes a model of the solar system caught the saloon keeper's eye. It was an elaborate mechanism with which one could make the moon circle the earth and the earth and planets circle the sun. My father suggested that a simple globe should be quite adequate for his small school district and was much less expensive. That was all that was needed for the president of the school board to show his cronies that he could spend big money. Dad could not dissuade him from buying the contraption which no doubt amazed several generations of schoolchildren of that remote outpost.

Two years in Duluth were enough. Dr. Woodberry and my father decided to seek a more stimulating life in New York City. Dad had always aspired to help make the world a better place, but he realized that he needed a practical skill to balance his tendency to have his head in the clouds, so he made up his mind to go to law school. Uncle Warner, as we called him, was optimistic that he could build a good dental practice in Manhattan. Their hopes must have been high when they set out together to take on the big city.

Because settlement houses were the pioneering social agencies of that day, Dad was glad to move into the University Settlement House on the lower east side. There, in exchange for his room and board, he led one or more boys' clubs and also conducted a study of social conditions. Some of his findings became incorporated into the tenement house law of 1901. He attended night classes at the New York Law School and was admitted to the bar in 1900. Fast work!

The boys' club attracted a bunch of bright youngsters who, unlike his students in Duluth, were eager to discuss everything under the sun. Several went on to outstanding careers. One of the boys was "Billy" Leiserson who, taking my father's advice to leave the city and go west for his education, went to the University of Wisconsin where he studied labor economics under John R. Commons. In the early twenties he became the first industrial arbitrator for the men's clothing industry in Chicago. A year or two later, in 1924, my father was chosen by the ladies' garment industry in New York to be its first arbitrator. When President Roosevelt set up the National Labor Relations Board he appointed William Leiserson one of its three original members.

In 1901, my father moved to the Maxwell House Settlement near the Navy Yard in Brooklyn. He had already begun working with the Citizens Union to prepare for a campaign against Tammany Hall in the city elections that fall. Probably they needed more manpower in Brooklyn for he took an active part in organizing a local fusion conference, which drew up a slate of reform candidates for the borough. Dad was nominated for magistrate-at-large and won the election becoming, at age twenty-six, the youngest judge on the bench. A reporter dubbed him the pink-cheeked philosopher. Unfortunately the judgeship lasted only six months as it was found to be an appointive rather than an elective position. The following year the Appellate Division made him a member of the Committee on Character to pass on qualifications of applicants to the bar. As it paid no salary, he went back to his law firm to earn a living.

The following eleven and a half years working for that firm were the most boring of Dad's life. He used to say that the only thing he learned of value was how to keep his desk clear.

Twice a month the tedium was broken by dinner at some restaurant engaged in lively discussion with some members of the "X Club." The club was started in 1903 by a few socialists and others including my father who were sympathetic to some of the concepts of socialism. Among the members were socialist Morris Hillquit, muckraker Lincoln Steffens, and several professors from Columbia including Charles Beard and John Dewey. They had plenty to talk about: overcrowded and unsanitary tenement houses, sweatshops exploiting child labor, political corruption, and especially, how best to remedy these social evils. This was a time when immigrants were arriving at the rate of 21,000 a day, unemployment was high, and workers were struggling to organize effective labor unions. The club continued to meet until we entered the First World War. One member, George Alger, said my father told him that the "X Club" discussions made a major contribution to his social philosophy.

Long walks with Uncle Warner provided weekend diversion. Sometimes they would take a train and head out for the country. Once when roaming around in Connecticut they became acquainted with a farmwoman. It turned out she had some legal problem over a will. Dad took on the case and was able to resolve it satisfactorily. In gratitude and because she was too poor to pay she insisted on giving him a family heirloom, an ornate silver fruit basket. We have recently passed it on as a wedding present to Gaysnee, my nephew Jon's wife.

Those years before his marriage were hard for my father. He felt stuck in his law practice but couldn't see any more compatible career opportunities on the horizon. I remember once after some young man had come to consult Dad about finding a job he remarked that he felt sorry for him because those first ten years after college were often the most difficult ones in a person's life.

Added to his discontent were family worries and obligations. Andrew's health had broken down and later his mother died. Dad contributed what he could to supplement Lena's salary and visited them as often as he could afford. After he met Mother no doubt he was torn between taking the train to Corning or the one to Warren. More troubling, he knew he could not support a wife in "the style to which she was accustomed," as they used to say. She, of course, was eager to get married and willing to live quite simply if she could not persuade him to use some of her money.

Finally in September of 1908 the big day arrived. My mother, dressed in a white satin gown with a high lace collar, was a stunning bride as a photograph of her descending the wide staircase of her parents home attests. She saved the dress, which I wore for my wedding as did my sister and niece for theirs.

Early Years of My Parents' Marriage

After their wedding trip to Mexico my parents settled into their new home on Cumberland Avenue in the Hill section of Brooklyn. They rented the top floor of a townhouse two or three blocks from Fort Greene Park beyond which lay the Navy Yard.

Because my grandmother had always had a cook my mother entered marriage lacking cooking skills, even though she had been called home from college to learn to keep house.

Dad must have been supportive of her efforts to learn, but perhaps it was slower and harder work than Mother had anticipated. In any case my aunt Grace told me of an early visit when a woman would come in to prepare dinner but leave before my father returned from work. Then at dinner he would boast to his sisters about what a good cook Marion had become. When I first heard of this deception I was shocked, but now it just seems sad that Mother should have been so insecure.

She was unsure of herself socially as well. Unsophisticated yet bold, this young woman from "way out west" must have seemed rather brash to the genteel first families of Brooklyn. She was always ambivalent about joining the socially elite, but in due time she found her niche among a group of forward-looking women, members of a study club which had been founded in 1898. Eventually most of them assumed leadership roles in various community organizations. Although they became her close friends, Mother always remained a little in awe of their intellectual abilities.

The club was started by Agnes Dennison, of the Dennison Paper family, when she was twenty-one. Her old-fashioned father did not believe in higher education for women, so, determined to educate herself, Agnes gathered a few friends together for that purpose. Their method was to devote a whole year to one country studying its history, culture, and politics. While I believe they all read the same books, the members took turns giving supplementary reports. I remember when Mother's turn came round our household would be in turmoil for days. Nevertheless she managed to hold her own.

By the time Mother met her, Agnes had been married for several years to a surgeon, Dr. James Peter Warbasse. They were both pacifists, Agnes being one of the original members of The Women's Peace Party. After World War I, Peter was kicked out of the A.M.A. for his pacifist activities. Fortunately, royalties on his book on surgical treatment made it possible for him to pursue his favorite cause: consumer-owned cooperatives. In 1919 he founded the Cooperative League of America and spent much of his time traveling about the country promoting the Rochdale Principles. They were both advocates of birth control. Quite likely it was through them that Mother met Margaret Sanger who set up her first clinic in 1913 in Brooklyn. Mother became her lifelong follower devoting many volunteer hours to the Brooklyn Maternity Center and later to Planned Parenthood and the Margaret Sanger Research Institute. She even attended an international conference on population planning in India when she was eighty-one.

Agnes was also a fine musician and all of her six children played musical instruments. We used to go to family chamber concerts in their large home on Washington Avenue. Mother marveled at how she could manage such a full life so efficiently. They became devoted friends.

I remember Agnes as a small woman whose eyes sparkled with vitality. Growing up I saw more of her than of her daughter, Vera, who was two years older than I. Then, in 1953, when Lyle and I moved to Ann Arbor, I looked up Vera. Instantly we reminded each other of our mothers! We enjoyed working together in the League of Women Voters, but after a few years she and her husband, Willett Spooner, moved to Rocky River near Cleveland. It was fun to reminisce again about our mothers when I called her the other night to fill out the details of this story.

Another lifelong friend in the study club was Mary Shotwell Ingraham. She was the first of her Quaker family to attend college, thanks to a mother who recognized that her daughter had more studious inclinations than her son. The Shotwell and Ingraham families were neighbors on Greene and Clinton Avenues, and Mary [Shotwell] and Henry [Ingraham] had been sweethearts for several years. Soon after she graduated from Vassar they were married in the same year as my parents, and lived near them on Adelphi Street.

The two couples started their families at about the same time. Mary (Polly) Ingraham was born in 1910, and my brother, Miner arrived in May of 1911. Henry Gardner Ingraham followed within a few months and his sister Winifred a year or two later. I entered the world in January of 1915. David, the youngest Ingraham, and my brother Raymond were both born in 1918 while our youngest, Marion, came in 1920. She always hated being the tag-along! We grew up as neighbors in Brooklyn and on Long Island in the summertime. Then, unexpectedly in 1917, we had a common uncle and aunt. That came about when Mother and Dad invited her brother Miner, then a confirmed bachelor of 41, and Henry Ingraham's sister, Edith, to join them for a few days of winter sport at Lake Placid, N.Y. It was love at first sight, and they were soon married. Their children, Winifred, Miner, and Horace, linked the Ingraham and Ingersoll children as cousins to cousins.

Mary Ingraham devoted years of volunteer service to the Brooklyn Y.W.C.A. Following World War II she became president of the national board of the Y at a time when that organization was at the forefront of desegregation. Later, in the sixties, she served on the New York City Board of Higher Education where she helped establish community colleges and a policy of open admissions. In a recent conversation, Polly told me that her mother, recognizing her husband's pleasure in gardening and fascination with plants, suggested that maybe he should have been a botanist instead of a lawyer. Henry replied that that would have led to his becoming a professor and to her being stuck in some small college town, so he had to be a lawyer to give her scope.

Polly also told me that she used to be frightened by my mother and was amazed that we seemed to be unaffected by her unpredictable behavior. On the other hand we were afraid of <u>her</u> mother whose dignity and air of calm authority seemed disapproving of us!

The right to vote was high on her friends' agenda. Mother enthusiastically marched with them in parades for women's suffrage both before and after the First World War.

How my parents spent their time together in the early years of their marriage, I can only speculate. No doubt Dad introduced Mother to reading aloud. I remember how he used to love to have her read to him as he lay stretched out on the sofa. He must have walked her legs off too, showing her different parts of the city, and taken her out to dine occasionally at some inexpensive restaurant. As evidence, my son, Tim, and Leslie tell of a visit to Mother at her New York apartment on Beekman Place soon after they were married in 1968. Mamo, as she was then called by her grandchildren, proposed that they hop on the subway and go down to Chinatown for dinner. On the way she told them that the restaurants of Chinatown were where the radicals used to meet in the early days.

At some point my parents acquired a car. Mother did not hesitate to drive it alone in spite of bystanders shouting, "Look at the lady driving an automobile!"

Golf was a recreation they shared when possible. Mother had taught Dad to play during his visits in Warren when he was courting her. They made a tradition of celebrating each wedding anniversary by playing at a different course. This was one of the several ways Mother used over the years to get Dad to take time off from work and politics. She loved to travel, and when she could not persuade him to go with her she often went on her own.

Politics heated up soon after my parents were married. In a new attempt to loosen Tammany Hall's grip on city government, a "Committee of One Hundred" was organized. My father became its campaign manager, and in the fall of 1909 election the Fusion forces gained control of the Board of Estimate. The Board of Estimate had greater authority than the larger Board of Alderman. It consisted of the mayor, the comptroller, and the president of the Board of Alderman who were elected city wide, and the five borough presidents.

Tammany retaliated by trying to push through a new city charter which would have stripped the Board of Estimate of its powers. My father took an active part in the fight to defeat it. This was finally accomplished in the state legislature with the help of a young senator, Franklin D. Roosevelt. In 1911 Roosevelt, my father, and a third man headed a delegation to Trenton to persuade Governor Woodrow Wilson to run for President.

Public indignation over a scandal about a murder led to revelations of city police protection of underworld criminals and to a clean sweep for Fusion in the 1913 elections. The new mayor was the outgoing President of the Board of Alderman, John Purroy Mitchel. He appointed my father Park Commissioner of the Borough of Brooklyn.

Dad certainly derived great satisfaction from the four years he served in that post. I remember when we took walks in Prospect Park he would often express his pleasure at seeing so many people enjoying the outdoors. While Park Commissioner, he improved neighborhood parks and playgrounds and developed new ones, adding wading pools, playing fields, and toboggan slides. By installing lights, he made nighttime ice skating and tobogganing available for working people. The introduction of children's gardens was a project he was particularly proud of. All this he accomplished while cutting costs by twenty percent, largely through substituting steady year-round jobs for less efficient seasonal employment.

Mother used to tell us of once when Dad was fretting over some park trees that seemed to be dying, she chided him saying, "You act as if you owned those trees." He answered, "If I did I wouldn't be so concerned."

Much of my mother's attention was taken up by her new baby, Miner (later renamed Jerry), who arrived on May 24, 1911. When they came home from the hospital they were taken care of by Miss Larson, a trained baby nurse. I remember "Larcy" for she came back to look after my baby sister, Marion.

About the time Miner was a year old my parents started building a house on South Oxford Street, only two or three blocks from their apartment. Long afterwards Mother told me of the fatal accident that occurred when a workman slipped off a scaffold above the stairwell and fell from the third floor to the ground. It was before workmen's compensation laws, but I understand that my parents provided a pension to the widow for many years. The tragedy left Mother terribly shaken, and she believed it caused her to have a miscarriage. She was able to bring her next pregnancy to term only to have the baby, a girl born November 3, 1913, die the next day. She had been named Elma after my father's sister who died when she was in her early teens.

Mother was very disheartened, but determined to have more children. She even tried adoption, but the little boy who was sent to them on a trial basis was so out of control that she quickly gave up. She said he climbed up the chains of the swinging settee in the living room like a little monkey.

Fortunately she soon became pregnant again, this time with me. By mid-December there were signs I might be coming too soon, so she was put to bed to stay through the holidays. Mother used to say that her best Christmas present that year was that I waited until January seventh to be born. However she still considered me to be two months premature, though she claimed that I weighed seven pounds, hardly a "preemie" by today's standards. Because her doctor had told her that the nervous system is the last to develop in the unborn child, she believed that my premature birth had caused me to be high-strung and nervous. To add to her distress, Mother was unable to breastfeed me. She hired a wet nurse, a source of conflict because the nurse complained that her own baby was not getting enough milk. I would have thought that infant formula was sufficiently advanced by that time to have been a better alternative. Her doctor advised her to wait a few years before having another child. She was willing as long as she could try for two more before she was forty.

I was named Agnes, but in my baby talk I called myself Asho. The family picked up the habit, which soon became entrenched. When I reached the mature age of thirteen my father said, "Look here, if you want to remain Asho the rest of your life, you should have your name legally changed. Otherwise you may have difficulties with such things as passports." So he took me to a notary public in some bank or office before whom I solemnly swore that my name change was for no criminal purposes. Of course when the time came to get a passport I did have trouble because the birth certificate had not been changed, but the gesture boosted my sense of autonomy.

Mayor Mitchel came up for re-election in November of 1917, but he lost to Tammany so my father's job as Brooklyn Park Commissioner came to an end. By that time the United States had entered World War I. Dad volunteered to serve with the Y.M.C.A. which, jointly with the *Foyer Du Soldat,* ran canteens for the troops near the front lines. The canteens provided small treats such as hot chocolate and tobacco free of charge. Dad was shocked that the Red Cross made the soldiers pay for such items.

My father became a regional co-director of the *Foyer du Soldat*, along with a Frenchman. Through this partnership, and staying with a French family, he quickly learned to speak well enough to get along. His host family, the Carpontiers, lived in the little town of Épernay on the Marne River. They could hear the gunfire during the second battle of the Marne. I wish I could remember more of the stories Dad used to tell of his experiences. I know he was impressed by the black troops of colonial Senegal, and by the amazement of the local population who had never seen black people before. On an appropriate occasion he delighted some children with the bright-colored hair ribbons and some suitable gifts for boys, which Mother had thoughtfully tucked into his baggage. Vegetables were very scarce, carrots being about the only ones available. Though not his favorite, Dad dutifully ate them for his health's sake, but after the war he never touched another carrot.

My father came to love the French people and the French language. His legacy to me was teaching me the Marseillaise, (I used to sing "allons enfants de apple tree-a,") and reading aloud with me my high school assignments in French literature. Sometimes, to hurry us children or my mother along, he would say "Let's go, tout suite!" adding for emphasis "the tooter the sweeter."

After the Armistice my father was invited to participate in the Paris Peace Conference. He attended some preparatory meetings, but did not stay for the conference because the pull to return home was too great. In retrospect he was sorry he missed this opportunity to be involved with international relations.

The summer Dad was in France, Mother took Miner and me to visit our grandparents in Warren. While there she received a telephone call from Washington. Fearing that if it were bad news she might faint and injure her unborn babe, she tossed some cushions on the floor and lay down on them before taking the receiver. The call was just an inquiry about how to get in touch with my father.

The baby, Raymond, was born on October fourth in a crowded, understaffed hospital at the height of the flu epidemic. At one point when Mother desperately needed attention, she threw some washbasins on the floor. The clatter brought someone in a hurry. I'm sure she was glad to get out of that hospital! She saw to it that her last baby was born at home, as I had been.

This was a difficult time for Mother. Raymond was only a few weeks old when I came down with a severe case of diphtheria. It was assumed that I caught it in a street crowd when a nursemaid took Miner and me to see a parade in celebration of the false armistice. I was quarantined in my parents' bedroom on the third floor for nearly two months. My earliest memory is of Christmas in that big bed.

Soon after my father's return from France in January, he looked into the possibility of working in the field of international relations. He consulted James G. McDonald, chairman of the newly formed Foreign Policy Association, on how he might contribute toward securing world peace. Nothing materialized in the way of a job, but Dad became a close friend of

McDonald and a strong supporter of the Foreign Policy Association. I used to attend their luncheon discussions with my parents when I was in high school.

For the next five years it was back to city politics for Dad, but this time as counsel and secretary of the Men's City Club of New York. He was also in charge of its public affairs program, which entailed frequent trips to Albany in support of various pieces of reform legislation. In the process he became well acquainted with Governor Alfred E. Smith with whom he worked on reorganizing state government and developing a system of state parks. Dad chaired Al's campaign committee when he ran for reelection in 1924. That same year he became the impartial chairman of the Ladies Cloak and Suit industry, its first permanent arbitrator. He stayed in that job for seven years.

This sketch of my parents lives brings me to the point where I had some awareness and grasp of what was going on with them and how they interacted with me. Now it is time to recount memories of my own life.

Chapter 2
Childhood

149 South Oxford Street: 1915-1925

The House

Since my earliest memories are of episodes in and around the South Oxford Street house, I shall start by describing it. Three stories high, it was a dark brown frame house with a wide porch across the front. Why brown? Probably to blend with the brownstones next door.

The inside was brown too, with dark woodwork, dark furniture and dark red carpets. The long front hall stretched back past the living room and the dining room on the right to a door to the pantry. On the left of the entrance vestibule was a small den and beyond that the stairs which turned after a few steps and ran up along the side wall. Past the newel post the hall widened to become a secondary living room complete with fireplace. It was here we had our Christmas tree and hung our stockings. Here too was my special niche, a small space between the foot of the stairs and the wall, a cozy retreat.

The living room was also dark except for a wicker swing, the size of a sofa, which hung in front of the fireplace by chains from hooks in the ceiling. It was too high for my legs to touch the floor to swing myself and, as we children were not allowed to push each other because we were too vigorous, an adult's company was needed for a nice gentle swing. Reading was better done in a large stationary chair by the light of the front windows. Some favorite storybooks and a set of the *Book of Knowledge* were in bookshelves to the left of the fireplace.

The dining room was brightened by the morning sun sparkling in a fish tank under the window. An old sepia photograph of me, my mother, Raymond, and Marion feeding the fish reinforces this memory as well as my impression of the brown interior. There was a round oak table in the center of the room, and a small table in the corner where we children ate our supper.

Breakfast was when we interacted most as a family. I would watch my father intently as he skillfully peeled his orange in a continuous curling strip. According to my mother's lore, if you swing the peel over your shoulder it would land in the shape of the initial of the person you would someday marry. Miner liked to take charge of the toaster. He had to watch it like a hawk so he could turn the slices at just the right moment by flipping down the sides. But often he was too late, so out to the pantry to scrape the black off if the toast wasn't totally burned.

The den was seldom used during the day when my father was at work, but even so I felt his presence at his well-ordered desk. There was also an upright piano where I reluctantly practiced with discouraging results. I remember being stuck on Schumann's "The Merry Farmer" forever. More rewarding was to sit at the keyboard and pretend to play, for this was a player piano. It was fun to watch the keys jump up and down in response to the scattered holes in the paper roller. One roll played Chopin's funeral march. Every time it came to the main theme, no matter what he was doing, little Raymond would sing out "Now the dead person is buried."

The most impressive part of the house was the long, narrow, open stairwell up to the third floor. From there you could look down over the railing to the front hall below, a scary distance. Upstairs the walls and furnishings were lighter. On the second floor at the front were a bedroom and a sitting/dressing room. Behind was the nursery and beyond that a sleeping porch. A hallway went to the back stairs and to two maids' rooms over the kitchen. There were three more bedrooms on the third floor and a large playroom across the front.

My earliest memory is of being in my parents' big bed in the largest third floor bedroom, when I had diphtheria. By Christmas, though still in bed, I was well enough to enjoy a tiny Christmas tree and a doll in a basket containing her clothes. But most of all I remember the metal cricket which clicked when I pinched it. Two weeks later I was allowed to come downstairs to celebrate my fourth birthday and see the big Christmas tree they had saved for me.

The four-poster bed was where on April 25 of the following year I first saw my new baby sister in my mother's arms. When I watched the nurse bathe her I was distressed to see a thing sticking out of her belly button. I was told it would soon drop off, but that seemed strange too.

I was never assigned any particular room in that house. Sometimes, perhaps when I was sick, I slept in the front room on the second floor, which also served as our guest room. There I could watch the shadows of cars high on the wall as they moved up the street. Occasionally I was awakened by the loud talk and raucous laughter of the Elks as they left their club across the street after a party. Usually I slept on the sleeping porch with Miner. There the disturbance was from fighting alley cats whose cries could sound quite alarming. Mostly though, I guess I liked the sleeping porch, except in the coldest weather. Then although I was wearing Dr. Denton pajamas and I slept in a home-made cotton flannel sleeping bag, it was icy cold when I first crawled in. To be sure I soon warmed up enough to drop off to sleep, but I always dreaded the first chill.

In the morning I'd dress in the sitting/dressing room with my parents. This was a pleasant room with a bay window and window seat. The flowered striped curtains were in burgundy and old rose hues, the same cretonne material covering a screen for privacy in undressing. Mother kept her dresses in a large closet where I liked to hide among their soft textures. My school clothes were always set out neatly on a chair the night before. They were kept in various built-in cupboards and drawers in the hallway. I can still smell the strong odor of brown laundry soap emanating from my underwear drawer.

Putting on that underwear was quite a long process beginning with an undershirt whose sleeves had to be pinned up with little gold safety pins if I was wearing a very short-sleeved dress. Next came the all-important pantywaist with its tiers of yellow, bone buttons on which were buttoned my panties and a white cotton or yellowed flannel petticoat. The theory was that constriction around the waist or legs cut off circulation so all clothes should hang from the shoulders. (I read about this in a child-care manual I later found on the family bookshelves.) Garters were also attached to the pantywaist to hold up wrinkled, ribbed stockings. You can see why it took me a long time to dress, though Mother said it was because I dawdled.

Finally I donned a fresh cotton dress and a hair ribbon to match. If yellow was the color of the day, Daddy would sing me a song about his "little yeller gal down Mobile." I now realize that referred to a mulatto. Another favorite song was "The Sunshine of Paradise Alley." He used to call me "Twinkle" and later "Twink" for short.

Where did I keep my toys and other personal possessions? I don't quite know, though I had some things at the far end of the long gray playroom. In spite of its built-in cupboards and toy chests the room was usually cluttered with a lot of stuff I didn't claim such as countless blocks and a big child-sized boy doll, named Jimmy. Miner's erector constructions and electric train took up a lot of floor space. Always ready to instruct, he tried to explain the function of the transformer and the nature of electricity, but I'm still mystified.

The kitchen was foreign territory, the domain of a series of unwelcoming cooks. Finally there was the spooky cellar with its bin filled with shining black chunks of anthracite coal. I can still feel the tickle of coal dust in my nostrils. A kindly colored man, named Joshua, came daily to stoke the furnace and shovel out the ashes, much to Raymond's admiration. Recently Ray told me that once in Joshua's presence he referred to him as a nigger. Joshua gently took him aside, and explained that he shouldn't use that word because it made people sad. Ray was deeply impressed and felt badly to have hurt the feelings of his good friend, Josh. He says he has never used that word since.

The Yard

The Oxford Street house must have been built on two lots because the yard was nearly as wide as it was deep, unlike the narrow ones of the neighbors. At the far end was a high brick wall, the back of garages that faced on an alley. I have no memory of the alley as it was off limits. A small one-room house filled the back left corner of the yard. It had been built for a little nursery school run by Agnes Warbasse. Miner was among the handful of children attending, but the venture was short-lived. All I remember was a bare, uninteresting room. The only other remnants of the Warbasse school were a large sandbox and a double width wooden slide.

The slide was remarkable in that one could walk up the wrong way by means of a narrow strip of exposed cross struts. During construction, before all the curved oak flooring boards were in place, the children so enjoyed climbing up the slope that Mother had the carpenter leave the last ten inches uncovered. The slide was wide enough for two children to sit side-by-side, a source of great joy to the Siamese twin boys, joined at the hips, who visited next door for a while. I do not remember them, but I often heard Mother tell of how well her invention served those Siamese twins. Eventually she donated the slide to some settlement house or child-care center where it could be indoors, protected from the weather.

When I was about seven or eight years old a rabbit hutch was built along the back wall of the yard for a pair of young cottontails that had been given us. We had been told that they were both males so we should not expect offspring. The rabbits grew big and plump on the carrots and grass clippings we fed them, along with their dry food. One morning when I lifted the lid of their bin, I was astonished to see four little blobs huddled together, three brown and one black. They must be baby rabbits, but how could that be? I was so bewildered that I didn't' know what to think or say, so I said nothing, and waited until others verified my secret. Until they did, I felt overcome by a strange sensation of awe and guilt.

The rabbits proved real enough. They were quickly named Blackie, Brownie, Darkie, who had a few black hairs mixed in with the brown, and Paleface. The first two outlived the other pair. The summer I was eight, I took them with me to camp. Mother saved the postcard I wrote home saying, "Tell Raymond and Marion Blackie and Brownie are fine." In time, only Blackie, who was my favorite, was left. I took him to our summer home on Duck Island where there was an extensive lawn. There we confined him in a circular, wire-mesh cage we had once used for Easter chicks. As it had no bottom, we could move it about and give Blackie plenty of fresh grass to feast on. One day, when fortunately I was not around, a visiting dog was quick to turn over the cage and seize the rabbit. I was told he had escaped, so was comforted by the myth that Blackie was enjoying his freedom in the woods.

About the time the first pair of rabbits came to us, the back yard was the scene of wanton destruction as Miner and I demolished my antiquated doll stroller. Made of wicker with a flat wooden seat, it once was painted white but had become grimy with soot. I never liked it as it was awkward and too big for any of my dolls. Even when I succeeded in getting one into a sitting position, it would slide right out under the strap as soon as we moved. Besides, I had my heart set on a doll carriage just like the pram my baby sister had ridden in the year before. In fact I had made it well known that I wanted Santa to bring me one for Christmas. I could just picture myself strolling down the sidewalk pushing my new carriage with its big wheels and collapsible hood that could be adjusted for sun or rain.

On the day in question, Miner and I were sent out in the yard to play, but there was nothing to do. We were bored. No doubt I had expressed my scorn for the stroller: so when he suggested that we take it apart I fell in line. Soon we were gleefully rolling the wheels around the yard. When Mother appeared and beheld the wreckage, she was quick to declare that Santa Claus certainly never gave doll carriages to little girls who deliberately destroyed the ones they had. My protests, that it was Miner's idea and anyway the stroller was no good and not at all the same thing as a carriage, were dismissed as irrelevant.

Christmas came and just as Mother predicted there was no buggy under the tree. Not till twenty-one years later did my wish come true. Then I proudly pushed my infant son, Tim, in a real baby buggy complete with hood carefully positioned to shade his eyes.

The Neighborhood

Most of our neighbors lived in narrow, attached townhouses made of a pinkish-brown sandstone, the dominant style of architecture in Brooklyn at that time. The steps to their high stoops reached out to the sidewalk. A wrought-iron fence and gate usually enclosed the tiny courtyard from which there were two or three steps down to the ground floor entrance under the stoop. I have a vague memory of not enjoying playing in one of these dark entranceways with some little boys who lived down the block.

In contrast to the brownstones stood the Elks Club, with its white stone facade flush with the sidewalk, directly across the street from our house. Further down on that same side was a large wide house that was converted to the Ethical Culture School the year Raymond turned four. He was a charter student and Marion enrolled two years later.

South Oxford Street was just one long block that sloped down from Fulton Street to Atlantic Avenue. Our house was only a few doors from the upper end. Fulton Street, with its trolley tracks, ran on the diagonal, complicating the intersection. Hanson Place came in from the west and became Greene Avenue when it crossed Fulton. The extension of South Oxford was Cumberland Avenue going north a few blocks to Fort Greene Park.

The park was the destination of many family walks. On the way my parents would point out the brownstone where they had lived in an upper floor apartment for the first years of their marriage. The park was small with no playground, just paved walks leading up a hill which overlooked the East River and the Navy Yard. There at the top of a long flight of steps rose a tall Greek column capped by a bronze ornament. My father always explained to our visitors that it was some sort of navigation instrument honoring the sailors of the Revolution who were captured by the British and held in prison ships anchored in the harbor below. On the way down from the monument, we children liked to slide on the polished granite walls that framed the steps. That was the only source of amusement in Fort Greene Park.

But Prospect Park, where we had to go by streetcar, had everything. It was even larger than Central Park. There was a large lake with ducks and rowboats and a refreshment stand where we bought Cracker Jack. In those days the prizes at the bottom of the box were really worthwhile, such as whistles, tops, rings, crickets, and magnets with little clowns that hung on to each other. I always loved to have Daddy take me rowing. Then I would share some of my Cracker Jack with the ducks. Usually, however, we just walked over the rolling meadow where sheep served as pre-mechanized lawn mowers. Here were some great sledding hills. There were hockey fields where I played in high school, and trails where I rode horseback as a teenager.

One of my earliest memories of Prospect Park was a traumatic ride on the merry-go-round. I must have been quite small for I was not allowed on the prancing horses, but was instead strapped onto a stationary swan. Soon after the carrousel started, a conductor came by and took my ticket. With each revolution I could see my parents in the watching crowd. However, when the merry-go-round stopped, I was on the side away from them. The other children got off, but nobody came to unstrap me. Soon other children settled on their mounts and we started up again. When the conductor asked me for my ticket, I was frightened and burst into tears. Around and around we went while I was crying so hard everything was a blur. I could barely see my parents as I whirled by, and of course they were helpless to rescue me. By the time we stopped I must have been quite hysterical. When we got home, Daddy helped me wash my face at the kitchen sink. He must have been joking to cheer me up for I distinctly remember the confusion of not knowing whether I was laughing or crying.

When I was into sidewalk games of hop-scotch, jacks, and roly-poly (bouncing a ball with variations), Mary, my only available playmate, was glad to show off her skills. I don't remember her last name but I think it was Irish as she was a devout Catholic. Mary was two or more years older than I, and her pesky little brother, Jimmy, was somewhat older than Raymond. The boys were good friends and Ray remembers visiting Jimmy at his home above a store at the corner of Hanson Place and Fulton Street. Mary, however, was inclined to hang out at our house. It was from her that I learned spooky things about religion, like the Holy Ghost and drinking blood, from which my free-thinking parents had shielded me. I was impressed by Mary's fortitude in giving up candy for Lent.

One day Daddy came home from his office with a wonderful surprise, a new invention called Eskimo Pies. As we clustered around him in the front hall, he handed out one to each of us, including Mary. We eagerly unwrapped the silvery paper and started to bite into the cold dark bar when Mary exclaimed that she couldn't eat it because it was candy. Even when we tried to persuade her that Eskimo Pies fell into a different category, she stoically played it safe and carefully peeled off all the chocolate before eating the ice cream. Though this dampened our joy of the moment, it left me deeply impressed by the power of religious conviction.

Summers at Centerport: 191?-1922

My early summers were spent at a place we rented from the Carters in Centerport on the north shore of Long Island. Located between Huntington and Northport, it was about an hour's commute by train into the city for my father. The white frame Victorian house had wide porches overlooking the bay. When visitors would exclaim that we were right <u>on</u> the water, I thought they were silly, because the house was firmly attached to the ground with a driveway and a strip of lawn between it and the beach.

On the south side of the house, a big maple tree shaded a lawn, which was partly enclosed by a grape arbor. We'd wait impatiently all summer long for those juicy Concords and Niagaras to ripen. The yard at the north end of the property was large enough for a small barn and a fenced in paddock. Beyond the barn the land sloped up a wooded bluff. In front on the beach were two little bathhouses, no more than five feet square. Near them a dock ran out into the water.

Once when I was quite small and had not yet learned to swim, I was standing on the dock with some of my parents' friends. One of them, a big man, told me to push him into the water. I complied, pushing with all my might. When he rewarded my efforts by diving, I fell right in after him. Of course I was promptly fished out in my sopping wet dress, but I hope that man was ashamed of his stupidity.

A path in the woods behind the barn led up the hill to where our friends, the Carpenter family, lived. One time when we were climbing the path to visit them, I was lagging behind. When some adult urged me on I answered, "I'm coming" which set me to singing the refrain of Stephen Foster's "Old Black Joe." I vividly remember the weight of sorrow I felt as I trudged up that hill with my head "bending low."

There were other expeditions that found me lagging, such as blueberry or bayberry picking, or to dig red clay for modeling at a clay pit. Sometimes Miner and I would cool off by sneaking into an icehouse at a nearby pond, carefully shutting the door behind us. It was quite dark in there, and the sawdust covering the blocks of ice was cold and wet. Soon we became downright chilly, and then we were glad to return to the hot summer sunshine.

But the most insufferable heat was once when I followed the suggestion of Miner and his friend Eric that we go in one of the bathhouses and take off our clothes. When we did, they jumped up and down jiggling their little things while I just stood there. It all seemed pointless to me. I was glad when they called it quits so I could get dressed and escape that awful heat.

Sometimes it was even too hot to sleep at night. After Marion's arrival, Raymond was graduated from the white iron crib to the iron youth bed. But he was only a toddler, not yet two, so, to keep him from wandering, they tied the drawstring of his nightgown to the end of the bed. He also wore aluminum cups over his hands, which they said was to keep him from scratching his mosquito bites or sucking his thumb. One night, when I passed his room on the way to the bathroom, I was distressed to find him sleeping with his head on the floor while his feet were tied up on the bed. I tried to lift him back into bed but he was too heavy. After much tugging and pulling I gave up and woke my parents. Raymond meanwhile slept through the whole episode, blissfully unaware of my heroic efforts on his behalf.

The joys of summer freedom were interrupted by the unavoidable afternoon nap, required until I was well past the age of six, because Mother still thought I was high strung and nervous. I would be shut in the downstairs guest room with the shades drawn, until someone came to release me. In answer to my protests that I could never sleep in the daytime, I was told to simply lie quietly on the bed and perhaps I would drop off. Of course I didn't stay on the bed, but found what ways I could to amuse myself in my hour of exile. One day I was jumping about the room when I heard someone coming. Fearing that I'd be scolded, I made a dive for the bed and closed my eyes in pretended sleep, unaware of the trap I had set for myself. Whoever it was tiptoed out of the room and quietly shut the door. It was ages before anyone came again. Finally the maid opened the door and announced that my mother was so pleased because I had slept a whole extra hour. Then it dawned on me that I had not only doubled the length of my imprisonment, but had forfeited my claim that I could not sleep in the daytime. There being no credible way I could admit my deception, I was stuck with it.

The summer Miner was ten and I was six, Poppy came to us. We had waited all afternoon on the porch for a special surprise. Finally a man came riding up to the door on a speckled Indian pony. At first I didn't realize that the pony was the surprise. Miner took charge of her right away, as he had learned to ride at Lake Mohonk boarding school. We named her Poppy, perhaps because of the pinkish-brown color of her spots. She spent most of her time in the paddock. Miner taught her to shake her head up and down to answer "yes" when he asked her if she wanted whatever bit of food he might offer her. Soon she was nodding her head every time she saw us coming. When saddling her he would duck between her legs, while warning that it was far too dangerous for me to do. In another few years, when I learned to ride her, I was boldly ducking under Poppy's belly too.

Naughty Mary Jane

Mother was the disciplinarian of the family. My parents did not believe in corporal punishment as they preferred sweet reason, but in desperate moments they had been known to administer an occasional spanking. Once when Raymond had been misbehaving at the dinner table, Mother sent him upstairs and my father after him with instructions to spank. Dad told him to lie on the bed, which he did, but on his back. Dad rolled him over to have access to the proper spanking spot. Quick as a wink, Raymond rolled to his back again. Dad made another attempt, but again his son was too quick for him. When his father started to laugh Raymond knew he had won the contest. Dad wisely called a truce, but suggested that it would be best if they said nothing about it when they returned to the table.

Devising appropriate penalties taxed their ingenuity. For instance, washing a child's mouth out with soap for biting or speaking bad words seemed logical at the time, though I think I would never have imposed it on my own children. Banishment to another room was their usual method of dealing with intolerable behavior. I have a vague impression of being shut in a closet, but I can't quite visualize it. Mario and Ray however have vivid memories of being locked in "the dungeon," a small empty storage room in the basement of the Duck Island house. Marion, who was afraid of the dark, was terrified, while Raymond outsmarted his captors by hiding a few small toys in there to help pass the time. However, imprisonment was not a feasible way of dealing with misbehavior away from home, such as when riding in a car.

Once when we were on some long trip in the family touring car, I was having a temper tantrum over some set-to with Mother.

"This can not be our good little Asho. This must be that naughty Mary Jane," she said using a familiar tactic. "Stop the car!" she told my father who was driving. "We must put Mary Jane out of the car."

My father complied, and Mother opened the door. But instead of shooing away the imaginary Mary Jane she put me, real live Asho, out on the side of the road. Then, to my horror, the car slowly started to pull away. It couldn't have gone more than a few yards, but I was terrified. Collapsed in tears, I was quite ready to promise to be good when they rescued me. My anger about this had always been directed against my mother. Not until I was also a parent did I realize that my father too had participated in this act of threatened abandonment. How could he have done this to me?

A few years later they tried the same trick on Marion, but it backfired. In panic and defiance she ran headlong into a cornfield. Jerry was sent after her and had quite a time finding where she lay hidden among the cornstalks.

My most unusual punishment was suffered at the hands of a French governess. Tall, angular, and without charm, Mademoiselle Vernarx was employed to look after the younger children and to teach Miner and me French. I doubt if I learned any French, for I avoided her as much as I could.

On an evening when my parents were out, Raymond and I were on the living room floor happily looking through old magazines for bears to cut out. Being older, I handled the scissors while he searched. We found quite a few in the advertisements as teddy bears had become popular in the early twenties. Our companionable project was rudely interrupted by Mademoiselle announcing Raymond's bedtime. When he resisted, I made the mistake of playing mediator. I promised to look for more bears while he was getting ready for bed, and then to bring them up to his room to show him.

Mademoiselle probably was not even listening, so did not appreciate how much I was helping her. Also I may well have taken longer than I realized. In any case, when I marched up to the third floor eagerly clutching my find, there was Mademoiselle standing in front of the door to Raymond's room.

"You can't go in there," she said sternly.

"But I promised," I protested.

"He is already asleep. Be quiet or you will wake him."

I did not believe her, and in righteous indignation I tried to push past her. She grabbed me. I kicked her in the shins. Declaring me to be hysterical, she picked me up and carried me into the bathroom. There she dumped me in the bathtub and doused me with cold water. By this time she was quite hysterical herself. That is the last I remember of Mademoiselle Vernarx.

My Broken Leg 1922

The summer I was seven and a half my parents had arranged to have my father's two unmarried sisters, Aunt Lena and Aunt Grace, join us for a short vacation in the White Mountains. They picked an inn at Randolph, N.H. because the Douglas Horton family had a summer home there. [He was my uncle Clare Crary's brother-in-law.] There would be cousins for Miner and me to play with and plenty of hiking trails. Leaving Raymond and Marion at home with a nursemaid, the rest of us took the train from Grand Central Station.

One morning soon after we arrived, I hurried down the front steps of the inn to where my father and aunts were waiting for me to go for a walk. For some reason Mother stayed behind in her room. I have always assumed that I had been upset by some quarrel with her, but was that why she did not want to walk with us? As I write this it occurs to me that, whatever may have overtly set us off, I was probably feeling my mother's unspoken jealously of her husband's attention to his sisters. Naturally I would have wanted to escape from her negative mood. In any case, I must have been quite agitated as I rushed to join my father and aunts.

As the four of us stood beside the driveway, I noticed as I glanced to the right that a car, an old Tin Lizzy, was slowly coming toward us out of the driveway. Suddenly, on an impulse like the proverbial chicken, I just had to cross that road. I dashed headlong in front of the car. It knocked me down and struck my left thigh. Right away I realized that I had violated the most basic safety rules. In my remorse and pain I kept screaming, "Don't scold me! Don't scold me!"

They carried me inside A doctor came. He had a kind of small sieve which contained ether. He told me to breathe in and then, if I didn't like the smell, to breathe it out just as hard as I could. It worked like a charm. After that vehement exhalation I couldn't help taking a deep breath, which quickly knocked me out. Next thing I knew I was riding in a truck or car on some improvised mattress on my way to the hospital in the small town of Berlin. There an X-ray showed that my only injury was a broken thighbone. I was rigged up with splints and a weight hanging off the end of the bed to give traction.

The hospital was run by a French Canadian order of nuns most of whom spoke no English. Many of their patients were fellow countrymen who had accidents while working in the local saw mills. The French sisters were delighted to have a little girl patient for a change, so my parents told me, and they gave me excellent care. One of them would play her violin for me.

After the first miserable day or two I was feeling fine again. What I needed was entertainment. First I was transferred from a small dark room to a sunny corner one. Then they engaged an English-speaking daytime nurse. Finding her last name difficult to pronounce, I simply named her Mrs. San because it rhymed with so many other words. I liked to tease her by kicking my right leg under the covers and telling her it was the broken one. She would respond with mock horror, exclaiming, "What will the doctor say?" Then I would admit that I was just fooling. Of course she knew I could not possibly have moved my broken leg, splinted and weighed down as it was.

Family members visited me daily, but before long it was time for Aunt Lena to return to her secretarial job in Corning and my father to his with the Men's City Club. Mother had to leave too as she was needed at home by the younger ones and to make countless decisions regarding renovations of our newly acquired house on Duck Island. Aunt Grace volunteered to stay on to keep me company. She came faithfully every day for the next few weeks to play games and read me stories. Years later she liked to tell of how a preacher came to call one day. In a solemn voice he asked, "And how is the little sick girl today?" to which I brightly replied, "I'm not sick. I just have a broken leg."

People sent me all kinds of presents till I had a whole drawer full of toys. The best was a series of tiny packets labeled with the days of the week so I could anticipate opening a new surprise each morning. Mother brought a crystal prism to hang in the window. I loved to follow the vivid scrap of rainbow it sent traveling about my room when it caught the sunshine. But my favorite toy was one I invented for myself. I asked Aunt Grace to go into the woods and find two sticks about a foot and a half long. She found just the right ones to serve as my violin and bow. I would saw away singing "Just a Song at Twilight" which Mrs.

San had taught me. I imagined I was swinging on the porch swing at Centerport looking out over the water at the dark clouds of an impending thunderstorm and feeling its electric excitement. We tied the sticks with lengths of string to the headrails of my bed so I could reach them whenever I wanted to play my violin.

Once Mother came to visit, bringing a box of grapes from Centerport. She described in detail how little Raymond had climbed up into the arbor to pick them and handed each bunch to Marion whom Mother held up high to receive them. Then their nurse took the grapes from her and laid them in the box. I was duly touched by my siblings' efforts on my behalf though it was Mother who had gone to all the trouble to stage the scene.

Finally the day came when I could go home. In preparation for the journey, a plaster cast was put around my leg and the lower half of my body. There I was, as stiff as a board, riding on my father's shoulder as we marched through Grand Central Railroad Station. Once safely home in Brooklyn the cast came off. Then followed the painful process of learning to bend my knee again. Each day the therapist would bend it a little more while I screamed. At last I could walk normally, though with all the traction the injured leg had become an inch longer than the other. To this day I have to turn up my right pant leg more than the left one.

By the time I was ready to return to school it was already October, well past starting date. To add to my difficulties, Mother had decided to send me to the school where more of her friends sent their daughters instead of to familiar Friends School where I had gone to kindergarten and first grade. So when I entered the second grade at Packer Collegiate Institute, an all girls school, I was very much the shy newcomer.

At recess one day one little girl kept stepping on my toes. The teacher told her she shouldn't do that because I had had a broken leg and so she should be kind to me. I knew that my broken leg had nothing to do with the case as I was completely recovered, but I could not defy the teacher by telling her so. That made me ashamed to be accepting her protection under false pretenses. I'm sure the other girl did not buy the teacher's argument either. I always felt like an outsider at that school.

Early Schooling: 1919-1924

"Come and play with me today." How could I ever forget those opening words of my first reader! They adorned the wall of my first grade classroom at Friends School. They were also printed individually on little yellow cards which we were supposed to arrange in the proper sequence. These cards were probably one of the many paper products made by the Dennison Company.

The other thing I remember in that reader was a picture of a child standing with an ear pressed against a telephone pole listening to the sound of the letter "L." This was a mystery I couldn't test out in the city because all wires were buried underground. Later, after we moved to Duck Island for the summers, I used to listen to the poles along the causeway. Whether they sounded like "L" is problematical, but they certainly sang. I believed that what I was hearing was people actually talking on the telephone until Jerry informed me that it was only the wind making the wires vibrate.

When I had attended the two years of morning kindergarten I took my afternoon naps at home, but in first grade I had to take them in the empty auditorium. Those hard pews in that large, darkened space were far from cozy. I felt forlorn and lonesome, believing that I was missing the best part of the day's activities. By the time I was transferred to Packer at second grade I was finally free of naps.

The best thing about second grade was the miniature Eskimo village of cardboard igloos covered with simulated snow. Our teacher read us the story of the Eskimo Twins, one of a series of books starting with the Cave Twins and going on through the Dutch Twins and several others, ending with the most exciting one, the Scotch Twins. I don't remember what else we studied in second grade, but we welcomed the mid-morning break for crackers and milk or orange juice. I was embarrassed to be the only one whose mother had chosen orange juice, but I must admit that it tasted good with a graham cracker.

In the third grade classroom I can see myself at the blackboard doing an arithmetic problem or at my desk laboriously trying to form perfect "l's" and "o's" at just the right slant. This was the Palmer method of penmanship. Although I never achieved a graceful, uniform slant, at least I learned to write legible small letters. It was the fancy capitals that threw me. The result is that I have always vacillated between cursive and printed capitals even in the same address. But it was spelling that was my downfall! Having learned to read phonetically, I resented the fact that English so often disregards its own phonetic logic. I hated to have to memorize spelling that made no sense to me. Arithmetic was so much more reliable, though often tedious. Not until I reached algebra did I find math really enjoyable.

Naturally, recess was the most important part of the day. There I strove ineffectively to acquire the skills of my classmates in jacks and jump rope. Playing house was distinctly a game of social hierarchy. First you had to be invited to join a group. Then it was a question of what role the leader, usually playing the autocratic mother, assigned you to. I hated having to be the maid, but never reached the point of starting my own group at school.

On rainy days we sometimes had directed activities in the gym. Then we played circle games like "The Farmer in the Dell." My favorite was a singing version of Sleeping Beauty. A child was picked to be Briar Rosebud, another to be the ugly witch who taught her how to spin, and another to be the handsome prince. The rest of us were the trees and bushes that grew up and "hemmed her in" after she pricked her "little hand" and slept for a "hundred years." The prince came and cut us all down, waking Briar Rosebud with a kiss on her hand. Then the pair rode off together. I'm often reminded of that song when I see a jungle of overgrown shrubbery overwhelming a house.

Although Mother eagerly tried to keep up with the latest theories in education and child rearing, she was quite indifferent to fashion in children's clothing. For instance, while my classmates wore knee socks, I had to wear long, cotton stockings. Many of the little girls' panties matched their dresses, which could be tucked inside the elasticized tops when they jumped rope. My panties not only didn't match but were buttoned to my pantywaist. Worst of all were my tightly fitted leather leggings, one for each leg, fastened by long rows of shoe buttons. I would spend what seemed like half the recess period left alone in the cloakroom struggling with those buttons. The other girls had wool leggings to match their coats—tapered trousers with only a short slit to get over their shoes. Of course these had a few buttons as it was before we had zippers, but they were much easier to manage and much warmer than my old-fashioned leather ones.

Mother also did not realize how segregated age groups had become in the larger schools compared to her country school of thirty-five years earlier. One day when I was in third grade she casually asked if I ever ate lunch with Vera Warbasse. I looked at her in astonishment and exclaimed, "But Mother, she's in the fifth grade!" It was evident that my mother had no idea of the social world in which I had to navigate.

Who did I eat lunch with? I have no idea. Perhaps with Martha Parks, the tallest girl in the class who was always placed at the end of the line behind me, the next tallest, or maybe with Elizabeth Carroll, an only child with long brown curls, whose mother used to arrange to have one or another of us come play with her after school. But most likely I ate lunch with my quiet friend, Edith Smith. Through us my parents became friends with her beautiful, widowed mother. They would invite the family, which included her brother, Alfred, who was in Jerry's class at Polly Prep, for an occasional weekend at Duck Island. In this way Edie and I kept up our friendship even though after third grade she went to Adelphi and I to Shore Road Academy.

Edie and I became neighbors when our family moved to Clinton Avenue in 1925 as she lived just two blocks down the street. Entering high school together, back at Packer, we clung to each other as we suffered being newcomers all over again. We certainly did eat lunch together that first dismal year—every single day in the noisy cafeteria. Eventually we made other friends and felt accepted. But our glory came when we joined the first class at Bennington where we shared in the excitement of helping to form a new college. Edie and I have remained close friends ever since.

Shore Road Academy 1924-1926

John Dewey's philosophy of education greatly influenced my parents, especially as Dad had known him in the "X" club. They were excited about his theories of "learning by doing" and "educating the whole child" which were being tried out in the new progressive schools that sprang up after the war. When the Smileys, a Quaker family who ran a resort at Lake Mohonk near New Paltz, NY, opened a boarding school for boys there in 1920, Miner was promptly enrolled. He was only nine and the youngest in the class. Likewise Raymond, at age four, became a charter member of the Ethical Culture School down the block from us on South Oxford Street. Marion went there later and at fourth grade entered Woodward School newly established two blocks from us on Clinton Avenue by my first grade teacher from Friends.

Her move was explained on the grounds that, in addition to being spared the trolley ride, Marion would be happier in the less intense atmosphere of the new school. Much later we learned the whole story. By the end of third grade Marion, who we now realize was suffering from dyslexia, had not yet learned to read. Her teacher had given up on her and told my parents, "You must not expect much of this child." My father, who rarely showed anger, was indignant that the school could not recognize his daughter's intelligence. Marion thrived at Woodward where she was given a wide range of activities and was appreciated for the bright child that she was. Somehow, before the year was out, she learned to read. She grew up to become the most highly educated member of the family.

My turn to be volunteered as a guinea pig came when our next-door neighbors, Miss Silver and Miss Goldsmith, started Shore Road Academy. They had found a spacious house in Bay Ridge overlooking New York Harbor. On its beautiful grounds was a greenhouse where each girl could have the hands-on experience of cultivating her own little garden plot. Perhaps that's what sold my parents.

The school started at fifth grade, but the fact that I was only at fourth grade didn't trouble anyone. My January birthday made me a borderline case anyway, and it was assumed that somehow or other I'd learn long division and whatever else is covered in fourth grade. A more serious difficulty was the distance, considerably farther than Packer on Brooklyn Heights. Instead of a short ride on the street car or a half hour walk with my father on his way to work, I would have to take the subway. It was a ten-minute walk down Hanson Place and across Flatbush Avenue to the Pacific Avenue station on the BMT, then a half hour ride to 82nd Street and a short walk to the school. At least I would be going against the rush hour traffic and Jerry could help me learn the way. He was attending Polly Prep and got off at Dyker Heights, the next stop after mine and the end of the line.

Nobody seemed concerned that I might miss my friends at Packer, perhaps because I hadn't shown evidence of strong friendships there. Most of the girls at Shore Road came from the area, so those who didn't already know each other had the possibility of getting together for play after school. Once again I felt like an outsider even though we were all of us newcomers.

In order to avoid my becoming too tired, arrangements were made for me to stay two nights a week with Mrs. Butler, a teacher who lived near the school. She and her grown-up daughter were nice enough. They let me help fix the salads for dinner with a blob of mayonnaise, which was new to me as we always had French dressing on our salads at home. I enjoyed whipping cream to top a pudding or other dessert. After supper there was time for only a short game before I had to go to bed. Mother had declared 7:30 as bedtime, an edict Mrs. Butler was more conscientious in carrying out than Mother was, or maybe I was just more compliant away from home. Consequently I would lie awake for a long time. On windy nights I could hear the bell buoy ringing out in the harbor. I even wrote a poem about it.

For the most part schoolwork went pretty well. In fact I got along better with the teachers than with the other girls. In their eyes, no doubt, I was the teacher's pet, which was another obstacle in my social life. For instance, there was the matter of my winning a prize for the best garden. It all happened by default.

Each girl was assigned a small section of bench in the greenhouse for her garden. We planted calendulas, nasturtiums, baby's breath, and other flowers. The sweet peas were always at the back of the plot where strings for them to climb on hung from a wire strung the length of the bench. There were variations in layouts with miniature paths separating the flowerbeds, but by mid-November, when our seedlings were only an inch or two high, there was little to distinguish one plot from another.

Then one girl got the idea of decorating her garden for Christmas by placing small ornaments along its borders. Others followed suit. The competition escalated. Stars, Santas, and angels dangled from the sweet pea wires. Some even covered the soil with artificial snow, smothering the parched seedlings. Meanwhile I continued to water my plants because I couldn't think up a stunning display to impress my classmates. Besides I had no opportunity to shop for decorations and surely would not think of asking Mother for some.

Just before Christmas vacation the prize for the best garden was announced. Much to my embarrassment, mine was declared the winner because it was the only one with healthy vegetation. I felt like a hypocrite. Those teachers didn't know how gladly I would have abandoned their pet project for the silly decorating game if only I had been invited to join in.

My real triumph at Shore Road came that spring. We were studying the ancient Greeks, and our teacher had been reading aloud *The Children's Homer* by Padraic Colum. She suggested that we put on a play about the Trojan War. To try out for the part of Achilles, she selected the scene where he is sulking in his tent after his quarrel with Agamemnon. Odysseus comes as an envoy to try to persuade Achilles to rejoin the battle because Agamemnon is in trouble. Achilles replies "Deem'st thou I grieve for Agamemnon's griefs, Odysseus?" After each girl spoke this line, in a bland little-girl voice, the teacher would protest, "No, no. Don't you see he is angry?" While I waited I was working myself up to such a state of imagined rage that, when my turn came, my face flushed red as I sputtered out those archaic words. That landed me the part of the great hero, the height of my dramatic career.

Going to School in Northport

I stayed at Shore Road Academy for another year before going away to boarding school for seventh and eighth grade. Meanwhile, I had three short intervals of public schooling in Northport, my only experience with co-education except for Friends. After settling in at Duck Island in 1923, Mother was reluctant to move back to Brooklyn at the end of summer, so she used to send us to the village school for a few weeks.

The first Northport school I attended was an old, beat-up building behind the church and monument on Church Street. The next year I went to a brand new brick structure on Laurel Avenue which housed all the grades through high school. A bus picked me up at the entrance to the causeway, half a mile from our house. While I do not now regret the experience, it was a difficult one for me at the time. As a summer person I felt like an intruder. I strove to learn new rules and procedures, and to make myself as inconspicuous as possible. Since I was there for only a few weeks, neither my parents nor my teachers took my studies seriously, but I did.

The crisis came in the sixth grade over geography homework. We were learning about South America. The assignment was to write the answers to questions at the end of the chapter, such as "what are the products of Chile?" By the time dinner was over and I turned to my homework, it was already late. I must have worked myself up to a state. Mother tried to convince me that the homework was not as important as getting to bed, and I tried to convince her otherwise.

The upshot was that I came to school with no homework. When the boy assigned to collect our papers came to my row, I slipped a blank sheet among the others as they passed. I hoped he wouldn't notice, but he did. In a loud voice he announced that my paper had no writing on it. I was overcome by embarrassment. However, the teacher just told the boy to go on with his job of collecting the rest. She never said a word to me about that empty sheet of paper, thus confirming my feeling that she didn't care.

380 Clinton Avenue—1925

My parents had always admired the handsome brick colonial house that their friends, the Leibmans, had built at the turn of the century, so when it came up for sale they jumped at the chance to buy it. I was inattentive to the preparations that had been going on for weeks, so the reality of the move did not hit me until the day itself.

On that fateful morning, as I was about to set off for school, I was reminded to come home to the new house. When I protested that I wouldn't know how to find it, my parents tried to assure me that I would because we had taken the five minute walk over there just the other day. No doubt they thought I had learned the route, but they couldn't convince me that I had. So they reviewed the directions: when I reach South Oxford Street cross Fulton to Greene; go past the Cumberland movie theater and on up Greene just a few blocks to Vanderbilt which has the streetcar tracks; the next street will be Clinton Avenue; turn left and the third house is 380.

It must have been late fall because by the time I got off the subway that afternoon it was nearly dark. I hurried up familiar Hanson place to South Oxford and crossed Fulton to Greene. Then began a close scrutiny of each street sign as I trudged along. After Cumberland came Carlton and the Adelphi. My anxiety rose with every block and the growing darkness. Surely Vanderbilt must be next, but no, the sign read Claremont. Thankfully, at the next corner there were Vanderbilt's car tracks, so I knew Clinton was only one more block. What a relief!

Then I wasn't sure I was at the right house. It did look different at night with lights shining through tall uncurtained windows. But there, etched on the glass in the arch above the front door, were the gold numerals, 380. Still, I felt uneasy as I rang the doorbell of this strange house that was to be my new home. I expected my family would be at least as relieved to see me as I was to find them, but I was greeted casually as if it had been an ordinary day.

It took me a long time to feel at home in that big house. It lacked the coziness of South Oxford. Most of the furniture was new. The old round oak dinner table and chairs were relegated to the kitchen. The new dining room table was an impressive, large rectangle, wide enough to seat two at an end when necessary. Together with the heavy chairs and sideboard, it had been acquired by Mr. Macomber, the architect who had remodeled the Duck Island house. He also found, or had made, four wrought iron candelabras each with five candles. Standing five feet tall at the corners of the table, they contributed an enchanting glow to Mother's dinner parties. They went to Mario who has given all but one away to special people in her life.

In time I came to love the Clinton Avenue house. Though large, it was well proportioned, actually wider than it was deep. Tall, arched windows flooded the living room with morning sun, and big windows throughout the house gave much more light than at South Oxford Street. From an ample entrance hall, the stairs turned up a square stairwell lighted by a skylight. The comfortably furnished living room was on the left with the dining room behind it. The equivalent space on the right was split between a more formal music room/parlor, a starkly plain office with my parents' two desks, and the kitchen. The pantry was behind the stairs.

Further description of the house will probably emerge when I recount my high school years, but first I want to tell about Duck Island.

Duck Island: 1922 ff

The acquisition of Duck Island was a stroke of good luck that fulfilled my parents' dream of owning their own place in the area where they had rented for a dozen summers. Lying directly across Northport Bay from the Centerport house, it is not really an island, but rather an offshoot of Asharoken Beach connected by a half-mile of causeway. The causeway and Duck Island itself gracefully extend the curve of the beach on the bay side. On the other side lies Duck Island Harbor, formed by Eaton's Neck which projects northward into Long Island Sound. The island, also a half-mile long, has wooded bluffs at either end and a low, narrow center section. All told it covers forty-four acres.

One day in the spring of 1922, Henry Ingraham, who had a beach house on Asharoken, phoned my parents to tell them that Duck Island had just been put on the market at a bargain price. Knowing that his sister and brother-in-law, Edith and Miner Crary, were also looking for a summer place, he saw Duck Island as ideal for our two families. Mother and Dad quickly conferred with Uncle Miner and Aunt Edith who agreed to the purchase. They set up the Duck Island Corporation to own and maintain the entire property. Then we bought from the corporation the existing house at the near end of the island and the Crarys bought the undeveloped bluff at the far end. The low price was attributed to a recent murder and suicide. The owner had been living alone in the big house, which she and her first husband, a Mr. Henderson, had built. She had told her gardener/caretaker, who lived in a small house near where Ray's is now, to protect her from her estranged third husband, Mr. Hemming. When he appeared the gardener shot him and then killed himself. However, the fact that the well had turned brackish may have had more to do with devaluing the property than the double murder. It had been dug six hundred feet deep back in 1890, but eventually sea water had seeped in.

Miner (Jerry), baby Agnes, Raymond, and Marion   Miner, Raymond, Asho, and Marion

Below: young Ray, Asho, Jerry, Mario on Poppy with Marion

Above: Mario, Jerry, Ray, Asho

Below: Ray, Asho, Marion, Mario

Water proved to be a more difficult problem for Uncle Miner than for us. We managed to dig three shallow wells that lasted until we got town water in 1929, although in dry spells we had to resort to using rainwater from the cistern to flush the toilets. After all attempts to reach fresh water at their end of the island failed, the Crarys had to wait for the town hook-up before they could start building.

Until they did, we had the freedom to enjoy their unspoiled woods. A steep narrow path led up to the point, the destination of our walks and pony rides. There we came out on to a small clearing and a wide view of Northport and Huntington Bays. That was the spot where Jerry and I camped out once. Below us an old seawall, topped with a layer of red sandstone, circled the point. It was fun to walk along it when the tide was high and came half way up the wall. In a heavy wind the waves would dash spray so high we could see it from our house.

That far end of the island seemed much larger and steeper before the house, garage, stables, and graded driveway took up much of the space. There was more extensive marsh too before the Crarys dredged out the tidal pond to form their garden and ball field. In those days Duck Island was, in proportion to our size, a vast territory inviting exploration.

This may be a good place to tell about my older brother's name change. He was named after Mother's brother, Miner, who had brought Mother and Dad together. When our uncle subsequently married and named his son Miner there was no problem because they lived far away in Warren. But after the joint purchase of Duck Island the prospect of three Miners in one place seemed confusing to say the least. My parents' solution was to change my brother's name to Jerry after grandfather Crary. That happened the summer we moved into the Duck Island house when he was twelve. I remember Dad took Miner on a train trip to see the west, and when he came back he was Jerry. Upon his return to school in the fall, a teacher persuaded him that "Jerry" sounded like a nickname and that he should have a real name which would be more dignified. So he became Jeremiah Crary Ingersoll. That was the same teacher who later told Raymond that he was not as smart as his brother. Ray and I think Jerry should have stuck with our grandfather's plain and simple Jerry Crary, because both the man and his name had ample dignity.

Renovating the rather ugly, nondescript house presented several problems to our architect, Mr. Macomber. He had many ideas for modernization while also achieving an early American look. First he tackled the driveway. The best feature of the house was its fine view of Northport Bay through the trees, but a circular drive took up most of the space between the house and the bank. By relocating the front door and the driveway to the north side we gained a larger lawn and a view unobstructed by automobiles. The driveway was shorter too as it was closer to the entrance road.

Next, nobody liked the way the house sat up high on its foundations, requiring several steps to reach the porch on the south side. Since we couldn't bring the house closer to the ground, Mr. Macomber proposed bringing the ground up to the house. This was an ambitious undertaking in those days before modern earth moving equipment. The job of transferring soil from an area below the slope on the west up to the house was accomplished by a team of horses dragging a big scoop. The driver would hold up the two handles at an angle so the scoop would scrape up enough dirt to fill it. Then he would pull down the handles and the team would drag the scoop up the slope to where the driver would dump it by tipping it over. Finally we had a fine front yard only one step down from a flagstone porch along the end of the living room. The excavated area became my mother's large vegetable and flower garden. Over the next few years we found several Indian arrowheads there.

On the new lawn in the square formed by the living room and the dining room, they planted a good-sized maple tree, a gift from grandfather Crary. I remember how Mother would line us up to ceremoniously water grandfather's tree. She was proud to tell anyone how they had laid around the tree a circle of drainage tile connected to the down spout to carry rain water from the roof to the tree's roots. The maple thrived under our loving care. It became a favorite climbing tree for us children and later for the grandchildren. With lawn chairs scattered under its summer shade, it was the center of our outdoor living.

A stone stoop ran along the full length of the dining room porch and attached to it was a low semi-circular wall enclosing a fish pond. The fish never did very well, but it was a fine place to launch our toy boats. However it was an awkward structure, so when the arrival of grandchildren made Mother aware of its hazards, she was glad to have it filled in and converted to a brick terrace. This gave her an excuse to further develop the "arbor" garden, a space around the corner on the east side of the dining room and partially enclosed by a grape arbor projecting from the end of the kitchen wing. Near the back door, which we used when we came in from swimming, was a footbath with a faucet. This conveniently provided water for a narrow ditch Mother had dug down the center of the garden. The "rill," as she called it, was edged with pretty flowers and ended in a small, ground-level pool. Water lilies and other water plants made this pond much more habitable for goldfish than the old one. The large outdoor fireplace over the edge of the bank was a much later project.

The house itself was the shape of a short-stemmed "T." A wisteria vine was planted by a trellis on the chimney to the right of the entranceway. Eventually it reached above the second floor windows bringing its delicious fragrance into the guest room. Inside the front door the living room was to the west of the center hall, the kitchen wing on the east and the dining room extended to the south. There was a screened porch at the end of each wing. Originally there were three chimneys, one at the north end of the living room, one on the east side of the dining room and one for the kitchen. However, Mr. Macomber did not like the position of the fireplace in the living room, so he turned it into a cupboard where we kept our home movie projector and reels of film. A new chimney and fireplace were built along the longer west wall. This not only made for better furniture arrangement, but was the setting for the lovely old pine paneling which had somehow been retrieved from an old house in New England. In places for which there was no paneling, new woodwork was cleverly made to match. With hooked rugs on the floor it all came together as a charming, warm room. The walls in the rest of the house, except for Jerry's small paneled "cabin," were left plain white plaster, which made for a clean, fresh look.

Attractive though the living room was, the dining room took the prize. A row of casement windows ran along the south end and around the corner to the east giving a fine view of the bay and the sound. A long oak table was placed parallel to the front windows where we always made sure our guests were seated facing the view. The table had been built right there in the house and was wired so that lamps could be set at either end. Thin pear-shaped pieces of wood, a temptation to play with, covered the two sockets, while the table was plugged into another socket in the floor. A bay window on the west looking out on to Grandfather's tree made space for a small, octagonal children's table. A high wing chair by the fireplace, an upright piano on the opposite wall and a sideboard completed the furnishings. Later Mother had a small writing desk and the fainting couch under the east windows. Ellen now has the couch and the octagonal table while Mario took the oak dining table to Squam. A second oak table, somewhat smaller, is in Ray and Elex's living room.

Upstairs there were plenty of bedrooms for our frequent guests. Two hallways diverged at right angles at the top of the stairs while a third, leading to the back stairs and maids' rooms, was closed off by a door. One hall went to my parents' room over the living room porch, passing my room and then Marion's on the left. To the right the guest room, later called the "bird" room, overlooked the front driveway. The other hall ended at the bunkroom over the dining porch. After two steps it passed another door to my room on the right and then jogged to the left. This corridor was lighted by a long row of windows looking out to the maple tree. Jerry's cabin, Raymond's room and a spare room all looked over the arbor garden and the marsh to the sound. There was a fireplace in the cabin and one in the guest room too. The special feature of my room was that it had a little drawer in a step in front of the door leading to the children's wing.

However, I much preferred sleeping in the bunkroom. It had a great view of the sound out its east window and of the bay through the row along the long south wall. Opposite these were two pairs of bunk beds placed end to end with a narrow set of steps between. One pair was a few inches shorter than standard length as they had been made to fit the space. Usually Jerry would sleep in the longer of the top bunks and I in the shorter, but whoever had a friend visiting was allowed to take over. Sharing confidences at night in the bunkroom was a very special way to solidify a friendship. Later, after my father died in 1940, Mother moved to the bunkroom. Because it was really quite narrow, she widened it by knocking out the wall to the spare room next door. The bunks were dispersed to the grandchildren and eventually to the next generation.

But why am I spending so much time indoors when outside is where the action was?

Jerry was the instigator of adventures, and I his happy follower. Sometimes he led me into situations that were scary. For instance there was the wild ride down the gutter. At the time we moved to Duck Island, a new concrete gutter had been made beside the road that went up the hill from the beach. It was about three feet wide and gently curved. That gleaming white path cried out for travel, but what could we use for a vehicle? The only thing available was the younger children's' kiddy car. Jerry found he could sit on it with his legs out straight in front of him. He had me give him a push, and off he went. After one or two spills he mastered the technique and made it safely to the bottom of the hill.

Then it was my turn. Jerry instructed me not to over steer and to be sure to keep my feet up so they would not trip me. Fearful that I would let my legs sag, I held my whole body tensely rigid. He gave me a little push. Sure enough, I found myself going too far to one side and I over corrected by steering too far the other way. The zigzags widened as the momentum increased. I was totally out of control. Before I knew it I crashed. In spite of scrapes and bruises I was thankful to be off that runaway kiddy car.

Another risky activity was melting lead. Of course we knew we needed to be very careful because it was extremely hot and could cause a severe burn. However we were innocently unaware of the dangers of lead poisoning. What the lead was doing there near the garage, I don't know, nor what sort of fire Jerry used. He handled the whole operation, while I was just an observer. As the dull lead came to a boil it turned bright and shiny like the quicksilver we used to catch in a glass jar whenever a thermometer broke. We knew mercury was poisonous and were careful not to touch it. Jerry used to sing a song on that subject to the tune of "The Last Rose of Summer."

> Little Johnny had a mirror, and he chewed the back all off,
> Thinking in his childish terror it would cure the whooping cough.
> Some days later Johnny's mother, sobbing, said to Mts. Brown,
> "'Twas a chilly day for Johnny when the mercury went down."

Once we had melted the lead, we looked for small containers to serve as molds. Seashells were good for this purpose, especially scallop shells. Sadly, when the molten lead cooled it became dull again. I'm sure some adult soon put a stop to our enterprise, but not before we made several scallop shell paperweights. Mother kept one of these for years.

All this reminds me of how much fun we used to have catching scallops in the early days. Unlike the more prevalent mussels, clams, and oysters, which stay on the bottom, scallops swim. Their two symmetrical, fan-shaped shells are hinged at the base and are connected in the center by a strong muscle. This wedged-shaped muscle is the part we eat. It enables the scallop to swim by rapidly snapping its shells together. The eyes are a row of many brightly colored dots in the fringe of soft tissue. Scallops fed on eelgrass, which grew low on the bottom of protected waters like Duck Island Harbor. Our search for them was near the narrow section of the island across the road from our dock and bathing beach. At about half tide we would wade in with our buckets and nets. If we were lucky we would come across a bunch of scallops. They would swim around our legs so fast that we had to act quickly before they got away. We would reach down and pick them up with our hands or scoop them up with our nets. Come to think of it, their fluttery motion is something like that of butterflies, only they don't open up as wide.

Jerry was our expert cleaner of scallops. He would pry open the shell with his knife, slice off the muscle close to the shell on one side, scrape the innards away, and then slice the scallop off the other shell. He could do this in record time as documented in one of our first home movies. Those small, delicate scallops, sautéed and served with bacon, were delicious! Unfortunately, the eelgrass disappeared from the bays and harbors of western Long Island in the early thirties, and the scallops with it. There still were plenty of clams, both soft shell for steaming and hard shell for chowder, as well as mussels and oysters.

In calm weather when the tide was halfway out, the clammers would appear on the bay, several right off our shore. Each clammer stood alone in his small rowboat working a pair of long-handled rakes. These had curved tines which fitted together to make a basket. When he had raked together a load the clammer would lift it out of the water and dump it in his boat. These were hard shell clams. Now-a-days the clammers use bright-colored tarpaulins for sails and drag a basket along the bottom. Oyster beds were marked by stakes further out in the water. They were leased from the county and seeded by an oyster company whose motorboats would harvest them at the proper time. The oysters are gone, but we can still dig for soft shell clams at low tide right on our own beach and gather mussels off the rocks at the Crary's point.

Walks along the beaches presented a fascinating variety of shells. I was particularly fond of some small, translucent, yellow and gold ones. Most were shaped like little bowls, but some were simply flat disks which we called toenails. We called another sturdier little shell a boat, because it had a shelf at one end like a seat. We found these, along with various snail, clam, oyster, mussel, and scallop shells, on the beach in front of our house. The sound beach, whose finer sand made it seem like an ocean shore, gave us special treasures. The most beautiful was the whelk. It is like a conch with a tapered stem. Dried whelk egg cases made fine rattles. They were coils of paper-thin disks with tiny baby whelk shells inside each one. Egg cases of the skate, black rectangles with log spikes at each corner, were aptly named devil's purses. Then there were razor clam shells and dried starfish.

Back on the bay side, in the tangle of brown bladder kelp which marked the high tide line, we often found horseshoe crab shells. The top is like an inverted shallow bowl and hinged to it is a tapered section ending in a long spike of a tail. The shells came in all sizes since the crab discards them as it grows. Naturally I preferred the delicate little ones. Sometimes we found dead horseshoe crabs, admittedly unattractive as they stank. My visiting friends were thoroughly repulsed by the dead ones and terrified of the live ones. The latter are rather startling when they appear as a dark shadow sliding along the bottom, but they won't hurt you because their claws are underneath. Jerry would even pick one up by the tail placing it upside down on the beach so we could watch how it used its tail to right itself. It would stick its tail in the sand, arch its back, rotate sideways, and flip over.

While the ugly horseshoe crabs looked threatening but were harmless, the beautiful pink umbrella jellyfish trailed mean stinging tentacles. Painful experience quickly taught us to avoid them, but we could play with a colorless variety which floated like an elongated ball with faint white streaks. These glowed with phosphorescence on August nights. When we scooped one out of the water it collapsed into a slimy glob. The same was true of the fragile forms of seaweed such as green sea lettuce and several branching types in shades of red. A neighbor, Cora Carter, used these to decorate stationery and greeting cards. She showed us the technique. First you soak the seaweed in fresh water overnight. Then you arrange a few pieces in a shallow dish of clean water. The trick was to slip a card under them, and then carefully lift it out without letting the seaweed slide off. As the card dried the seaweed would meld into it, but my clumpy creations never achieved Mrs. Carter's artistry.

We tried fishing off the float at the end of the dock. Once Jerry had been pulling in several flounders, when much to my surprise I found one on my line. At dinner that evening I proudly ate my first fish, but it must have been my last as I can't remember ever having caught another. Ray reminds me how the blowfish would puff themselves up with water to look fierce when we frightened them. We would herd them toward the shore where they would become stranded on the beach, collapsing as they spluttered out the water. He also tells of skinning eels. A nail would be hammered through an eel's head on the side of the barn and a cut made in the skin just below the head. Then, using a piece of sandpaper to grasp the slippery skin, it was pulled down like rolling off a silk stocking, but I'm sure I avoided that scene.

The most unusual marine creature we ever encountered at Duck Island appeared soon after we moved there. One day the collie who belonged to Mr. Steele, our caretaker, came limping up to the house with a bleeding leg. We wondered how he had been wounded. A few hours later we saw a strange lump, like a large stone, slowly moving across the front lawn. It was a huge turtle nearly two feet long. It stood high on sturdy legs, not flippers like a true sea turtle, and it had a domed back. Nevertheless it was presumed that it was a sea turtle, rather than a land tortoise, and that it had bitten the dog and followed the trail up to the house. When we saw how easily it snapped a stick in two, we kept a respectful distance from its powerful jaws. We kept him in the fishpond by the dining room porch for a few days. Then he disappeared. I would like to think he was returned to the water, but suspect that Mr. Steele may have cooked it up for soup.

The tides, like the seasons, gave predicable variety to our lives, both visual and practical, such as marking the best time of day to go swimming. Usually we swam in the bay, either at the dock or at the foot of the hill below the house. The beach starts at the top with a narrow strip of sand, then small pebbles grading to large stones and finally to muck at low tide. Sharp shells embedded in the mud add hazard to its "uckiness." Given the fact that at low tide one had to wade out much further to reach a swimmable depth and that even the float at the end of the dock was in shallow water, we always tried to swim at or near high tide. However, we did occasionally swim in the sound as the bottom there was sandy even at low tide. We entered across the road from the entrance to our causeway. Ours was the last driveway on Asharoken Avenue, and from there on the beach stretched for a good mile to Eaton's Neck, unmarred by any houses. We did not swim in Duck Island Harbor as our end of it was too thick with marsh grass, but it was ideal for ducks and herons.

Mother was quite expert at identifying each of the several kinds of ducks that frequented our waters. Birds were her life-long love, but I did not share her enthusiasm as I was too impatient to notice fine distinctions or to learn to use bird glasses. Although I have never mastered the binoculars, over time, in my own way, I have come to love birds too. It is always a thrill, returning to Duck Island, to spot a white egret or a great blue heron in the mud flats.

For a while Jerry was the budding young ornithologist of the family. When he was about fourteen, Mother hooked him into bird banding. He became one of the thousands of volunteers registered with the proper bureau in Washington to track bird migrations. They supplied him with record sheets and numbered aluminum bands. His other equipment consisted of a pair of small pliers, a bird trap, and bait. He became adept at gently holding a bird lying on its back in the palm of one hand while putting a band around its leg with the other. We younger children would let him know when we saw a bird in his trap. Often it was one he had already banded who was just coming back for more food. Towhees, which we called chewinks, were frequent repeaters and he came to know them as individuals. But the real excitement came the next summer when some of his old friends returned.

About this time Mother formed a Woodcraft group with some of our younger teen-age neighbors, including Polly and Gardner Ingraham. Woodcraft, largely based on Indian lore, was started by the naturalist and artist, Ernest Thompson Seton, in 1902. Many of his ideas were adopted by Colonel Baden Powell when he founded the Boy Scouts in England. The two men worked together to establish the Boy Scouts of America, but after a while Seton broke with the organization because he found it too militaristic. The Woodcraft League became co-educational after the war.

My parents had attended some of Seton's popular lectures in which he told stories of animals he had observed in the wild, and Mother had gone to a few meetings of the Woodcraft League, but I doubt if she was any better prepared for her undertaking than I was when I became a Cub Scout den leader. At least my den was part of an established troop, but she was on her own with only the *Birch Bark Roll* as her guide. However, Ray remembers Mr. Seton actually came to Duck Island once, so maybe she had more help than I was aware of. Her project must have been brewing for some time, because when we built (or remodeled) the stable and workshop by the garage she had built a rather large room at one end. It had tall windows on three sides looking out onto the woods and she called it the Woodcraft room. Weather permitting, the group met in the council circle, a clearing in the woods halfway between the garage and our picnic point. They were supposed to earn little embroidered feathers called coups for various accomplishments.

What the Woodcrafters actually did in their council meetings I do not know, for unfortunately I was too young to be a member. By the time I was old enough they had long since ceased to be. I had to content myself with imagining all the ingenious things I might make to survive in the woods like the boys did in Seton's *Two Little Savages*. That book absorbed me for the whole summer when I was ten.

One other small compensation came my way. Some of those same big kids formed their own club called "The Terrible Ten." Perhaps their primary purpose was to think up good initiations which could be why they decided to let in some of us younger ones. The initiations took place at the Shotwell farm belonging to the Ingrahams' grandparents. One of the boys had to jump off a beam in the barn into the hay, but Winifred Ingraham and I were to be tossed in a blanket. With some apprehension I managed to get up on to the blanket, which was held on four sides by the club members. Then with a shout of "One, two, three, heave" up I went. It turned out to be fun!! Another two or three tosses completed my initiation. Polly's assertion that I had done well raised my triumph to pure joy.

When we moved to Duck Island of course Poppy, our speckled Indian pony, came with us. She had a paddock along the side of the road between the end of the garden and where the tennis court was eventually built, at which time a new one was fenced off behind the garage and stable.

Poppy was strong-willed and clever. For instance, she soon found that a certain apple tree had a low, horizontal limb just high enough for her to go under. Whenever anyone except Jerry rode her, she would make a beeline for that tree and dash under the limb, effectively pushing her rider off on to the ground. After a few tumbles I learned that if I paid close attention and used all my strength on the reins, I could keep her away from that trap. Visitors, even though forewarned, usually got dumped.

For a while we had a second Indian pony, named Marble Cake, because of his large, brown and white patches. He was more docile, but slow and reluctant. When Jerry became too big for ponies, we traded Marble Cake for a horse. Woody was a high-spirited bay with a silver mane and a silver tail. We were told he had played polo in his younger days. He was a challenge, even for Jerry, and eventually for me. At some point I too outgrew Poppy, so we sold her, to a caring family, I trust, and bought another horse. By the time I reached high school and Jerry was away at college, that horse too was gone. All we had left was Woody, my solace and soul mate.

During Jerry's high school years riding provided us with a very special companionship. We would keep the horses at a trot along the causeway, but when we reached the shore at the east end of the harbor away we would gallop. On our return we would always slow down when we came to the lone cedar, which had acquired a Japanese look. We rode all over Eaton's Neck where dirt roads ran through woods and past fields. Our destination might be the lighthouse or the old sand excavation, which we called Sand City. A favorite spot was the sluice near Winkle Point where the tide rushed in and out through a narrow channel. We would sometimes tie the horses to a tree and take a swim in the current. Eaton's Neck had only a scattering of summer homes then, but now the entire area has become suburbanized.

I was always impressed by Jerry's superior knowledge and glad when he passed some of it on to me, such as how to tie a square knot instead of a sissy granny knot. I completely trusted him, except when he teased me. An example of my trust was the time we camped out on the Crary's point. I had already settled into my sleeping bag when Jerry realized he had forgotten some essential item for breakfast. He would have to walk the half-mile back to the house to get it, but first he asked if I would be afraid.

"What is there to be afraid of?" I asked.

"Nothing," he replied.

Assured that there was no danger, I sent him on his way. Later Mother told me how proud Jerry was of me for not being afraid to be left alone so far from home. Though pleased by his praise, I was puzzled that he should think me brave when he had told me I was quite safe, and wasn't Mother herself always fearless?

Jerry trusted me too. One day I discovered two perfect little hiding places in my bedroom. After removing the small drawer from the step at one of the doors, I found a little compartment on either side of the opening. I shared my secret with Jerry and let him have one side in which he hid a box marked "Private, Keep Out!" Well, of course curiosity got the better of me.

Guiltily I opened the box to take a peek. There, to my surprise, was a booklet on the anatomy of sex. My curiosity came to an abrupt halt. Handling the box like a hot potato, I hastily returned it to its hiding place, and never touched it again.

Early on, Jerry learned the way through the attic to the trap door to the roof and soon had me following him. Stairs in the back hall led to a floored attic under the high pitched roof of the dining room wing, but the area under the flat part had no floor boards and only a dim light at the near end. Stepping very carefully on the beams so as not to break through the ceiling below, we would grope along until we came to the ladder. What a relief when Jerry climbed it, pushed off the lid and there was the bright sky! It was a thrill to be way up high looking out over familiar territory from this new perspective.

The flat section of the roof was covered with copper. It was an area about ten by twenty feet over the center parts of the front hall and living room. Wood shingles sloped off the two sides and the west end to the living room chimney. At the east end was the start of the peaked roof of the dining room wing. At first it was excitement enough just to be up there, but after a while we found that we could slide down the short distance to the living room chimney. With our feet braced against it, this was a comfortable hideout as the shingles were not as hot as the tin roof. This was plenty good enough for me, but Jerry felt compelled to venture out to the dining room chimney, which required straddling the peaked roof and hitching oneself along for quite a distance. It really did take courage to follow him as the ground on either side looked mighty far away. The thought of rolling down that steep roof kept me from trying it again.

When Mother saw what a good time we were having on the roof she decided to improve access so she and our guests could enjoy it too. Fortunately the ladder in the attic was directly above the hall leading to the west bedrooms, so it was an easy matter to put a trap door in the ceiling and install a set of steps that could be raised or lowered by a pulley. In addition to its fine view, the roof was a great place for stargazing. I remember especially how Mother would settle down with blankets and pillows to watch the August meteor showers.

Mother's hospitality was expansive as well as expensive, but she prided herself on her informality and simplicity. She staged great steak cookouts at the picnic grounds on the north point beyond the Woodcraft circle. Stones of the right size were collected and a big fire built over them. When hot enough, they were raked out and spread along the bank. After brushing off the ashes and applying a little grease, each person was given a steak or hamburger to cook to his or her own taste. The feast ended when Dad, flourishing a big butcher knife, cracked open a luscious watermelon which had been chilled in a washtub of ice water.

A rare treat was making maple sugar. A kettle of maple syrup was hung over the campfire to boil down. Mother would keep testing it by dripping some into a cup of cold water until the drop formed a soft ball. Then she would ladle the thick syrup into small bowls. After letting it cool a while, she gave us each a bowl and a spoon and told us to start stirring. If we could keep beating long enough we would be rewarded with a smooth maple cream, but fatigue and temptation usually won out. Even so, that sticky, sugary mess probably tasted better to us than the more delicate cream did to the grown-ups.

One great advantage Duck Island had over our rented place at Centerport was that we could go there year round. We spent frequent weekends there in the spring and fall and many wonderful Thanksgivings and Christmases. That was when we really appreciated the fireplaces, coming in from a windy walk along the sound beach or popping corn after supper. In the coldest weather we could skate on a fresh water pond that was near where the Long Island Lighting plant is now.

Whatever the season we usually had guests, often whole families. We might not know the children though the adults were friends. I remember once when remote relatives, the Darlings, were visiting, and their two or three children ate with us at the children's table while the grown-ups dined at the big one. As we were sipping our water waiting for Dad to finish carving, Jerry and I learned that our young guests did not know how to gargle. We promptly proceeded to teach them, much to the consternation of our elders. Later Mother told us she was "mortified" at our behavior.

Mother saw to it that no guest departed empty-handed. She would ply them with flowers and vegetables from her ample garden, or, in off seasons, with fruit, branches, or jars of beach plum jelly. She had a special way of wrapping flowers: first she put wet paper towels covered with wax paper around the stems and then she wrapped the whole bunch in several layers of newspaper. Since her bouquets were of generous size in the first place, they became quite bulky bundles. This was all very well if her company had come by automobile, but rather awkward for those who had to take the train and subway. Mother couldn't understand how one teen-aged visitor could be so selfish as to refuse to take flowers home to her mother, but Ray recalls how he enjoyed picking quantities of tulips one spring vacation and, when he drove back to Swarthmore, handing them out to surprised women classmates.

The garden was Mother's pride and joy. Covering nearly an acre of ground below the west slope of the lawn, it was approached by a path through a double row of pink flowering dogwood. Three or four steps down was a terrace eight feet wide along which were planted grape vines. Those grapes, by the way, took an inordinate amount of attention for the few scraggly bunches that escaped hungry birds. On the lower level two privet hedges extended horizontally and wide flowerbeds bordered the central path. The space on either side was laid out in fan and wedge shapes planted in vegetables and flowers. Mother thought the vegetables, especially plump purple eggplants, looked pretty mixed in with the flowers, though this probably made harder work for the gardener.

Early on, Mother found Florence Baker, a landscape architect, to help her. They became fast friends and would spend hours together in the garden planning the blend of colors and the seasonal sequences of bloom. They also developed projects of decorative stonework. The first involved replacing the steps entering the garden, and constructing an octagonal of flagstone on the terrace enclosed by four stone benches. This Dad labeled "Mother's Folly Number One." Folly number two was another circle at the lower end of the central path and extensive stonework, including a fishpond, around the tennis court. Several more follies followed, but the new plantings surrounding each project eventually made the stone blend into the surroundings with charming effect.

Mother was always eager to show off her garden to visitors and annually to the Asharoken Garden club. It was the setting for Mario's summer wedding, when, escorted by Uncle Andy, she followed her many bridesmaids up the center path to the octagonal where Joe was waiting. Four of the nine grandchildren were also married in various parts of the garden. In later years Mother delighted in riding her guests and grandchildren around it in her electric golf cart. By that time she was known to all as Mamo, the name given her by her first grandchild, Andy.

Elex tells of a wild time she and her friends, the Hirths, had helping Mamo plant tulip bulbs. Although nearly ninety, she had ordered as huge a supply as ever, and was determined to supervise their placement. Knowing that this would be an exhausting task, Elex devised a strategy. Al was to drive Mamo in her cart and stop to plant each bulb just where she wanted it. While he was patiently following her instructions, behind their backs Elex and Dee were frantically running around the garden poking bulbs into the ground at random. Before Mamo had a chance to become too fatigued, miraculously all the tulips were planted.

When we had to sell her property after Mother died, I bought the garden to shield Ray and Elex and the tennis court from the big house. This purpose is well served by a tangle of shrubbery at the top of the terrace and by bushes planted along a fence Ray built out to the road. The garden is now mostly in grass, but Elex has kept up the small circle of herbs surrounding the birdbath with the duck faucets. Two beds of rose bushes and some mounds of untrimmed box remain as well as the privet hedges, the quince trees, and the two apple trees Mario and her friends planted to fulfill Mother's wish. Although the garden' s glory is gone, it is still a lovely and peaceful place.

Boarding School 1926-1928

Mother was a great believer in boarding school as a way to foster independence. Her brief stay at Bucknell when she was fourteen and her year or two in Northampton before entering Smith College had been liberating experiences. So she saw to it that each of her children received the benefit of two years of schooling away from home. The results were mixed. Jerry had a rough time at Mohonk, where as a nine-year old he was tormented by a bully. On the other hand, Raymond at ten got along well at Eaglebrook, a school for young boys in Deerfield, Massachusetts. Marion hated Brownmore in spite of horseback riding in its beautiful mountain setting near Santa Fe. She missed the close friends she had made in her four years at Woodward. Most of her girl classmates had gone on to Packer where she was glad to rejoin them in her junior year. But this time I was the lucky one, because boarding school gave me my first best friend.

Holmquist School, on the outskirts of the small artists' community of New Hope, PA, appealed to Mother because it was in picturesque Bucks County. Miss Karlene Holmquist ran the school assisted by her sister, Miss Louise. They lived by the canal, which ran alongside of the Delaware River, in a barn that had been converted into a residence and small dormitory. Across the road was an old mill, which served as a theater for the New Hope community and as a gym for the school. The other school buildings were nearly half a mile up the road on a spacious walled estate with grounds large enough for a hockey field. The original residence housed most of the boarding students while a few lived on the second floor of the newer classroom building.

On the day Mother took me to Holmquist I was quite apprehensive. We were told I was to live in the barn and that Betty McCreery would be my roommate. Would this Betty person think I was a dim wit, I worried. When we found my room, a large one with windows on three sides, there she was sitting on her bed looking bright and friendly. Her mother had already settled her in. Suddenly I was impatient to have my mother leave for fear she would say something embarrassing. When at last she left, I nervously sat down on my bed opposite Betty. Something made her laugh and I joined in. It was instant bonding. From then on our giggles were ready to burst out on the slightest provocation. To this day I marvel at Betty's ability to find something amusing in any situation.

We quickly discovered that our birthdays were two months apart. It was fortunate we hit it off so well as we were the only boarders in the seventh grade that first semester. Our other five classmates were day students, among them Christina Holmquist, niece to Miss Karlene and Miss Louise, as well as Barbara Braden and the Folomsby girl, whose fathers were local artists. Consequently outside of classes Betty and I were constantly together. Once someone misspoke our names calling us Ashy and Betto. From then on Betty was always Betto to me, but I'm glad I didn't become Ashy.

Delightfully free of anxiety, Betto seemed to embody all the traits and skills I lacked. I admired her wit and boldness, her horsemanship and her speed as a runner. She was definitely the leader of our duo. I was happy to fall in with her adventurous schemes, like borrowing trays from the kitchen to go sledding after "lights out" or taking a forbidden swim in the polluted canal on a sweltering day in June. That is probably how I contracted a case of typhoid fever.

Our mischief notwithstanding, we were actually good students. Betto hated math so wondered how I could enjoy it, while I envied her ability to devour three books in the time it took me to plod through one. She loved romantic novels such as *The Three Musketeers* and *Lorna Doone*. We were both fans of Zane Gray, his *Riders of the Purple Sage* being our favorite. The only argument I remember having with Betto was over who was the greatest president. George Washington was her hero and Abraham Lincoln was mine. History later became a favorite subject, but all we had in seventh and eighth grade was social studies, a mishmash of current events, civics, geography, and whatever might occur to our rather eccentric teacher.

Our English teacher commanded more respect. She helped us clarify our writing by teaching us how to diagram sentences. I'm grateful that she assigned memorization of poetry because recalling snatches of verse continues to be a source of pleasure for me. Of course we always found something to laugh at. The stage direction in Shakespeare's *Julius Caesar*, "Thunder and lightning, enter Caesar in his nightgown," struck us as hilarious.

When it came to the extras Betto's mother chose art classes for her and mine selected sewing for me. So two afternoons a week, while Betto had the privilege of walking into New

Hope with one of our classmates to take art from her father, I was stuck in a classroom with our French teacher and poor, dumb Sylvia. She was a big girl of fourteen who must have been somewhat retarded. All the girls teased her mercilessly. Once, believing as I did at the time that a virgin was simply a holy person, she denied that she was one, so they pinned a sign to her back saying "I am not a virgin."

Although I felt sorry for Sylvia, she was no fun, especially under the stern eye of Mademoiselle. Our every stitch was monitored to ensure proper use of our thimbles. Now I can't sew without one. My project was a dress for six-year-old Marion made of a cotton print with little pink roses on a mauve background. I had to embroider pink smoking on the front and sew French seams. That is once with the wrong sides together and back again with the right sides together, all in tiny stitches. Not until twenty years later did I learn to use a sewing machine.

Other afternoons we had riding. Our riding master, Mr. Ely, trained us to ride in drill formation. I never understood how to make my horse change its lead, but Betto was very good at it. She could jump and do circus stunts riding bareback too. Her mother was an accomplished horsewoman and her sister, Honour, a senior at Holmquist, received first prize for horsemanship.

Sundays we walked up the road in our best dresses to a little church, Episcopal I suppose, because we recited the Apostles Creed. This made me feel like a hypocrite. I could not believe it was literally true that Christ "sitteth on the right hand of God," but nobody helped me to understand it as metaphor. However, I always enjoyed singing the hymns even though I can't carry a tune. In the evening we sang more hymns at our own vespers service in the living room of the main house. Christmas caroling was exhilarating as we walked in the snow past moonlit fields.

But Saturday was all for us, free to do as we pleased. What pleased us most was to go exploring. We would follow the creek past the old mill and through a tunnel under the canal to where it emptied into the river. We could walk up the towpath for miles, but that was too monotonous. More challenging was climbing along the top of the wall that surrounded the school grounds. This entailed coping with tangled vines and overhanging branches. Most often we headed west across the fields beyond the school. Sometimes our destination was a stone quarry a mile or two away. Wherever we went we invented an adventurous scenario. Once we imagined that we had been trekking across the desert, we were out of food and water and one of our horses was lame. When we finally reached our room we plopped on our beds in utter exhaustion, relieved to be back to civilization at last. I wish I could remember our other escapades as vividly.

After Christmas vacation that first year, we returned to find another bed in our room and Betsey Waters, our new roommate. We really didn't like her, and felt she was an intruder. She taught us our first dirty jokes. Betto drew a cartoon sketch of a girl in a bathtub filled with black water which she captioned "Dirty Waters in the bathtub" and posted in the bathroom. Of course she was reprimanded for being unkind, but we thought Betsey deserved it. When Betto came home with me for spring vacation at Duck Island, we confided in Mother that we didn't like Betsey, and that she had done things with a boy that we knew were not right. Mother later told me she had called Miss Karlene who in turn called Betsey's mother. The report came back that she was grateful to have been alerted to her daughter's need for guidance. True or not, the upshot was that Betsey did not return to school.

Betto and I were again free to pursue our imaginative adventures. That spring we appreciated our friendship more than ever. Betto gave me confidence to expand as a person. The fact that she found my attempts at humor funny made me feel witty too. However, when my family paid me a visit I was caught in a terrible dilemma. How should I behave? My family knew me as rather serious and shy, though given to sudden outbursts of emotion. Somehow I was afraid to reveal my tentative new self to them. Yet what would Betto think of me if she saw what a dimwit I had reverted to? I felt like a split personality and was overcome by confusion.

All this didn't bother Betto at all. She remembers that visit as the exciting time we had riding around in a car without a door. In those days car doors were hinged on their rear edge to provide easy access. It happened that Mother, not realizing that a rear door was open, had driven too close to some obstacle, which ripped it off. Betto thought it was great fun riding in the exposed back seat with Jerry and watching the amazed expressions on the passers-by. She admired my mother's evident enjoyment of the novelty, but I was embarrassed by her making such a conspicuous fool of herself.

That summer I visited Betto at her family's country home near Cornwallville in Greene County, New York. Although their horses were too skittish for me to ride, we had a lively time exploring her favorite haunts. Then one morning a red spot on my shirt revealed that my first period had arrived. Mother had conscientiously explained the physiology and even anticipated the event by slipping a sanitary napkin into my suitcase, but I didn't know how to use it. Fortunately Betto had been initiated a few weeks earlier and turned to her mother for help. I was deeply grateful to Mrs. McCreery for her comfortably matter-of-fact instructions which eased my embarrassment. She advised not doing anything too strenuous, so Betto and I spent the day lolling about in a hammock trying to feel as grown-up as this milestone was supposed to make us.

In eighth grade Joanne Ball moved in with us. Though not very bright, she was amiable, and we three had fun together. I was heartbroken that I couldn't return to Holmquist the following year, because my parents wanted me home again.

In compensation, our parents arranged a reunion for the three of us the summer after ninth grade, on a six-weeks riding trip in Yellowstone Park and the Tetons. It was a highly organized expedition for sixty or more girls run by Valley Ranch, which had a similar trip for boys. At the end the two groups returned to the ranch for a farewell dance greatly anticipated by many of the girls, but which I found the least enjoyable event of the summer.

While we rode the trails accompanied by counselors and cowboys, another crew drove the chuck wagon and trucks with our duffel to our new campsite where we would find our tents set up in a neat circle. Sometimes they would build a magnificent bonfire around which we would sing cowboy songs along with the usual repertoire. Since we changed tent mates every few days, I didn't see as much of Betto and Joanne as I had anticipated, but I certainly saw some beautiful country! The high point was a gem of a lake way up in the Tetons fed by a glacier in which I took a fleeting dip.

Before starting out from the ranch, each girl chose her own horse. Betto had an experienced eye, but she proved to be too good a judge because each horse she picked already belonged to one of the cowboys. In the end all the good horses were taken and she was stuck with a nag. Meanwhile I spotted a horse with a friendly look in his eye and that was good enough for me. He proved to be quite peppy and kindly responsive to my requests. It was a turnaround to have Betto envying me my mount!

The following summer Betto and her family moved to California, and we didn't see each other again for more than twenty years. However, Mother, believing in the importance of keeping up friendships, wrote her annually and relayed news to each of us. She liked to imagine that long ago in Scotland the Crarys and the McCreerys belonged to the same clan.

Betto was ready for a change as Holmquist left her unchallenged and bored. This led to bolder mischief and finally to a week's suspension. Since her parents were not about to interrupt their annual duck hunting trip to care for a wayward child, she had to stay in the strange household of our social studies teacher while her cohorts were enjoying themselves at home going to the movies.

In California she attended Scripps College and went on to earn a masters in archaeology, digging up evidence of early Indian settlements. She still continues her interest in ancient and modern Native American cultures. During World War II she joined the WAVES, she says to satisfy her mother's wish to carry on the family tradition of sending at least one member to serve in every American war. She was stationed in Portland, Oregon for two and a half years after which she met and married Jerry Everall. He was a store manager for Sears Roebuck, who moved him around frequently.

By the time our two Steve's were five-year olds, Jerry was managing a new store in Wilmington, Delaware, the closest we had ever lived to each other. So I treated Steve and myself to a train ride and a visit. Betto's son called mine Steve Crayon. Not long after, the Everalls, including younger sister Eve, came to see us in Bethesda, but the next year we moved to Ann Arbor.

Our paths did not cross again until 1969 when we were in Washington for Lyle's year with the National Water Commission and Jerry was managing the Wisconsin Avenue Sears. Through us they had become acquainted with Erwin and Cynthia Hannum, and the six of us enjoyed several dinners together. That summer Jerry took early retirement and he and Betto headed for the small ranch they had bought in Prescott, Arizona. When we and the Hannums took our southwestern trip in rented R.V.s in 1978, naturally we visited the Everalls who gave us good advice concerning washed out roads. Ten years later Lyle and I had a pleasant day with them in Green Valley. Then last fall (1993) I had a wonderful five-day visit in Prescott when Betto and I caught up on all these reminiscences.

Chapter 3
High School Years
Packer Collegiate Institute

Re-entering Packer's "old gray ivy walls" at thirteen I felt even more an outsider than I did when a seven year old. Although I recognized some of my former classmates they had become strangers who had much to talk about among themselves but not with me. How could I greet them as if I knew them when we had led such different lives? Then there were all those intimidating new students because the class doubled in size at the high school level. Many wore silk stockings and heels while I stuck with bobby socks and loafers. Worst of all I was fat! I was sure everyone was looking at me with disdain as I hurried through the crowded halls to the safety of my assigned seat in my next class. I usually lingered to the end of the line going into morning chapel because I was too shy to ask someone if I could sit with her. Once it dawned on me that perhaps the other girls were too preoccupied with what others thought about them to notice me, but this revelation was small comfort. I wanted to be noticed, in a nice way, of course.

The day I wore a little glass-studded donkey pin to school I was noticed all right! Everyone jumped on me.

"How can you be for Al Smith, that Catholic?" "He says *ra-adio* instead of *radio*." "Don't you know the Pope would rule the country?" "Who would want Mrs. Smith in the White House?"

My feeble protests that my father knew Governor Smith had done a lot of good things for our state fell on deaf ears. As for the Pope, I realized I was ignorant of his powers, but I knew they did not extend to our government. I'm sorry to say I did not have the courage to wear that donkey pin to school again.

Thank goodness politics played no part in my friendship with Edith Smith, also a returnee after four years at Adelphi. We were disappointed not to be in any of the same classes, but every day we ate our lunch together in the crowded basement cafeteria, too depressed to converse. After school we would come to life on the streetcar ride home, often visiting each other as our houses were only three blocks apart on Clinton Avenue.

As its name implies, Packer Collegiate Institute offered two years of college. Founded in the mid-1800's for the education of young ladies, it reeked with tradition. The building, on Joralemon Street in Brooklyn Heights, seemed nearly that old too, though an addition including a gymnasium must have been built in this century. The ceilings and windows were high, the woodwork dark, and the well-worn floors creaked. Its proudest features were the chapel and the garden. The latter extended to the next block and was planted in flowering trees and shrubs, but we were allowed to walk only on the path which enclosed a central square of grass reserved for graduation day. Games and jump rope were confined to a paved terrace at the back door, perhaps twenty by thirty feet. In later years a flat area on the roof was caged in as play space for the younger children.

The chapel was on the second and third floors where services started our day. Every morning we would enter singing a hymn, listen to a scripture reading, recite the Lord's Prayer, sing another hymn, endure words of wisdom from Dr. Denby, our principal, and file out on the third hymn. On Fridays a fourth hymn was added after a flag salute and student assembly. Actually I enjoyed singing those hymns, believing that my off-key efforts would be drowned out by the other voices. When I was in second and third grade we sat downstairs in the side pews and left during the second hymn. We ninth graders, called the first academic class, sat behind the second "Acs" in the center balcony while the third and fourth "Acs" filled the back of the downstairs center sections. The front pews were reserved for the so-called juniors and seniors, actually the two classes of the junior college. The seniors even wore caps and gowns to chapel.

Those juniors and seniors took all the glory away from us high school students. They presided over student government, the school literary magazine, the yearbook, and what hurt me most, they put on the junior and senior plays. I would have loved to have acted in a full fledged production. We were even deprived of a graduation ceremony! Ironically, Packer had gained the reputation of being the best college preparatory school for girls in Brooklyn, so most of the high school students went away to four-year colleges.

For all I know the college section had the best teachers too. Although I had a few excellent ones in my last two years, most were fuddy-duds. Under their uninspiring tutelage I plodded my way through four years of French and Latin, hating Latin all the way. At least in French we were finally rewarded by some literature I could relate to, but I had no interest in Caesar's self congratulatory accounts of his military conquests, nor in Cicero's political orations or Virgil's ornate epic poem, the Aeneid. One month of respite came the last year with Ovid's mythical tales, the Metamorphoses. Why did I have to suffer four years of Latin? It was considered a good discipline in itself, a foundation for English and the Romance languages and an aid in getting into college. Well I admit there was a certain satisfaction in successfully decoding a difficult passage and I did gain a firmer grasp of grammar, but I have always maintained that vocabulary building could be taught in one semester in a well-designed course combining some linguistics and etymology. As for college, although I was accepted at Smith and Vassar, I ended up at Bennington, which deliberately shunned rigid entrance requirements.

Algebra had been a favorite subject at Holmquist, but at Packer algebra and geometry were taught together over the span of two years. I was utterly bored with the repetition of the algebra, and so turned off by the fussy teacher that she spoiled the geometry for me too. When I drew her the second year Mother appealed to the principal to have me transferred to another class. Dr. Denby refused saying I had to learn to get along with all sorts of people in this world, so I was stuck. That teacher may have taken credit for my score of 100% on the Regents' exam, but I attribute it having taken the course twice. Fortunately a good teacher the following year restored my love of math, but I did not continue further because at Packer three years of math were considered sufficient.

In the fourth "Ac" I took physics, my only science in high school. I found it fascinating, though what we were taught then was probably little more than children get in grade school today. I had an outstanding teacher, Dr. Brandt, in ancient history and enjoyed the subject, especially the first semester covering Egypt, the Middle East, and Greece, but found the second tedious, building the Roman state and empire. American history passed me by because at Packer it was given in eighth grade. Being a state requirement, I had to pass a test before entering Packer, so that summer I studied the textbook on my own, but managed to get through only the first half. The morning of the test Dad tried to give me a cram course in the Civil War and some major subsequent events. Fortunately the test was an oral one given by a friendly teacher. I sailed through the first half dreading the imminent exposure of my ignorance. Miraculously, the teacher, after shuffling through her papers, said she couldn't find the rest of the questions but I had done so well she would pass me anyway. What luck and what a relief! I suspect she had more important things to do than administer a perfunctory test, but at the time her failure to find the "mislaid" questions seemed like divine intervention.

In terms of creativity and benefits in later life, I got the most out of English classes. My writing improved, especially in the last two years, under the guidance of two excellent teachers who thoughtfully critiqued my weekly themes. I enjoyed précis writing, an exercise of reading or hearing a paragraph and reducing its main ideas as concisely as possible into complete, grammatical sentences. This has proved useful in taking lecture notes, though the habit of using few words constricts me somewhat in creative writing. My last year we had to write research papers complete with footnotes and bibliography. I did one on morality plays in the Middle Ages and another on the Manchurian crisis. The latter was about control of the Mongolian railway when the United States was resisting Japan's threat to taking over Manchuria, a remote and rather boring subject for me, but as he told me later, a very real one for Lyle. That was the time, a few months after arriving in Tokyo to teach school, when he felt a sudden hostility by the Japanese toward Americans.

Poetry gave me the greatest pleasure. I loved Shelly and much of Wordsworth whose following fragment resonated with my restless spirit:

> In youth from rock to rock I went
> From hill to hill in discontent
> Of pleasure high and turbulent
> Most pleased when most uneasy.

Once when we were studying Milton's *Il Ponseroso* and came to the line "Then to the spicy nut-brown ale!" Miss Ingels asked us what senses this appealed to. One girl volunteered "taste" and another "sight." I, remembering holiday dinners sipping our prohibition era homemade wine, suggested "a warm feeling." When asked what I meant, I added "a sort of glow." Much to my embarrassment, Miss Ingels commented, "You see this passage appeals to sight, taste, and, to some of us, sensation!"

Declaiming poetry took place in Oral English which we had once a week for all four years. The class was conducted by Miss Wade, whom I remember as a large and rather ridiculous person. She made us do voice exercises using our diaphragms, but I never could find mine. However I threw myself into the recitations with gusto. Snatches of the many poems I memorized remain with me and are an integral part of my thinking.

On the whole I did well in academics, but my downfall and shame was spelling. My diary of February 1931 records a crisis when Dr. Brandt marked a history paper down from an "A" to a "C" because of misspelled words, and called me in after school to talk over the problem. Although she was nice about it, her "bawling out" only made me feel all the more discouraged. Then two weeks later in English class a test was returned graded C [-] with the comment that it was worth a B except for spelling mistakes. This felt like the last straw and I must have shown it for Mrs. Harkness told me not to feel so bad about it. Her kind words started me crying, much to my embarrassment. Mary, a somewhat patronizing friend whom I didn't really like, was sitting beside me. When she tried to be consoling, I was so mad at her that I muttered through clenched teeth "shut up." At least my anger stopped my crying! After school Mrs. Harkness told me to buy an eighth grade spelling book, saying that if I learned a word a day by June I would be able to pass the state's Regents' exam as far as spelling was concerned. She may also have been the person who arranged for me to be tutored once a week. I remember how I used to sneak out of study hall and wend my way through the darkened chapel to my secret appointment, hoping no one would notice me. Whether the tutoring improved my spelling I cannot say, but I suspect my resistance to its lack of logic was still high. Had I remained in Packer for all of elementary school no doubt I would have been thoroughly drilled in the subject, but perhaps it would have broken my spirit. In adult life I have managed to get by with constant reference to the dictionary. Now I gratefully rely on my computer's "spell check" for reassuring support.

Sometime during the first year Sally Dodd and I found each other. We were among the few who still wore socks and "sensible" shoes and the only ones who carried book bags. She had some of Betto's zest and love of sports. She even admitted to liking gym which most of the girls, including Edith Smith, did their utmost to avoid, though we were united in hating the required uniform of bulky navy blue serge bloomers and white middy blouses. Sally and I went out for hockey together. We played on a field in Prospect Park reserved by the school. I remember how the sharp autumn air hurt my chest as, in the position of "inside," I would desperately run to keep up with the rest of the forward line. Whenever the ball came my way I treated it like a hot potato and passed it as quickly as possible, leaving to others the responsibility of trying for goals. The same was true in basketball where I played guard. In girls' basketball in those days guards were not allowed to throw baskets. The court was divided in half with the two forwards and center at one end and the guards confined to the other. I would jump around waving my arms ineffectively. It all seems rather pointless now as I really wasn't competitive, but I guess I just enjoyed the exhilaration of physical activity.

By the time I was in third "Ac" I felt more at ease with the other girls and was part of a small circle of friends. My election as class treasurer that year and as secretary the next made me realize I was generally well liked. The last entry in my diary, dated January seventh, 1932, my seventeenth birthday, sums up my state of mind, saying, "For the first time since I can remember I have been happy and self-assured over long stretches of time . . . I don't worry or even think about myself half as much as I used to . . . These days I'm awfully busy, but enjoying myself immensely."

Before leaving the subject of Packer Collegiate Institute I want to tell about two episodes which reveal its stuffiness. The first has to do with flag salutes and the second to the way the principal handled our misbehavior in chapel.

Flag salutes were given on Fridays, usually by a Junior or Senior, but sometimes by a high school student. Often they were also written by the presenter, as we were all encouraged to submit our original compositions. You can imagine the pompous declamations of high-flown praise of the greatest nation on earth. They all seemed so false to me that I was impelled to write my own in a humbler and more realistic vein. I put my heart into my piece, pointing out that we were a young country and could learn much from the older ones if we worked with them. Perhaps I even advocated joining the League of Nations. In any case my flag salute was turned down, no doubt because it was considered not sufficiently patriotic.

The other event evolved from my suggestion to my friends Sally Dodd and Ellen Mayo that it would be interesting to see if we could put expression in the hymns as if we really meant the words we were singing. The experiment proved to be too successful. Our dramatic expressions were not only in our voices, which might have been drowned out by the others, but also on our faces, along with poorly concealed amusement. Of course we were spotted by a vigilant teacher, who nabbed us as we left chapel and sent us to the principal. We were kept waiting in his outer office for quite a while which heightened our anxiety. Finally Dr. Denby called us in. First he declared his dismay at our disrespectful conduct and lectured us at some length. Then he spoke to each one in turn. Whatever he said to Sally reduced her to tears. To Ellen he threatened to refrain from writing a letter of recommendation for college. Then he turned to me saying, "Miss Ingersoll, until now I had considered you a model student. How do you account for yourself?" Confronted with this specious reasoning, all I could do was simply deny I had ever been a model student. I felt good about my encounter with Dr. Denby, but indignant at his unfair treatment of Sally and Ellen.

Afternoons

After school Edith and I would catch our Gates Avenue streetcar in front of Borough Hall as it ran along Fulton Street, a street darkened by the elevated structure which carried trains to and from Brooklyn Bridge. The "El" was an eyesore that not only spoiled the view of Borough Hall and its potentially attractive plaza but made for rather seedy conditions underneath. A hodgepodge of shabby stores and office buildings lined the street, and just a few blocks further on was a burlesque theater. By the time my father ran for Borough President the opening of a line of the city-owned Independent subway made the Fulton Street elevated obsolete. He campaigned for its demolition and after he was elected succeeded in getting rid of it. Ray still has the cartoon from "The Brooklyn Eagle" showing a giant hand lifting the disintegrating structure and captioned "Get the 'El out of here!"

This digression is by way of explaining that Fulton Street was not a pleasant avenue for sauntering schoolgirls. However Edith and I frequently did just that. The best window shopping was at Abraham and Straus, Brooklyn's finest Department Store, on Atlantic Avenue, the next street over. A greater attraction was a record store on Fulton Street, which had small booths where we could listen to the latest song hits. On days when I was tied up with music lessons, Edith would go in there and listen by the hour and finally leave with a new record. She would play it for me the next time I went to her house. I particularly remember how thrilled we were by Rudy Valle singing "The Stein Song," the University of Maine's rousing drinking song. Another favorite was "Smoke Gets In Your Eyes." Others like "My Sin," "Body and Soul," and "Love For Sale" were not really as risqué as their names imply. Edie reminds me that we even took our wind-up Victrola with us the time we camped out on the point at Duck Island.

But we did other things besides mooning over love songs. Sometime in the fall of our first miserable year at Packer Edith spotted an advertisement for Fireside Crafts' Correspondence Course. She was enchanted by the array of cute things, like doll house furniture, we could learn to make in only ten months. All we had to do was pay five dollars a month for the ten lesson kits. Each kit would provide us with the materials we needed for that lesson, and every month the completed assignment was to be mailed in to Fireside Crafts for comments. Then, upon receipt of another five dollars, the company would return the corrected lesson along with the new kit. At the end of the course we would be eligible to buy any of their materials at a discount. It sounded easy and like something fun we could do together after school.

The instructions warned us not to send cash. Perhaps Edith's mother wrote out a check for her, but I, knowing the money had to come from my allowance, would walk several blocks out of my neighborhood to the post office so I could exchange my five dollars for a money order. That was only the first difficulty. Next, the first kit proved to be disappointing as it contained only a few small tubes of oil paint, a couple of brushes, and a floral design to be filled in. It seemed hardly more difficult than a child's coloring book—until I started using the paints! I found that unlike crayons, I couldn't control the brush to keep the paint within the lines of the pattern. Well, I mailed it off hoping for better luck next time. It was returned with a comment that I should be more careful and a new lesson with a more intricate design. Hard as I tried to be neat the results were always messy. Knowing that Edith was doing better than I, I soon avoided doing Fireside with her. Where was the fun?

A few months rolled by. Somehow I couldn't find time to keep up with the assignments; the walk to the post office became more and more burdensome, and I had other needs for my money. So I simply quit.

Then came the letters from Fireside, polite at first but ever more demanding. When they threatened to take me to court I was really scared, for I was sure I had committed a crime. No longer able to keep my predicament to myself, I showed the letters to my father. He hit the ceiling. Far from finding my default illegal, he said the company had broken the law by entering into a contract with a minor. It was his turn to write a letter threatening court procedures! That did the trick, and I was gratefully relieved to have Fireside out of my life.

Somewhere along the line Edith must have quit Fireside too, but we didn't see as much of each other as we would have liked because of my afternoon singing lessons. Twice a week after school I would walk a few blocks to Mr. Sprackling's house on Brooklyn Heights. He quickly discovered that I couldn't carry a tune and that my range was quite limited, so he settled on simple folk songs from around the world. Actually I became quite fond of some of them, but not daring to sing where anyone could hear me, I never practiced at home. After a year or so I think Mr. Sprackling must have persuaded Mother it was a hopeless cause so she let me drop the lessons. When I asked her years later why she had subjected me to them when she knew I couldn't sing, she replied that was just the point: she thought I could be taught how. She too could not carry a tune and perhaps she regretted never having had voice lessons to remedy her deficiency.

Not long after I was free from singing instruction I had to endure the ordeal of tennis lessons. This time Mother wanted to help me enjoy the new tennis court which Uncle Miner had put in at the time he was building his house on Duck Island. My weekly lesson was just a few blocks from school at the Brooklyn Heights Casino, a private club with two courts, which doubled as a dance floor for debutante balls and other social events. I found this setting intimidating and the instructor more so. For a desperate half hour he would bombard me with balls and rapid commentary: "Watch your footwork." "Too late." "Where's your back swing?" "No follow through." "Throw the ball up higher on your serve." "Keep your eye on the ball!" That last admonition was the most important, but I was so preoccupied with making my arms and legs behave that I couldn't focus on the ball, much less deliberately aim it. The instructor may have assumed that I practiced with friends during the week, which certainly would have helped, but such friends as I might have had either far outstripped me or did not belong to the club.

The upshot was that while the emphasis on form made me look like a graceful tennis player I remained too defensive to become an effective one. Jerry and Mario, with less instruction, had the true competitive spirit, and became quite good. Ray soon gave up the game, preferring soccer, but I kept struggling on in spite of embarrassment. Gardner Ingraham gave me encouragement by sometimes inviting me to be his partner in doubles. He was an excellent player, not too intent on winning, and gracious enough to overlook my errors. Uncle Miner, on the other hand, took his tennis so seriously that none of our generation wanted to team up with him, although he never seemed to rattle my father. In fact Dad was the only one who put me completely at ease. His approach to the game was the direct opposite of mine. While I dashed breathlessly about the court, he would calmly take no more than three or four steps to reach for a ball. He returned nearly all of my shots, often neatly placing them just beyond my reach. When I did manage to get one past him he was generous with his compliments, but, more important, he so obviously enjoyed playing with me that I felt great.

One free afternoon Edith and I had a bold adventure. We had often wondered what kind of entertainment took place inside the burlesque theater we passed daily on our way home. Although I don't remember ever raising the question with an adult, I had the impression that it was considered not nice, and certainly unsuitable for young girls. Naturally we resented exclusion on the basis of our youth or gender, and we felt quite capable of judging for ourselves what was nice or not nice.

One sunny afternoon, (we must have been about fourteen), curiosity got the better of us. With our schoolbooks tucked under our arms, we walked right into the theater, stepped up to the counter and purchased tickets. I'm surprised now that nobody stopped us, but business was slow and they probably needed the cash. In the dim light we could see a few men slouched in the back row. Edith and I headed for the center where we became a small island in a sea of empty seats. Then we observed our surroundings. The theater was dingy and drab, the air stale and hazy with tobacco smoke.

The show itself was utterly boring. First a couple of guys told some stupid jokes and engaged in childish slapstick. After a while a weary looking woman, too old to be called a girl, wandered on stage. She sang a languid song while slowly taking off one sleazy garment after another until she was down to a g-string and a bra which hardly covered her nipples. That was all! Then came more slapstick followed by another tired woman going through the same slow routine. It was a far cry from the sparkle and pep of a Broadway musical. The only act that appealed to us at all was a trumpet soloist who, standing bare naked on a runway that projected into the audience, raised her trumpet high and blasted out a familiar tune.

At the intermission we ducked out of there in a hurry. As we turned to go I could see that more men had filled the rows behind us. This time I noticed their sullen looks, which I found unnerving. It was a relief to get out into the sunshine and breathe fresh air again. On the ride home Edith and I were too depressed to talk much, but we agreed it all seemed shabby and sad and certainly not nice. We wondered what those men got out of the show. Surely *we* would never want to watch *men* taking off *their* clothes!

The whole experience left a bad taste in my mouth. As soon as I got home I brushed my teeth with soap, and felt better for the penance. Later I told my parents what we had done. My father couldn't understand why we would want to see the seamy side of life. He told me that when he was in Paris at the end of the war he saw ugly and sordid things he would rather forget. What they might be I had no idea, but I was impressed by his solemn concern for my welfare. I was sorry that my naive escapade had caused him distress.

Living With the Family

In spite of the misery of the first two years at Packer and my longing to be back at Holmquist with Betto, I gradually grew accustomed to living at home with my family. During those four years before going off to college I became better acquainted with them, especially my father whom I came to know as a person in his own right and not just as my indulgent daddy.

It took me a long time to feel at ease in the Clinton Avenue house. It seemed too big and I couldn't find a cozy spot to settle down in, but then, being restless and discontented, I might not have felt at home anywhere. Even at Duck Island I was happiest when outdoors. A favorite retreat was an easily climbed pine tree which leaned over the sea wall. I have a vivid memory of being perched there on a warm spring day and suddenly becoming quite chilled as I read the grim ending of Edith Wharton's *Ethan Frome*.

The city house was also a source of embarrassment. Once when I brought a new friend home she exclaimed, "Oh, you live in a big house!" which made me wary of bringing others. The same was true of the Duck Island house, though its informal style and natural setting were less formidable. There was also the problem of introducing members of my mother's large household staff. Because of considerable turnover, I established personal relations with only a few of them and the rest seemed like intruders.

I guess I felt most secure while doing homework at my father's desk in the "office." It was a narrow, dark room with my mother's cluttered desk near the window and my father's bare one beside it. These were painted green, as were the file cabinets and a bookshelf against the opposite wall. In fairness to Mother I should note that Dad did most of his work at his office while she handled the household bills, personal correspondence, and charitable contributions, as well as a crowded social calendar. Looking at my own messy desk today I can better sympathize with her. When I was sixteen Mother converted the guest room to my use with handsome new furniture procured by Mr. Macomber, elegant rose and beige drapes, and a delicate dressing table which I never used. What did please me was my own large flat-topped desk where I henceforth studied.

Mother worried that I was too studious. Once I came home from school and joyously announced, "I made the honor role!" but she was preoccupied and did not respond.

"Aren't you glad?" I insisted.

"You know grades are not important," she replied.

"They are to me. You just don't care!"

"I do care, dear. It's because I care about your happiness that I want you to realize there is more to life than working for grades."

"You don't understand!" I wailed, and dashed up the stairs in tears to brood in my room over how Mother's ideas about my happiness were not mine. How could I explain to her that getting on the honor roll was the only way I knew how to be somebody in that big school? Another time, when I exclaimed vehemently that I hated Latin, she told me I shouldn't hate because it sent poison through my system. I didn't care about her physiological theories. I just wanted her to understand how I *felt*. She seemed to have a knack for making irrelevant remarks that set me off.

Mother tried her best to encourage me to be more sociable. Before I went to boarding school she had enrolled me in Miss Hepburn's Friday afternoon dancing class. This was to assure a place in Brooklyn society and the privilege of "coming out" at age eighteen. When the time came both Mario and I shunned that opportunity. As ten and eleven year olds we had to be dressed up in party clothes complete with white gloves. Miss Hepburn spent more time drilling us in proper manners than in teaching dance steps, an ordeal for all of us but probably harder on the boys. On entering high school I advanced to Heppie's Saturday night assemblies where I felt awkwardly over-sized and painfully inarticulate. There, instead of partners being arbitrarily assigned, the girls sat on a row of chairs along a wall waiting to be asked for a dance. Although an equal number of girls and boys were enrolled there always were extra girls left unchosen and sitting on the sidelines. Probably some of the boys simply found ways to avoid coming in the first place, but I learned from my brothers that those who came liked to congregate in the men's room. From time to time Miss Hepburn would send in a reluctant boy as emissary to order them out, but her efforts did little to rescue this wallflower.

When Jerry was a senior in high school Mother staged a hobo party for him. He and his friends enjoyed being dressed up like bums, a welcome relief from the strict dress codes of school and Miss Heppie's. Flushed by her success and knowing how much I had enjoyed my summer at Valley Ranch, Mother had the inspiration to throw a Western party for me. She went to elaborate lengths to decorate the house in cowboy style and to devise carnival type games and contests. The guests were each given a little bag of toy money which they could squander as they pleased. The sons and daughters of Mother's friends, whom I scarcely knew, reportedly had a good time, but I was only fourteen and not ready for a party. It was more rewarding for nine-year-old Marion who was put in charge of the candy store. When the party was over and no one thought to retrieve the unsold stock she quietly hid it in her closet. That cache of Snickers bars satisfied her sweet tooth for weeks.

Marion was my only sibling at home when I returned from boarding school as Jerry had gone off to Amherst College and Raymond for two years at Eaglebrook. She was in third grade at Ethical Culture School, which had relocated from South Oxford Street to Prospect Park Slope, a short ride on the Vanderbilt Avenue street car. She found it scary to take the trip alone without Raymond to accompany her, but she was a spunky kid and never told our parents about her apprehension. She probably didn't tell them about how it felt to be the only child in her class who couldn't read, either. At least I was unaware of her troubles, being utterly absorbed in my own. When Marion transferred the following year to Woodward down the street, she not only flourished in her school activities but quickly acquired new friends in the neighborhood. One of her classmates was David McLain who lived next door and had been her sidekick from the time we first moved into Clinton Avenue. Dad used to call them the Gold Dust Twins, after a well-known ad for cleaning powder.

Although my little sister was saucy and bright and contributed sparkle to our family life, the more than five year gap in our ages meant we lived in separate worlds. Her efforts to join mine as peacemaker between Mother and me were rebuffed as unwelcome meddling in my affairs. I dubbed her "Little Miss Fix-it." Once she accused me of using big words just to show off, but I knew she would be quick to interpret any attempt I might make to speak more simply as talking down to her.

It was Pokey, a lively Toy Boston Bull Terrier puppy, who provided a common interest. Marion and I taught her such tricks as begging, rolling over, and jumping over a stick, but the best trick of all Pokey taught herself. She had already learned to catch a tennis ball in midair when we were playing once with a balloon and she jumped up attempting to retrieve it. Instead the balloon bounced back to us. We soon improved on this game of catch by finding a small beach ball, which worked very well. It was amazing how high that little dog could jump. She remained our favorite family pet and lived about fourteen years, long enough to walk down the garden path during Mario's wedding ceremony.

In due time Marion and I had our joyful and tender moments together, as documented in my diary entry of March 2, 1931. After telling of having had fun joking with her and of my surprise at how much she knew and understood, I wrote, "When she is getting undressed at night and wants me to come up with her, I read to her whatever homework I happen to have, (English especially) and she really seems to enjoy it. Even though some things probably go over her head I think it is best to treat her just as a pal or rather a roommate. We both enjoy it!"

Bedtime was when I came to be close to Raymond too, after he returned from Eaglebrook. He had not been easy to get to know, for even as a little boy his self-sufficiency and stubbornness set him apart from the rest of the family. Boarding school made him all the more independent which Ray attributes to the boxing class Mother set up for him and three other seven-year-old boys in our gym on the third floor soon after we moved to Clinton Avenue. Having learned to punch straight forward rather than swing his arms around wildly, he was able to win the frequent fights he became embroiled in so by the time he entered Polly Prep he had enough self confidence to no longer need to fight.

He was only twelve, but my parents gave him a lot of freedom, although they worried when he was sometimes late for dinner because he had dropped in at the Cumberland Avenue Movie Theater after school and stayed to see the feature twice. All they could do was trust him and let him go his own way. Actually he has always had good practical judgment and caution, unlike Jerry who was inclined to take risks.

Raymond's room, which he shared with Jerry when he was home, was near mine with a bathroom between so I was aware of his getting ready for bed while I was studying at my new desk. Sometimes, after he was in bed, he would call to me.

"Asho, come here. I want to ask you something."

The interruption to my homework being not unwelcome, I would go into his room and sit on the side of his bed.

"What's the question?"

"Oh, I forgot."

Then I'd wait and in his slow and deliberate way we would get into a conversation about most anything. Once he told me, "I like to talk to you. I don't get a chance to talk to Dad, Jerry's away at college, and you know how Mother is. She always changes the subject."

"Yes, I know! How about Marion?"

"Oh, she's all right, but she's just too quick!" It was true, for she would jump in and finish his sentences before he was half through.

Once when I was in a crunch with homework I offered him a dime to trace a map for me in my ancient history workbook. He did a careful job and enjoyed doing it, so from then on we had a deal. I reasoned that this arrangement was justified since the main point of the exercise was to enter places on the tracing leaf preparatory to locating them on the original blank map the next day in class. Raymond had a talent for drawing which he later used to advantage in his career as an engineer, but as a boy he specialized in cartoon characters. I was witness to the creation of his *magnum opus* of this period one time at Duck Island. His friend, Jinks Carson, was visiting from boarding school, and naturally they wanted to go to the country. None of the rest of the family were able to go, so just the three of us boarded a train at the Long Island Railroad station at Atlantic Avenue. Roger Hennesy, the caretaker, must have met us at East Northport and I suppose that his wife, Alice, prepared some simple meals for us, though we may have tried our hands at cooking too. Anyway, for the most part we went our own ways.

It was a rainy weekend and the boys spent a lot of time closeted in Raymond's room while I became absorbed in a book. In the evening when I was ready to turn in, it occurred to me that I should exercise some adult responsibility and try to persuade the boys to go to bed. I knocked on their door and they invited me in. To my astonishment they had covered the white plaster walls with humorous pastel chalk drawings and were working on the ceiling. Raymond was putting the finishing touches on a 1930's science fiction version of a space rocket which whizzed past the gates of heaven and animated astronomical bodies. One, labeled "Impertinent Planet," was thumbing its nose. Fanciful creatures decorated the walls. Jinks had sketched a huge, grotesque insect about to attack a little man with a squirt gun sitting on top of a tall cactus. Captioned "Quick, Henry, the Flit!" it was obviously inspired by a series of subway ads for an insect repellent created by Theodor Geisel long before he became Dr. Seuss of storybook fame.

There were many other comical drawings which made me laugh. Since the deed had been done, there was no point in worrying about what Mother would say. It turned out she too was amused. In fact she was so taken by the idea that from then on she invited her houseguests to autograph the walls of the spare room next door with their own artistic creations, thus adding to her reputation for being an innovator. Eventually she had the walls sprayed with something to keep the chalk from smudging. Recently [1995] Ray was surprised to learn from the latest owner that his drawings were still there. We had assumed that they had long since been painted or papered over.

In addition to his aptitude for drawing, Raymond also had a good singing voice and was said to have perfect pitch. At an early age he was started on the violin soon abandoned, but he took up clarinet in fifth grade at Eaglebrook. I doubt if Polly Prep went in for music or art, as their extracurricular activities focused on sports. However, he joined the chorus at Swarthmore College and has greatly enjoyed singing in choruses ever since. Mario also had a lovely voice and learned to play the guitar while at boarding school. She would lead us in song and delighted in picking certain sentimental ones she knew would make me cry. I'm glad she could fulfill our mother's desire to have a musical daughter.

When it came to help with homework I would turn to Dad rather than Mother as he was less inclined to overwhelm me with too many suggestions. If I showed him a draft of an English theme, for instance, his comments would be few but pertinent, usually related to cutting down on excess verbiage. By the time I had advanced to real French literature he enjoyed reading it with me. I particularly remember our sharing *Les Pêcheurs d'Islande*, by Pierre Loti.

Most important was Dad's support in rescuing me from self doubt and the shame of tears after tangles with Mother. He would invite me for a walk and patiently listen to my grievances. Then, as we talked, my spirits would rise and I would again believe that I was in fact a rational and capable person. Once he told me that in some respects I was more mature at age sixteen than my mother was when he met her when she was twenty-five. We had many good conversations while walking as Dad always took an interest in my thinking and I was readily excited by "ideas." Sometimes I joined him for his before-bedtime stroll around the neighborhood and sometimes, if I was prompt enough in the morning, we would walk the two miles to school where he would take the subway to his office in Manhattan. The best walks were, of course, at Duck Island.

I wonder now if Mother might have felt jealous at being left out, although she had plenty of opportunities to walk with Dad alone. However there were other things we enjoyed doing together like reading aloud. I remember listening to her reading Walter Lippmann's *A Preface to Morals* while Dad lay stretched out on the couch. Although we were not church-goers, we liked to listen Harry Emerson Fosdick's sermons on the radio. We also went together to some of the Foreign Policy Association's Saturday luncheons and occasionally to the theater. One particularly pleasant time for the three of us was a leisurely Friday evening described in the following diary entry of March 6, 1931.

"Dad came home from Washington tonight. Everything seemed so happy and peaceful and everything went off smoothly. At dinner the conversation was interesting and afterwards Mother, Dad and I went into the living room and talked. Nothing really happened, but everything was in such perfect harmony that it made me realize what a happy family we are. Dad was telling me that we were much more fortunate in our family life than most people. I love it when Dad talks that way. It makes me feel so happy and encouraged and for a while at least afterwards things seem to run much more smoothly. I like encouragement not only for myself but also for the world in general and I think other people need more of it too."

This diary was resumed the end of January after a lapse of two years. My first effort had lasted less than two months, most of its entries being brief and factual, but nevertheless revealing of my everyday life during that short period. It started out bravely thus: "January 6, 1929. Sick in bed since New Year's. Resolutions: not to let my feelings get hurt, not to talk so loud, not to eat so much, to work harder and to keep a diary."

In contrast, my return to the diary at age sixteen was for the deliberate purpose of confiding my private thoughts and feelings, "to say what I darn please." This time I kept it up for eight months, and what an emotional roller coaster ride it was as it ranged from the joy of an exhilarating ride on Woody to the humiliation of rejection on the dance floor. Though I'm tempted to quote at length, I don't want to interrupt the flow of my story, so instead I plan to add the diaries as an appendix. However, the following two examples will give a flavor of my troubled thoughts.

One day I come to the dismal conclusion that I am a "fake" because most of what I said and did was not really true to myself and even my private thoughts were not always true. I wrote: "Even though I know nobody can ever know what I admit to myself I still try to cover things up. Why should I want to lie to myself? I don't think I really lie but often it is hard to dig out the real reason I do something and the top one usually is so much easier that I just let it go at that. But I know it is wrong; it is like cheating at solitaire. I would never think of cheating somebody else but when it is myself I know about it so it is all right. When I come to think of it, more than half of the things I think and say are not true, true to the way I really feel I mean, and yet the last thing in the world I want to be is a hypocrite . . . Am I so very insincere or does everybody do the same? If so why should they? I should think they could at least admit things to themselves in the privacy of their own thoughts. It is hard though." The next day I declare that I changed my mind because most of what I actually say is true, but I simply leave lot of my thoughts unsaid out of politeness or to avoid hurting some ones feelings. Then I add, "However I have not yet figured out the part about lying to myself but I am inclined to think it is so, unfortunately."

Another time I am restless and "in quite a stew" because I have no plans for the future. Having lost my enthusiasm for Vassar, I don't know where to go to college. I say, "it seems that I'm just standing on air and it is certainly a desperate feeling," adding "It has just dawned on me that I am really just a child! I shouldn't be at my age but I know I act like one . . . I don't even have enough independence to make up my mind about where to go to college. It is just terrible! I wish I didn't feel so mixed up. The first minute I wish I never did have to grow up ever and I rush around like a fool and act quite childish. Then the next minute I have a sudden passion to be grown up and be so independent and self confident just like all the people I know who go to college . . . Perhaps I need Jerry to encourage me and make me feel better. He is such a comfort in that way." I consider writing him a letter but know that by the time an answer comes I won't be feeling this way. I conclude with "Anyway I'll go to school tomorrow and study horrid old Latin and won't have any time to worry about college or anything else!" The very next day I write, "oday I feel quite the opposite . . . joyful and decidedly foolish. I've just had a grand time joking with Marion."

My diary reminds me of how I was caught in the middle of a conflict between Jerry and Mother over the time he spent with his girl friend during his semester break from college. My mother considered Jean to be an "older woman" who was leading her brilliant but naive son astray. Ironically, Mother was responsible for their meeting two years previously when Jerry was a seventeen year old college freshman and Jean an aspiring pianist of twenty-one. That fall Mother thought it would be nice for eight year old Marion, no longer needing a governess, to have a music student live with us who could help her with her piano practice. In response to her inquiries, Julliard sent Jean Picket who had come to the big city from Wilkes-Barre, Pennsylvania. Although rather quiet she seemed to fit into the family well enough, but when Jerry came home for Christmas vacation they promptly fell in love. This had not been in Mother's scenario! Not surprisingly Jean did not live with us the following year, but she and Jerry continued to date. They were always nice to me and the next summer I was happy to be included in a visit to her home. While they would wander off, Jean's younger sisters were left to entertain me. What I remember best about the visit was sitting on the front porch with her father listening to his dramatic description of a recent flood as we looked out over the Susquehanna River.

At the time Jean came to visit for Jerry's mid-year break they had not seen each other in nearly five months, because our family had spent the entire Christmas vacation at a ski resort in Canada. No wonder they wanted to be alone together, but, as recounted in my diary, Mother complained to me that it was inconsiderate of Jean to have stayed the whole five days so the family had no time alone with Jerry. He, in turn, confided that Mother had made them feel very uncomfortable about this, and I added my observation that she said little things that hurt Jean. I wrote I had gotten both sides full blast, but although I felt sorry for Mother, I knew I would always be on Jerry and Jean's side. I concluded with "This has taught me a lot about life and love in general and maybe it will help me later. At any rate I'll always know I can confide in Jerry about all such things for he has told me everything and we understand each other!"

The following June our whole family set sail for two months in Europe. Jean was there on the dock to wave good-bye to Jerry. It proved to be a final farewell for after that they drifted apart. Poor Jean had more than age going against her. The double role of being employee and "one of the family" made her relationship with Mother ambiguous right from the start.

Journey Abroad

The trip to Europe was the only major one we undertook as an entire family. Three years earlier we had expected to spend the month of August together at Ernest Miller's ranch in the southwestern corner of Montana, but Dad never made it. While he was tied up for all of July with the 1928 Democratic National Convention, Mother and we four children stayed in Uncle Clare's house located behind my grandparents' garden in Warren, Pa. Our Duck Island house had been turned over to Uncle Miner's family for the summer. It was a somewhat boring time for me as I was on crutches from having broken my ankle by skidding on the carpet at the top of the stairs, (no walking casts in those days). I missed Dad and was impatient to start our vacation in the wild West. However, when Al Smith was nominated for president, Dad was too deeply involved in planning the campaign to join the family, so we boarded the train without him. It was a three-day trip and Mother had her hands full, especially as I was still on crutches. She used to tell of how helpful the Pullman porter had been to us and of the quantities of our baggage he handled, but in all the confusion of getting off the train at Bozeman, much to her shame, she forgot to tip him.

Once we reached the ranch we all had a wonderful time! Mostly we took day rides, but Jerry soon went off with some other teenagers on three-day pack trips. I was included on one of these, and later Mother, Raymond, Marion, and I went on one just for us when it rained the whole time. Mario, who was only eight years old, remembers the misery of a downpour in a dark woods where our horses had to pick their way over fallen trees, and I can picture us huddled in our damp tent listening to Mother read one of Albert Payson Terhune's "Lassie" stories. The glorious climax of the summer was the last pack trip, which the five of us and two cowboys took to the headwaters of Tumble-down creek, a high valley, a cirque, surrounded by sharp peaks. As we looked up at the brilliant stars we promised ourselves to bring Dad back there someday. That dream came true ten years later. It proved to be our last family trip before Dad died in February 1940.

In 1931 my father was free to enjoy a long summer vacation because that spring he had decided to resign as arbitrator of the cloak and suit industry. He believed seven years in one job was enough, and knew he had "sucked that lemon dry." Now, as he said, all he had to do was "wind the clocks and set the mousetraps." Over the course of the next year he would come home from time to time with the announcement that he had found a new mousetrap to set which would turn out to be some committee or other having to do with reform city politics.

Mother took charge of planning the logistics for the big trip. Because the prospect of traipsing about Europe for two and a half months with four children ranging in age from eleven to twenty seemed a bit daunting to my parents, they determined to split us up. A new travel agency called the Open Road that specialized in student tours had just the ticket: for Jerry a four week study-tour of cooperative housing in Scandinavia, Germany, and Austria led by Harry Laidler of the socialist League for Industrial Democracy, and for me, during the same period, travel in Germany and short stays in Geneva, Venice, and Paris with the dean of a small southern girls' college and four of her students. Meanwhile my parents would be provided with a car, a driver/guide to tour western Germany and see the castles on the Rhine with the younger two. Their destination was Lake Annecy in the French Alps where Marion and Raymond would stay at an American children's camp while Jerry and I would drive through central Germany with Mother and Dad.

Near the end of June we all set sail on the S.S. Bremen, a new ship which had introduced a tourist class in place of third class. Our quarters were cramped, to say the least, but we kids didn't mind and Mother and Dad were good sports. In fact sneaking up to first class was an exciting challenge for the young people on board.

Jerry and I ate our meals with our tour groups. His was an assortment of interesting and broad-minded people among them Olive Stone, a teacher at a small college in Alabama, through whom he and Min met two years later at a farm school on wheels. My Winthrop College group was more limited in both size and outlook, and, since they were considerably older than I and already knew each other, I felt quite the outsider. Their favorite topic of table conversation, besides their campus social life, was food. Once in the presence of our German guides they got off on the subject of how much their families had suffered and how rich they would have been if it had not been for the war. I was shocked that they could refer to our remote civil war as the war in the presence of our hosts whose country was suffering so acutely from defeat in the recent world war.

The trip was saved for me by Annemarie Rudiger who traveled with us for the first week until we reached Berlin. She and her friend, Marta, who was our guide throughout Germany, boarded the boat when we docked at Bremerhaven. Right away Annemarie and I were attracted to each other. I soon developed a full-blown crush on her. (Do girls have crushes these days, I wonder, or do they start dating so early they pass over that stage? Perhaps their natural impulses become confused over the issue of lesbianism. If so, too bad.) Anyway I was thrilled that a married woman of twenty-five should care about me, but it must have been evident to her that I took more interest in learning about her country than did the Winthrop girls. Annemarie and her husband had each lived for a while as students in the United States, and so were motivated to offer hospitality to Americans. They graciously entertained our group in their apartment in Berlin where Herr Rudiger and his friends played string quartets for us. Later they invited me to join them and some friends for an afternoon boat-ride on a large lake outside the city. I was sorry to have to say good-bye after knowing them for less than three weeks, but promised to see them when I returned to Berlin with my parents in September. My joy in Annemarie's friendship is described at length in my diary.

My other contacts with Germans brought the discovery that despite the language barrier I could feel at ease with boys. In Breslau one evening I got into a lively discussion with our student hosts about the difference between the Boy Scouts and the German youth movement, (precursor to Hitler's). Upon departure next morning, I was flattered that one young man asked me to correspond with him. Another time on an outing in the mountains I had a long and delightfully unself-conscious walk with a boy I liked very much.

Traveling with the Winthrop college group was quite a strain; how much I didn't realize until we reached Geneva and I found what a relief it was to be reunited with my parents. Jerry joined us there, and after some sightseeing in the area and looking in on Marion and Raymond at their camp, the four of us set out on our motor trip through central Germany. It proved to be quite strenuous, and tension mounted. I now believe Mother felt left out of Dad's conversations with Jerry and me. She expressed her resentment by trying to give me the silent treatment, but after two days exploded in a big blow-up vividly described in my diary. I had been earnestly trying not to let her get on my nerves, but rather than crediting me with restraint she accused me of merely tolerating her. I wrote, "It was as if she were hitting me over the head with a hammer each time she said something especially the word tolerate." Calm followed the storm and the rest of the trip went smoothly enough.

In Berlin tea with the Rudigers seemed like coming home, but I was sorry we were spending only one day in the city. Imagine my joy when I learned that Mother had invited them to drive with us to Hamburg! Four flats along the way did not dampen our spirits, and that night I was happy to once again room with Annemarie and confide in her. She assured me that she too had difficulty in getting along with her mother. Next day, after fond farewells, we boarded our ship and the Rudigers took a train back to Berlin.

Meanwhile Raymond and Marion, whose camp had closed, were shepherded to Paris where they were confined for a few days in somebody's home before being taken to La Harve to meet our boat. (Ray still feels cheated that he never got to see the Eiffel Tower.) By the time our ship reached La Havre it was already evening and we were impatient for the tender to meet us. Dad had already packed a suitcase in preparation to go ashore in case the children missed connections. Suspense grew as we peered through the darkness. Finally we saw lights approaching and after a while the outlines of the tender. Then Jerry yelled, "Hello Raymond!" and back through the night came a welcome shout: "Hey Jerry!" Relief was followed by anxiety. "Where is Marion?" "She's all right; she's just bashful!" Raymond yelled back.

The voyage home provided a significant encounter with a boy. Emmet was a quiet lad of eighteen about to enter Yale. At first I felt awkward with him because I couldn't think of anything to say. When I told Mother about this difficulty, she said he was probably as shy as I was, and I could expect lots of silences with him, which I shouldn't let bother me. Her advice helped, but I soon found out he was not the bashful boy she thought him to be. After dinner Emmet and I would go up on deck to watch the phosphorous in the waves. One evening, as we stood there, I felt a slight pressure across my lower back. Realizing it must be his arm, I didn't dare move, but nothing more happened. However I knew this came under the category of necking, so next day I conferred with Jerry about the rights and wrongs of necking and kissing, a subject I had discussed at some length with my girl friends. He confirmed my opinion that it wasn't half as bad as some thought and that a kiss did not necessarily mean two people loved each other. He predicted that the first time I was kissed I'd either fall for the guy or be disappointed. As I wrote in my diary: "His warning came in the nick of time for the next night when Emmet and I went out on deck to cool off he calmly without a word kissed me. I certainly was surprised it lasted so long but I wasn't thrilled at all. I was really quite surprised at my calmness and coldbloodness [sic]." In fact I remember thinking how big his nose looked at close range. There was however a thrill of sorts in the thought that I was no longer "Sweet sixteen and never been kissed." My next kiss didn't come until three years later when I was on a student tour in Russia, but that one was far from cold-blooded.

Anticipating College

Soon after returning for my last year in high school I abandoned my diary, no longer needed as a confidant. Life was too full for brooding thoughts, and besides I had more friends to confide in. My relations with Mother improved as she became less prone to try to improve me. Perhaps she gave up the project because, now that I was happier, she was simply more satisfied with me. Also I was not quite as quick to interpret her every suggestion as a criticism. When she would broach a touchy subject with careful diplomacy I always knew that she had first talked the matter over with Dad, but calm reasoning was hard for her to sustain, and often she would blurt out some remark that would spoil her well-planned strategy. However our blow-ups were less intense and less frequent, and there was always comfort in the thought that next year I'd be away at college.

I still didn't know which college I preferred, but since my classmates were all worrying about where they would be accepted, I felt less alone in my uncertainty. So I applied to Vassar and Smith and left the decision to fate. Once Hamilton Holt, a friend of Dad's who had served with him in the *Foyer du Soldat*, came to call. He had recently become president of Rollins College in Florida and he tried to sell me on the place, but it had no appeal. I associated Florida with visits to my grandfather in St. Petersburg, and, being boy-shy, I was leery of co-education.

Then we heard that a new progressive college for women was going to open in the fall at Bennington, Vermont. It sounded interesting and certainly more exciting than the "Seven Sisters" colleges. From time to time Dad would return from his various political meetings around town with tidbits of news about Bennington. Most important to him was that the board of trustees was headed by Dr. William H. Kilpatrick, a former student and colleague of John

Dewey. At that time Kilpatrick was president of Teachers College at Columbia which had been running the Lincoln elementary and high schools to put Dewey's theories of progressive education into practice. Other universities had set up similar demonstrations, such as the Lab School in Chicago and University High at Michigan, but there was not yet a full-fledged college founded on progressive principles. Although Sarah Lawrence, a women's college in Bronxville, claimed to be the first, it was then only a junior college. Actually Dewey was a firm believer in co-education, but Bennington's founders believed parents would be more willing to take educational risks with their daughters than with their sons.

In due time we obtained a prospectus of the new college and learned it would have no grades or formal examinations and no required subjects. Each student would make her own study plan under the guidance of a faculty advisor who would also be one of her teachers in the field she had chosen as a "trial major." It all sounded like freedom to me! It would be fun to be in the first class and help create a new college. By late spring Bennington had won me over. I took the College Boards anyway, probably just to go along with my classmates. When both Smith and Vassar sent acceptances, I asked for a year's postponement on the outside chance that Bennington might not live up to my expectations.

Meanwhile I felt sorry for Edith being left out of all the excitement as she still had another year to go at Packer. Upon entering high school at age twelve she had been put on a five-year track because it was thought that she would be too young for college when she reached sixteen. Actually she turned out to be more mature and capable than most of us. It was a sad time for her too because her brother, Alfred, had died in an auto accident at Hamilton College just a month or two before he was to have graduated.

That summer I went to a drama camp somewhere in southern New Hampshire or Vermont expecting to act in Shakespeare plays. Instead we spent hours rehearsing a romantic pageant of the Children's Crusade, the annual finale of the camp's season. The few speaking parts went to "old" campers while the rest of us dutifully marched along as crusaders, occasionally responding in unison to our leaders' noble words. Nevertheless my parents planned on attending the performance when they came to drive me home. They decided to make it more of an outing by inviting Edith and her mother to come along, and to take a look at the new Bennington campus on the way. There they met with the director of admissions. Miraculously, after only a brief interview, she offered Edith one of the last three openings in the class that was about to enter in just a few short weeks. Just as miraculous was her mother's willingness to let her take it for which Edith has been eternally grateful. In retrospect, I doubt if it all happened as suddenly as we were led to believe. I can imagine Edith's mother had given the possibility much thought and had talked it over with my parents. She may well have made the appointment with the admissions director in advance and sent her Edith's high school record. In any case I was surprised and overjoyed that Edith would be with me to share this great adventure of launching a brand new college.

Before I leave home and family, I must report a significant event: Jerry's one year's suspension from Amherst for driving a car within the forbidden radius of twenty-five miles from the college. He had been keeping his car in a farmer's barn just beyond the limits and was caught when he had to bring it to a garage in Northampton for repairs. Naturally my parents were very upset at the news, and especially sorry that he would be deprived of graduating with his class only a few weeks away. They recognized that Jerry had taken a risk in circumventing the rules, but attributed the harshness of the penalty to his having loaned the car to his German exchange student roommate who had an accident in which a Smith College girl was seriously injured.

The question now was how should Jerry constructively spend his time before returning to Amherst the following February for his final semester. Whatever my parents' suggestions might have been they were ignored in favor of one from Hal Ware, a socially concerned professor at Amherst. He put Jerry in touch with some farm organizers who were helping to form a farmers' union and were looking for volunteers. This was 1932, the depths of the depression from which farmers had been suffering long before other segments of the economy. Jerry joined with three or four others to tour around the Midwest to talk with farmers. They called themselves a farm school on wheels. It was an exhilarating and radicalizing experience for Jerry and certainly influenced the course of his life.

Chapter 4
College Years
Bennington

Endowed with my mother's adventurous spirit and my father's social conscience—a mixed blessing that has inspired and frustrated me all my life—I set off to college at the depth of the great depression eager to take on the world. That so many were suffering dire hardships while I was among the privileged few who could attend an expensive college troubled me. I wanted to find out what could be done to right these wrongs. No wonder I decided to trial major in Social Studies even though I had a bent for math and science.

Bennington was more than ready to expand my horizons. There, on an open hilltop in Vermont, the young faculty was just as excited about starting a new progressive college as were the eighty-seven girls who made up our freshman class. Together, in small classes and weekly tutorials, we had unprecedented freedom to teach and learn creatively. It was a heady experience for everyone. Our excitement was shared by the community as a whole at frequent evening meetings, many with outside speakers. These stimulated much discussion, which often spilled over into the dining rooms the next day, and opened my eyes to unfamiliar subjects, especially to the arts. As the 1932 presidential campaign was underway when the college opened I was particularly interested in hearing representatives of the two major parties and the Socialist and Communist parties. In a straw vote taken at the start of the series most of the students favored the Republican incumbent, Herbert Hoover, while a majority of the faculty went for Roosevelt. Following the speeches the faculty vote remained Democratic, but the students switched over to the Socialist, Norman Thomas, whose spokesman gave a lively and visionary talk that appealed to our idealism.

My advisor was Lewis W. Jones from whom I also took a class in economics. He and his English wife, Barbara, constituted the Social Studies faculty that first year. Lewis graduated ten years earlier from Reed College in Portland, Oregon where our college president, Robert Leigh had taught. He and Barbara met as graduate students at London University and had just finished writing the report of the National Committee on the Costs of Medical Care when they came to Bennington. Neither had taught before, but in different ways each proved to be an excellent teacher and together they made a well-balanced team. Lewis had a contagious enthusiasm that fed mine and encouraged my propensity for discussion, but it was Barbara who helped me focus on disciplined writing. Although she loved teaching, she had to give it up nine years later to avoid the appearance of nepotism when Lewis became president of the college following Leigh's resignation. Lewis went on to the presidency of Rutgers, and sadly Barbara never had a chance to teach again. The Joneses not only inspired me as teachers but became close and supportive friends.

One of the tenets of progressive education was to begin with the here and now leaving history and theory until the student came to see their relevance. Nevertheless, Lewis Jones, no doubt needing a prop, started off his introductory economics class with Sumner Schlichter's thick textbook on the subject. From it we learned about supply and demand, Gresham's law that bad money drives out good, and some of the complexities of foreign trade and the business cycle, but often our wide-ranging class discussions would revert to the depression and what might be done about it. When spring came and Roosevelt launched his New Deal, Schlichter was abandoned in favor of studying the proposals that were being put forward in rapid succession. Our class divided into teams each selecting one agency from the "alphabet soup." Virginia Westwood, from Nebraska, and I chose the AAA (Agricultural Adjustment Act). Her interest arose from having lived in the heart of the farm crisis and mine from my brother Jerry's recent volunteer work with the incipient Farmers' Union. She analyzed the provisions of the legislation while I dug into the background, mostly from current periodicals. I learned that the depression in agriculture had started in World War I but stemmed from causes going far back in history. In response to our report our classmates readily agreed with us that there must be a better remedy for the farmers' problems than plowing under crops and killing little pigs while city dwellers were going hungry.

My interest was also captured by a course on scientific method taught jointly by our three science faculty. The first unit on astronomy presented by Paul Garrett, the physicist, thrilled me as I learned about galaxies: our own within the Milky Way and more astonishing the inference from known nebulae that there were countless more galaxies beyond us in outer space. Subsequent mind-boggling discoveries of our astronomical century could never match the elation I felt as I pored over astronomy journals in the library or on the many nights I looked up at the stars in the expansive sky above our hilltop. I remember nothing of the units on chemistry and botany, but biology presented in terms of human physiology satisfied my curiosity about how our bodies work. When we came to the reproductive system, partly taught by the College physician, Dr. Wilmoth Osborne, the class really took off. It amazes me how lacking in such basic information my previous schooling had been.

Other freshman subjects were less memorable. At first I enjoyed German with a charming young woman direct from Germany who began with reading children's books and singing Christmas carols, but as the words rapidly became longer and more complicated I was discouraged from continuing. A course in the modern novel, often covering one a week, nearly did me in. Always a slow reader I seldom finished one book before having to rush on to another. That was one class where I kept my mouth shut! Even worse was music appreciation the following year where we had to analyze one movement a week. I could barely distinguish the pattern of themes in a simple Mozart symphony to say nothing of recognizing their developments or transitions from one key to another. From then on I stuck to social studies, a broad enough field to offer much variety. The one exception was a wonderful class in poetry with Genevieve Taggard, a distinguished poet herself whom we all loved. I can still relive the passion with which I immersed myself in Robert Burns and then in Shelley while preparing reports to give in class.

Nevertheless I absorbed considerable appreciation for the arts and literature from frequent exhibitions, lectures and concerts and indirectly from my classmates. Many talented students were attracted to Bennington because, unlike other liberal arts colleges, it gave full credit for the visual and performing arts. I stood in awe of these artists and musicians and would have loved to have taken acting, but the drama students also seemed out of my league. Edie, having done well under conventional art instruction at Packer, started out trial majoring in art, but was dismayed when expected to paint freely from her own imagination. She soon transferred to social studies where she felt comfortable and competent. Fortunately I was not scared off by recreational dance offered as an alternative to outdoor sports and so had the privilege of studying modern dance from Martha Hill. A former member of Martha Graham's concert group she was a well-loved teacher who introduced the whole college community to modern dance and organized a summer school that drew outstanding dancers of the day.

Most of my classes and the library were in a remodeled dairy barn newly painted red. The campus had been a working farm on the estate of the Jennings family who came to the rescue with a contribution of 140 acres when the college trustees had to retrench from the original plans for elegant structures on the slopes of Mt. Anthony in Old Bennington. The chicken coops were converted into music studios and the farmhouse into faculty apartments and a nursery school. A colonial-style brick Commons, the only new building besides a cluster of four small student houses, was the center of our social life. There we ate our meals in the several small dining rooms on the second floor, attended performances and community meetings in the theater above and mingled at all hours in the large lounge on the ground floor. This room was graced with a fireplace at one end, a lattice of mailboxes at the other and a row of tall windows. Along the windows were several small maple tables and chairs where we would often sit and look out across the campus and the Walloomsac River valley.

And how that view grew on me! Through all the ups and downs of college life it seldom failed to lift my spirits. In the first place we were on a wide open hilltop so night and day I was aware of the expansive sky. Mt. Anthony, about two miles to the south, was hardly more than a hill whose nearly perfect cone-shaped silhouette gave it a picture-book charm though somewhat marred by the obelisk commemorating the Battle of Bennington and the brave Green Mountain Boys who ambushed the British. A long, high ridge lay to the east of the campus and to the west nearby fields sloped gently upward.

An experience that has always stayed with me was walking up those fields in early spring with a friend whose art assignment was to become aware of colors in her surroundings. The day was perfect for our purpose—trees were in their young foliage, the grass was newly sprouted and the sun was pleasantly warm. At the top of a field we settled ourselves on a spot with a broad outlook and gazed across the landscape. Of course green was the dominant color, and at first we simply noticed its various shades, but the longer we looked the more excited we became as we discovered patches or flecks of other colors within the greens like an artist's paint strokes. That informal lesson in art appreciation was the best one I ever had.

Behind the campus on the outskirts of the village of North Bennington lay the part of the Jennings estate still in private ownership. A few years after I graduated, Mrs. Jennings gave the rest of the property to the college, including her massive stone summer residence, a large carriage barn, and a gently curved and graded driveway. Until then cars approached by way of a rough dirt road that took two right angle turns around a little cemetery before climbing steeply to the flagpole in front of the Barn. However Mrs. Jennings did not object to our walking on her tree-lined driveway, though I doubt if she knew how her sturdy maples tempted me to climb them at night when no one was looking.

Student living quarters were in a quadrangle of small clapboard houses each with twenty-one rooms and a faculty apartment. They were placed below and slightly to the west of the Commons. An identical set of white boxes were built on the east side in time for the second class and two more quadrangles of similar style were put up for the third and fourth classes. My freshman year I lived in Booth House named after the pastor of the Congregational Church in Old Bennington whose dream initiated the idea of a new women's college nine years earlier. An attractive living room that sometimes served as a classroom was in the middle and a four-room suite at either end. My room on the second floor, like most of the others, was on a corner with two windows and was quite spacious for one person. Furnished with simple early American maple bureau, desk and bedstead from the Cushman factory down the road and an easy chair from home it was a relatively quiet retreat for study. Not so any more, for all the rooms are doubles now.

Edith and I had decided to live in separate houses the better to make new friends, but at first we stuck together for meals sitting at one or another of the small round tables. We were shy with our older and apparently more sophisticated and talented classmates some of whom had waited a year or two for Bennington to open, understandably so as I was only seventeen and Edie at sixteen was next to the youngest in the class. However we soon gravitated to some less intimidating girls from Boston who used to sit at one of the two tables for eight in the back dining room. Atossa Herring, also in social studies, may have been in the group. We referred to ours as the Boston table and the one in the opposite corner as the lipstick table. Eventually I discovered friends among the lipstick crowd and even went on a trip to Russia with two of them at the end of our sophomore year.

The food was exceptionally good and plentiful, and we ate with hearty appetites. When gingersnaps were on the menu we connived with our student waitresses to bring us an extra plateful so we could top off the meal with gingersnaps soaked in cream. No wonder our class gained an average of ten pounds that first year! One night at dinner someone suggested we serenade the faculty and on the spot our Boston friends made up a song. Then we gathered some more recruits and trooped into the faculty dining room. Our professors were appropriately surprised and amused though it was really a silly song. As I recall it went something like this:

> We like the beginning of college
> We've acquired so much knowledge
> We know it's all just due to you.
> Life, love, religion and marriage
> We're all in the same carriage
> When it comes to cream spinach soup.
> Now any night when you hear much noise

Dear faculty please remember
It's only due to Williams boys!

Not surprisingly a new women's college only fifteen miles away was a great attraction to students from all-male Williams College just over the state line in Massachusetts. At the start of their semester, a week or so after Bennington opened, hordes of them came to check us out at all hours of the day and night. Bennington was not prepared for the invasion, but a hastily installed entrance gate and a night watchman partially solved the problem. Thereafter only guests who had been invited by specific students were admitted. However it didn't take long for a few boys to make contact with girls who were glad to sponsor them and arrange blind dates for their respective friends. By this social custom the number of guests expanded rapidly. I tried a couple of blind dates, but found them far from fun, as I didn't know how to flirt. My ill ease and their vapid conversation threw me back to the miseries of Miss Hepburn's dancing school.

Perhaps my first experience with flirting, although I didn't recognize it at the time, was with a red-headed intern at the American Hospital in Paris where I was laid up with a case of jaundice in February of my freshman year. It happened because Mother, always on the lookout for an opportunity to get Dad away on a trip somewhere, suggested we take advantage of Bennington's Winter Field and Reading Period to travel in the Mediterranean. The idea of a mid-winter vacation appealed to Dad because by summer he expected to be involved with the New York City Fusion Party's campaign to elect a reform mayor and other city officials. He had wanted to visit Greece ever since he was a philosophy student in college and I too was enamored of the Greeks. All three of us thought a boat ride up the Nile would be an enjoyable way to see Egypt, and that we should end our trip in Italy.

Thus the new year of 1933 launched us aboard a ship headed for Marseilles. We arrived there on my eighteenth birthday and sailed on to Alexandria the next day. On an excursion out of Cairo we rode camels and climbed a few giant steps up the Great Pyramid. The tedium of the boat trip up the Nile was relieved by watching peasants on the bank raising water from the river with the same long levered poles as were depicted on the monuments of the pharaohs. When we finally reached the Valley of the Kings, we were overwhelmed by massive sculptures and temples and more history than we could absorb. Greece was a refreshing change with its graceful white marble columns and sparkling blue seas. The high spot, literally, which we achieved after our driver plowed us through the muddiest roads I'd ever traveled, was the temple to Apollo at Delphi on a steep slope of Mount Parnassus. We were enchanted by the view of olive orchards below us with the Gulf of Corinth beyond and pretty purple anemone at our feet.

Not until we reached Italy did I even think about my college assignment. Bennington's recess between two unbroken four-month semesters was originally intended to give both faculty and students relief from the cold and isolation of Vermont winters. There was little guidance at first as to how students might best spend their time, but Lewis Jones suggested that I write a report on Fascism in Italy. Actually I was better prepared to appreciate antiquities, thanks to an excellent high school course in ancient history, than I was to sort out conflicting information and opinions about Mussolini's dictatorship. In 1933 all that most Americans knew about him was he had made the trains run on time. I didn't learn much more as a tourist in Rome, but hoped to get an inside view from a visit with the parents of Nikka Tucci whom Jerry knew at Amherst when Nikka came there as an exchange student two years previously. Then the day before we were to have dinner at the Tucci's home I came down with an awful stomachache. A doctor at our hotel prescribed ether capsules to allay the pain. I arrived at the formal dinner party all dressed up and smiling bravely while feeling miserable and reeking of ether. Needless to say I barely managed to carry on a minimum of polite conversation much less to engage in a discussion of Fascism. I was still in acute pain the next evening when we boarded a night train for Paris. Upon arrival there we went directly to the American Hospital.

So that is how I came to spend a week in the hospital while Mother and Dad were having a lark taking in the sights of Paris during their unplanned extended stay. My affliction was diagnosed as acute jaundice, probably what is now called hepatitis, an infection I may have picked up in Greece. Twenty some years later I was screened from giving blood to the Red Cross because they had learned that hepatitis was passed on to our soldiers from donors who had been infected by the disease. I have wondered how many poor soldiers suffered from my patriotic donations during World War II.

Whatever the treatment I was soon feeling fine. Nowadays I would have been discharged without delay. To stave off boredom, I amused myself by folding origami cranes and other paper objects which became a topic of conversation among the staff. One nurse showed me how to make a new kind of bird. Two interns, or maybe they were residents, used to drop by frequently, one a dark-eyed Argentinean and the other, the redhead from the United States. I suppose I was actually flirting with them. At least I enjoyed their attentions, especially after being confined to the company of my parents for so long. One day the Argentinean told me I was wholesome, but I protested that the word reminded me of drab whole wheat bread. He replied that to the contrary my wholesomeness made him want to rape me. I blushed in confusion and alarm thankful that I was safely ensconced in a hospital bed. Thereafter I shunned him in favor of the non-threatening redhead. At my departure we exchanged addresses and promised to write.

Back on campus I was thrilled to receive a letter from him, and thereafter we kept up a restrained correspondence. In the fall he returned to the United States and asked to come visit me. I engaged a room for him in a tourist home in nearby North Bennington and arranged to double date with some supportive friends with whom I had shared my long-distance potential romance. I had told them he was tall and nice looking with a good sense of humor. When we met at the train station I was taken aback. He was not nearly as tall as I remembered, nor as young and good-looking. There was nothing to do but go bravely on with our plans for the week-end. I was embarrassed, but confessed my disappointment to my friends, for they too could see that he was pathetically antiquated and dull. He must have felt awkwardly out of place on a girls' college campus. After the weekend was over and I had seen my redhead off on his train, my friends and I laughed at how I had been taken in. Boredom, the horizontal perspective of a hospital bed and wishful thinking had certainly distorted my perception.

As far as I remember that was the only dating I did during my sophomore year, but I was happy enough without it. Classes, visiting speakers and evening performances continued to make life interesting. Besides, the college had doubled in size with the addition of new faculty and the second class of students offering more courses and new friendships. Among these were Tom Brockway who taught history and Ruth Dewing and Polly Swan both social studies majors. At the end of the year Ruth and I requested rooms next to each other for the following fall.

Of the many stimulating lecturers who came to campus the one who stands out in my memory is Buckminster Fuller, a charismatic speaker who charmed us all. He showed us diagrams of his dymaxian house, a forerunner of his geodesic dome, and his dymaxian car. The house was somewhat circular and was suspended from a central core, which, like the dome, contained all the utilities. He convinced us that it was much more efficient than a conventional home. But it was the car that really intrigued me. A teardrop shape reduced wind resistance, my introduction to the concept of streamlining. Best of all, the car could turn on a dime because it had only three wheels. I have been told that the design never took hold because after a prototype collided with another vehicle it was discarded as unsafe, although the possibility of driver error or faulty construction was never investigated. Recently I saw a tricycle wheelchair that reminded me of the dymaxian car. The large wheels were placed ahead of the single small one, and their tops were tilted inward. The owner said this made it both stable and maneuverable and well suited for basketball and other sports. I like to think that Buckminster Fuller, who became fondly known as "Bucky" to later generations of admirers, got his start at captivating the imaginations of the young with us Bennington girls.

I studied with both of the new Social Studies faculty members: historian Tom Brockway, and sociologist Andree Emery whose personalities were completely opposite. Miss Emery, an exuberant and unpredictable Hungarian with illusions of grandeur, had a hard time teaching statistics and I had a hard time being her pupil. She would become so distracted by her own digressions that she would make some simple arithmetical error in a problem she was working out on the board. Then I would cringe as she headed for disaster having discovered that if I tried to rescue her by pointing out the mistake she became hysterical. About all she succeeded in teaching me was the bell-shaped curve and the difference between the mean, the median, and the mode. She had her run-ins with college staff too, such as ordering an inordinate number of books for the library and attempting sweeping inroads of her colleagues' territories. I heard about these when I served on the Student Educational Policies Committee as a representative of the Social Studies division. Our committee made its recommendation that she not be reappointed for another year and the powers that be came to the same conclusion. Her place was taken by George Lundberg, a well respected sociologist who made significant contributions to the college both academically and socially.

In contrast to Andree, Tom Brockway was stable and modest with a gentle but incisive wit. In his American history class we used a recently published text by Charles and Mary Beard that examined the policies of our founding fathers as related to their economic and social class, an eye-opener for me after the stereotypes presented in high school. He was also my counselor with whom I met once a week to talk over my work. Sometimes, when I was unable to carry on an informed dialogue because I had not done as much reading as intended, Tom would fill the gap by casually discoursing about one thing or another and interjecting wry comments. Unfortunately my ill ease, earnest seriousness, and lack of sophistication too often prevented me from appreciating his fine sense of humor. I envied my good friends, Atossa Herring and Ruth Dewing, who came back from their winter field trip to Mexico with tales of how much fun Tom had been. Their group was under the guidance of Atossa's father, a professor of South American history at one of the Claremont colleges in California, and Tom with his wife, Jean, and baby daughter had come along to assist him.

My appreciation of Tom grew over the years as he and Jean were always there to greet us when we returned to Bennington. The first occasion was the twenty-fifth anniversary of the opening of the college when Lyle and he hit it off right away. Thereafter Lyle would feel equally included as I by their warm welcome when we would drop in to see them at their home not far from the campus. Tom, who had served as dean for nine years and as acting president three times, continued his close ties to the college after his retirement in 1965. Before long he undertook writing a history of the college from the earliest hint of Reverend Booth's dream in 1923 to Dr. Leigh's retirement in 1941. During the process Tom sent me, and countless others, postcards in his fine handwriting that probed our memories and solicited comments as he came to each section. Many quotations from our replies enliven the book, published in 1981.

The last time I saw Tom was at my sixtieth reunion in 1996 when Atossa and I visited him at the small nursing home where he had been living since Jean's death a few years earlier. Though nearly 98, he was as jovial as ever and laughing about the good time he and Atossa had in Mexico. In December 1998 he celebrated his one-hundredth birthday at a grand party and died the following month. I was touched to read the tributes given to him at a memorial gathering that revealed how well loved he was by all who knew him, college friends, neighbors, and townspeople alike. He personified the continuity of the college and served as a link to the surrounding community. Nearly everyone mentioned his genial humor and his playfulness. Ruth wrote of an incident in Mexico when, after their group had attended a bullfight where they defied custom by cheering a bull who refused to budge, they repaired to a cantina to celebrate. At one point in their revelry Tom got down on his hands and knees on the dance floor and gave a wonderful imitation of a bull while Jean, unruffled, continued dancing.

Much as I would have enjoyed the trip to Mexico, I was committed to staying home for my winter break. I had missed out on the excitement of the Fusion campaign to elect Fiorello LaGuardia mayor of New York and my father Borough President of Brooklyn, I wanted to be around for the launching of the new regime.

My Father and City Politics

Politics was a frequent topic of conversation in our household, but most of it rolled over my head until I reached high school. Then, upon reentering Packer in the fall of 1928, I felt the intensity of bigotry in politics on the day I wore the little glass-studded donkey pin to school, and everyone jumped on me for favoring Governor Al Smith for president.

After Smith was defeated by Hoover and Roosevelt became governor, Dad resumed attention to city government which had been under the firm grip of Tammany Hall since 1917. I heard much talk about corruption by Tammany and the scandalous behavior of mayor

Jimmy Walker, a dashing and popular playboy who trusted his friends to run the city for him, no questions asked, while he lived it up. One of his favorite partying places was the Casino in Central Park. Walker had leased the sixty-year old building to a friend and encouraged private investors to make extravagant renovations including two glitzy ballrooms. Prohibition was circumvented by charging a three dollar cover charge and three dollars for a bottle of soda water to be mixed with liquor brought in by the customers. My father was shocked that a facility owned by the people should have been turned into such an elitist restaurant and swanky night spot. Fiorello LaGuardia made it a campaign issue when he ran against Walker in 1929, but his accusations fell on deaf ears, and the jaunty, wise-cracking mayor won again. Not even the stock market crash a few days before the election could dampen Jimmy's popularity. The following fall LaGuardia was again elected to Congress having already served five terms in the previous fourteen years. A maverick Republican, he resumed his role as a scrappy crusader for social welfare legislation.

Back in New York some Republican legislators and eventually the major newspapers were calling for an investigation of corruption in the Walker administration. At first Governor Roosevelt resisted proposals for widespread "fishing expeditions" against the mayor because he did not want to alienate Democratic voters, but in August 1930 he requested the Appellate Court of the boroughs of Manhattan and the Bronx to investigate the municipal courts within its jurisdiction. Retired Judge Samuel Seabury was chosen referee of the first of three investigations.

Judge Seabury, who came from a distinguished family, was learned, upright, and aloof. I know my father had high regard for him as a man of utmost integrity. They had worked together in the Fusion campaign that elected John Purroy Mitchel mayor in 1913 when Dad became park commissioner of Brooklyn. The Seabury investigations were carried on during my last two years of high school, but of course I can't recall the details. I had to wade through a laudatory biography of Walker just to ascertain the few facts mentioned here. However I remember that Seabury's final report in June 1932 accused Jimmy Walker of "malfeasance, misfeasance and nonfeasance." Walker was entitled to a hearing before the governor on the charges, but F.D.R. put it off until after the Democratic National Convention, as he didn't want to stir up Tammany opposition to his nomination for president. I was away at drama camp when the hearings took place in August. The upshot was that Roosevelt could not pin any wrongdoing on the mayor, only nonfeasance, i.e. neglect of duty. Expecting that the governor would remove him from office and taking the advice of Al Smith to resign for the good of the party, Jimmy Walker sent his resignation to the city clerk on September 1, 1932. A few days later he sailed off to Europe with his actress-sweetheart, Betty Compton.

Before long Judge Seabury and Dad were once again working together for a Fusion slate with a group of civic leaders consisting of liberal Republicans and independent Democrats unaffiliated with Tammany. They met regularly during the spring and early summer of 1993. Seabury was the informal leader of the group and everyone's first choice for mayor, but he firmly declined. Both Robert Moses, then park commissioner for the state, and LaGuardia wanted to run. Moses dropped out of the race when he realized that neither Seabury nor Al Smith would support him, but LaGuardia persisted. In spite of "The Little Flower's" brash, impulsive and loud manner, Seabury finally was persuaded that he was the only candidate who could win. His decision was also influenced by his good friend A.A. Berle, one of the early advisors to President-elect Roosevelt. Berle had asked LaGuardia to lead the fight for some New Deal legislation in Congress before the inauguration in March. As a "lame duck" congressman LaGuardia was free to give the project his all. He succeeded in rounding up the votes to pass an amendment of the bankruptcy laws and the creation of the Farm and Credit Home Bank. These measures enabled F.D.R. to move swiftly to meet the banking crisis as soon as he took office.

With LaGuardia's nomination assured by Seabury's support, the Fusion group turned to choosing candidates for the rest of the ballot. As far as I know they were unanimous in their choice of my father for Borough President of Brooklyn. He told me he couldn't refuse after twisting other people's arms to serve and knowing the shortage of good people.

The campaign began in earnest in September. Ray, a sophomore in high school at the time, tells me that often at dinner Dad would ask him if he had finished his homework. He always assured him he had.

"In that case, would you like to go campaigning with me tonight?"

The answer was always "Yes." A car and driver provided by the campaign committee would be waiting to take them to scheduled speaking engagements. These were held before small groups in storefront meeting rooms, union halls, or churches, but sometimes there would be a large gathering where LaGuardia would be the main speaker. Ray stayed quietly at the back of the hall and never seemed bored by hearing essentially the same speech over and over again. He says the only place he felt uncomfortable and out of place was in the churches. After they arrived home, usually about ten, Ray would go straight to bed. Sharing those evenings on the campaign trail meant a lot to him and I'm sure to Dad as well. My opportunity to participate in campaigning came four years latter when he was up for reelection.

In that 1933 election LaGuardia won with 40% of the votes in a three-way race against Tammany and the Recovery party newly formed by Roosevelt supporters. All the major Fusion candidates were voted in. Afterwards a reporter who came to our house to interview Dad confronted Mario, then thirteen, with "What are you going to do now that your father is Borough President?" "Keep him from getting a swelled head," was her quick reply.

Not that our father needed such monitoring as he was noted for his modesty, but I know he delighted in her sassy wit. It was about this time that he confided in me that far from being modest he had a good enough opinion of himself that he felt no need to "blow his own horn." He didn't mind if others took credit as long as their common goals were achieved. Nevertheless Dad was pleased when LaGuardia accepted his suggestion that they all take the Athenian oath of citizenship following the usual swearing in ceremony on New Year's Day. Upon coming of age the youth of ancient Athens pledged:

> To bring no disgrace to the city by dishonest act
> To fight for the ideals and sacred things alone and with many

To desert no faltering comrade

To revere and obey the City laws and to incite respect and reverence in those above us who are prone to annul or set them at naught

To strive unceasingly to quicken the public sense of civic duty

To transmit this city not less but better and more beautiful than it was transmitted to us.

Dad was glad to have me home for the two months following Christmas and to resume our conversational walks. As my project was to study city government I dutifully attended meetings of the two elected bodies: the Board of Alderman and the Board of Estimate. The first was made up of representatives from each of the city's many wards, and the second consisted of the three citywide officials: the Mayor, the Comptroller, and the President of the Board of Alderman, and the five Borough Presidents. Because the Board of Estimate initiated policy for the city as a whole Dad found serving on it more interesting than his limited duties as Borough President. However, as I must have confessed to him, I found the meetings boring as nothing much happened. Things were at a standstill as the bankrupt city was facing a serious financial crisis. Without a balanced budget (it was $30 million in arrears) bonds could not be sold nor federal grants obtained for public works to relieve unemployment such as completion of the new subway.

The real action was taking place elsewhere in Albany and Washington. LaGuardia lobbied for a state bill that would give him emergency powers to reorganize the city bureaucracy including elimination of nonessential jobs and pay cuts. He overcame Governor Lehman's objections that the proposal gave the mayor dictatorial powers by agreeing that these be vested in a majority of 10 of the 16 votes of the Board of Estimate. His fight for votes in the legislature called upon all of his dogged determination, political skill, and willingness to compromise. In the end a considerably watered down version of the bill passed on April 9, 1934. By that time I had long since returned to Bennington.

Although LaGuardia was impulsive and scrappy his boyish exuberance endeared him to many followers as they knew his concern for the common people came from his heart. He is still fondly remembered for his dramatic radio readings of the Sunday "funny papers" to the city's children during a newspaper strike.

In contrast Robert Moses, the new city-wide park commissioner and director of the Triborough Bridge Authority, though admired for his accomplishments, was arrogant and ruthless. As park commissioner for the state under Al Smith he had developed an extensive parkway system and built Jones Beach State Park on the south shore of Long Island. The ocean beach was very popular among people who owned cars, while those without had to content themselves with Coney Island at the end of the old subway line in Brooklyn. Moses moved rapidly ahead in both his new jobs developing new city parks and playgrounds and improving old ones. Although most people sang his praises not everybody appreciated his massive concrete "improvements." But Moses was no compromiser and not afraid to step on toes. Inevitably his high-handed attitude led to many clashes with the mayor.

Dad used to say that the hardest part of his job was trying to keep peace between the two prima donnas. Over the years Moses became more and more dictatorial and difficult to deal with, while Dad's friendship with LaGuardia deepened. In 1937 the LaGuardias rented a summer cottage on Asharoken Beach adjacent to the beginning of our causeway and about a half mile from our house. He liked to walk the beach to pay us a visit, sometimes bringing his wife, Marie, and their two young children along. Once when he dropped in to talk with Dad about some situation that agitated him Ray overheard his father saying, "Keep your shirt on Fiorello!"

Unfortunately the LaGuardias stayed at the cottage for only two years, driven out by the famous hurricane of 1938. Marie was alone with the children that weekday afternoon in mid-September when Long Island was struck without warning. The furious wind and huge waves were frightening enough, but then after the wind subsided and the bay was calm the tide, augmented by the storm surge, continued to rise up the beach above the usual high tide mark. Marie watched in alarm as the water relentlessly spread across her front yard, entered her house and covered her living room floor.

On Duck Island mother had been unfazed by the fury of the gale, but afterwards was dismayed to see that the tops of several of the tall oaks silhouetted against the bay had been snapped off. None of us remember if the phones were still working or if Marie called mother, but in any case mother set out with Roger Hennessey, the caretaker, to see what they could do to help her. By that time it was near dusk. Since the causeway was flooded they could not drive so they had to wade through the water. When they reached the LaGuardia's house they found Marie and the children on the second floor. She was utterly terrified. Whether or how she was able to communicate with Fiorello I do not know, but eventually he arrived having driven out from the city with a police escort. Marie was so shaken that she never wanted to risk facing another hurricane.

Meanwhile Mother and Roger had to make their way back through knee-deep water. The night sky was clear and lighted by the moon and brilliant stars. However, Roger was really scared and insisted upon using his flashlight. Mother was unable to persuade him that they could see the few cedar trees that marked the edge of the road much better if he'd just turn the "pesky" thing off. She was enjoying the adventure and kept exclaiming over the phosphorescence they stirred up in the warm water. Finally, in exasperation, Roger blurted out, "I don't give a damn about the phosphorescence!"

Actually mother was very lucky She and her birding friends had planned to drive out to East Hampton that day to look for migrating shore birds and spend the night at a hotel on the beach, but the forecast of rain led them to cancel their trip. Later the birders were shocked to see in the *Times* a picture of a demolished hotel, the very one where they had intended to stay. The storm had taken everyone by surprise because it moved north over the ocean very rapidly, and, unlike most hurricanes that strike land further south, it didn't reach shore until it hit Long Island. Today weather satellites would have provided more advanced warning. Ray was lucky too. He had driven Mario up the Connecticut valley to Northampton where she was entering Smith. After he got her stuff unloaded and into her room he decided to return by way of the Hudson River parkways so he could look up a girl at Vassar. He found the college had not yet opened so missed the girl, but he also missed the hurricane, which was roaring up the Connecticut valley. Though he ran into patches of heavy rain he made it to my apartment in Greenwich Village without any trouble. Mario told him later about how frightened she was walking back from a freshman orientation meeting to her dorm as she struggled against a howling and overpowering wind while tree limbs cracked and crashed around her.

Russia and Romance

In November 1933 Roosevelt recognized Russia and lifted the ban on trade and travel that had been in effect since the Bolshevik revolution in 1917. Not long thereafter the first student study tour to the Soviet Union was announced for the following summer. I was immediately eager to go. I wanted to see firsthand how Russia's "socialist experiment," as it was often called, was fulfilling the promise to improve living conditions for all her people. The fact that the trip was sponsored by the Anglo-American Council reassured Dad who had great respect for one of its board members. In retrospect I'm sure that the American Communist Party was the undeclared sponsor, but no one mentioned that possibility. The upshot was that two classmates, Janet Summers and Ellen Knapp, and I signed up. Dad jokingly predicted that I'd probably fall in love with a Russian.

We set sail in late June on a seaworthy ship whose name has long since been forgotten. Its third class cabins were very cramped, but that didn't bother me as I was cheerfully prepared to put up with anything. Our group numbered about seventy, mostly college students with some of the older members in leadership roles such as conducting seminars on board. We docked in Hamburg and took a train to Copenhagen where the high spot was an enchanted evening in Tivoli, a charming, low-keyed amusement park. After another brief stop in Stockholm we boarded a boat to Helsinki. (My memories of these cities blur with those of a longer trip to Scandinavia three years later with Ruth Dewing and her mother.) From Helsinki we took a train to Leningrad, now returned to its original name of St. Petersburg. My only clear recollection of that city was trekking through long corridors of the Imperial Palace where the rich art collections of the Czars were displayed. We passed so many paintings of lavish banquets and voluptuous women that by the time we reached the French Impressionists I was too weary to give them the attention they deserved.

Finally an overnight train brought us to Moscow where we expected to spend a month at the university mingling with Russian students. Instead, our group was tucked away in some obscure corner, and the only students we saw were three or four English-speaking ones who were assigned to us for the length of our stay. Classes were held in the one large room where we also ate our meals. They covered Marxist theory, the history of the revolution, the invasion by the White Russians and their foreign allies, and the severe hardships the people encountered while trying to establish a functioning economy. Most of all we learned about the Soviet Union's achievements. The country had just embarked on its second five-year plan having completed the first in 1933. Everywhere we heard the same refrain: "We accomplished the five year plan in four and a half years." They were also very proud of their conquest of illiteracy and their creation of an extensive health care system.

Our daily field trips to factories, collective farms, clinics, and schools invariably followed the same pattern. The director or some other high ranking official would give us an effusive welcome and then launch into a description of the enterprise weighed down with statistics of production quotas met, number of persons served, and goals surpassed. Presumably these details fitted neatly into the grand master plan for the entire country. At the end of the presentation, doubly long for having to be translated by our guide/interpreter, we would be conducted on a tour of the premises. Invariably there would be a wall newspaper displayed in some prominent spot. I was impressed that day care was provided on site for the workers' children where mothers came on their breaks to nurse their babies.

We were well entertained by classical opera and ballet and by performances of folk dancing and singing. My favorite recreation was wandering about in the "parks of culture and rest" where we could mingle with crowds of people all enjoying themselves.

When it came to social life Janet, Ellen, and I went our separate ways. While I gravitated toward the older more serious students, they formed a group of younger, fun-loving ones. Some of them got up a mock wall newspaper entitled "The Wailing Wall," an assortment of in-jokes referring to daily life within our group of Americans. Janet, the artist, contributed a cartoon showing some of us women lined up for our turn at the shower room. Most of us found their stunt an amusing and harmless diversion, but not so the higher-ups. In no uncertain terms they reprimanded the pranksters for offending our Russian hosts and, by implication, disrespecting the Peoples' Revolution. That put a damper on our spirits! I was sorry they could not share our sense of humor and laugh with us, but I have since observed that inability to appreciate another's humor usually reflects underlying differences in basic beliefs.

After the month in Moscow two weeks remained for travel to other parts of the country. I had intended to go with Janet and Ellen on a trip that included Kiev in the Ukraine and Odessa on the Black Sea. That is until Howard, a philosophy professor and our group's authority on Marxism, invited me to join him and a few others who were privileged to be the first foreigners to visit the nearly completed White Sea Canal linking the White Sea to the Baltic. I was flattered that Howard had chosen me. How could I turn him down, even though a canal in the remote north was not as appealing per se as swimming in the Black Sea?

The expedition turned out to be a long monotonous train ride, about 1800 miles round trip. First we returned to Leningrad. From there we skirted the south end of Lake Ladoga, the largest lake in Europe, then turned north to Lake Onega, another large one. We followed its shoreline northward and that of a smaller lake until we came to the start of the canal that would connect this chain of lakes to the White Sea two hundred miles due west of Archangel. The canal, stretching fifty miles across desolate country, was still an empty ditch when we saw it. The Russians considered it an engineering marvel as well it might have been, but I was more concerned that it had been built by prison labor. Our questions regarding the working and living conditions of the prisoners were evaded by discourses on how useful work was a more effective method of rehabilitation than sitting idly in a cell. The implication was that after a season of labor many offenders would be ready to return to society. No mention was made of what happened to the rest of them during the bitter winter months when they could not dig the frozen ground nor of how many might have been political prisoners. It has since been revealed that of the 300,000 convicts who built the canal 100,000 perished. Looking back I'm amazed at how naive I was then. Of course it was before the world learned of Stalin's famous trials of 1935-38 that ruthlessly purged the party of alleged heretics and the army of potential traitors.

Whatever political doubts I may have had were swept aside by Howard's personal attentions. Not only was he our respected leader, but he was eleven and a half years older than I, so no wonder I was somewhat in awe of him. He and I had many conversations while riding the trains, but most included others of our group. The only way we could be alone was to stand in the outside space between the railway cars. When we reached Kiev after our trip north we took advantage of greater opportunities for privacy. In those last two or three days together, while Howard kept telling me that I was beautiful, I was rapidly falling in love with him. In my euphoria I could not foresee the ensuing emotional turmoil that would disrupt my last two years of college.

Before leaving the country our groups reunited in Moscow for a farewell celebration. Of course many speeches were delivered by the American leadership and our Russian hosts. On rather short notice I was asked to make a few remarks from the point of view of a student, so naturally I exclaimed over how much we had enjoyed learning about their beautiful country and their great undertaking. Then I expanded on the point that as a student I felt a kinship with the Russian people who were also eager learners with good reason to be proud of their accomplishments. I'm sure I expressed appropriate gratitude for their hospitality. Afterwards when I asked Howard how he thought I did he said something to the effect that I was so charming it didn't really matter what I said. I was crushed. Had I been too simplistic or not sufficiently laudatory? Now, in this day and age, I'm appalled by his patronizing attitude.

Since Howard and I had different itineraries we did not see each other again until some time after we arrived home. I had arranged to return by way of Berlin so I could visit Annemarie Rudiger, the friend I made in 1931 when she hosted the Open Road group of southern girls I was traveling with. Although we were glad to see each other we failed to capture our original mutual attraction. She no longer seemed the vibrant and inspiring person I remembered her to be, and I was no longer a lonesome and adoring sixteen year old. Even so we might have bridged the gap had it not been for Hitler. I carefully refrained from expressing my enthusiasm for the Soviet Union, and tried to confine our conversation to personal matters. After confiding that she and her husband were hoping to start a family soon she told me with sadness that his string quartet had disbanded because two of its members were Jews. My face must have registered my dismay when she attempted to justify the exclusion of Jews with the analogy of a mother pig who has more piglets than she can suckle so must kill one in order for the others to survive. I was so shaken by her statement that I shudder every time I think of it. Thereafter our friendship lapsed to an occasional exchange of Christmas cards. However, when it became possible to send Care packages at the end of the war, I sent her several anonymously. Annemarie expressed profuse gratitude on behalf of her family that now included six children. Naturally she wanted to know who her benefactor was and wondered if I might be one of the friends she made while a student in the United States before we met. Somehow I could never bring myself to reveal my identity.

Last Year at Bennington

The greatest pleasure of my junior year was my developing friendship with Ruth Dewing facilitated by our living in adjacent rooms. Miki, as she was then called, and I loved to exchange lofty ideas. The youngest of three sisters, she too had grown up with stimulating table conversation. Her mother, in 1906, was the first woman to earn a Ph.D. in philosophy at Harvard where her parents met in a philosophy seminar conducted by William James. Her father went on to become Harvard's eminent professor of corporate finance.

Miki and I would talk long into the night and often became so excited that after saying our "good nights" one of us would feel compelled to pop into the other's room to add just one more thought to top off the discussion. One of our on-going topics centered on the difference between education and propaganda. Miki was a staunch believer in education as a remedy for our social ills. I valued education too, but thought she was too idealistic in believing it could be purely objective and neutral. I claimed that in reality much of education was biased and therefore propaganda. The subject's many ramifications, including issues of truth, deception, and social goals, thwarted our efforts to arrive at clear and consistent definitions. When our discourse spilled over into our psychology class taught by Ted Newcomb who had joined the faculty that fall, he suggested we pursue the subject as an independent study project. However, even with his enthusiastic encouragement I still couldn't tame the lion I had by the tail, for I was wrestling with my own conflicting political and philosophical convictions.

At this time alarm over the rise of Hitler and the growing fear of war in the country at large was reflected on college campuses where many convinced pacifists declared their refusal to fight in any war by taking the Oxford Oath. Radical politics came to Bennington in the form of proselytizers representing various student organizations. One was Diro, a dynamic young man from Dartmouth who rather overwhelmed us with his compelling arguments as to why we should join the National Student League (NSL). More soft-spoken delegates came from the Student League for Industrial Democracy (SLID) with known ties to the Socialist party. It was rumored, but not admitted, that the NSL was fostered by the Communist party. Both groups claimed the same broad goals of opposition to war and fascism and support of peace and democracy. The few of us who turned out for these visitations persisted in asking for explanations of the differences between the two groups, but we received no satisfactory answers. Finally, in frustration, we formed our own organization, the BUF, the Bennington United Front. We were quite pleased with ourselves when subsequently the national NSL and SLID reached the same solution by merging to create the American Student Union.

Meanwhile, that fall Janet Summers and I accepted Diro's invitation to attend a meeting of his NSL branch in Dartmouth. He gave her quite a rush and she succumbed to his charms, but within a few months she was able to separate her attraction to him from her attraction to his beliefs. She rejected the man, but kept the politics. It took me another year to do the same, for I was head over heels in love.

In fact I was practically commuting to Howard's apartment in Greenwich Village every second or third weekend, a four hour drive each way. I don't know how I did it! One rainy Sunday evening it was after eight o'clock when I hit the road back to college. Much of the way I drove through heavy downpours guided only by the blurred taillights of the truck ahead of me. Tense and tired, I stopped at a roadside restaurant for a cup of coffee, but was too unnerved to relax. When I reached Bennington sometime after midnight I was utterly exhausted. Next day I wrote Howard a vivid description of my ordeal to which he replied with sympathy and amazement. Since he didn't drive he had no idea of what an undertaking it was to drive alone at night in the rain.

Not only was the travel back and forth a strain, but so too was the shift from one mode of thought to another. Bennington's encouragement to think independently increased my self-confidence, but while with Howard I felt humble and looked up to him as the voice of authority. This inequality in our relationship made me uneasy, but I attributed the problem to his being so much older than I and hoped that in time I would catch up to him. We agreed that we would wait to get married until after I graduated. In this decision I was fortified by my parents' subtle support. Although they were not happy about my liaison with Howard, they wisely refrained from saying so. Once, before they had met him, I poured out my admiration for Howard on a walk with Dad. He listened patiently until I was finished, then after a thoughtful pause remarked, "Now that you have told me all his good qualities what are his faults?"

I was taken aback and could only stammer, "I suppose he has some, but I don't know what they are."

During the winter field and reading period I elected to stay home and work as a volunteer teacher's aide at Woodward School where Marion had gone. It seemed like a good way to explore teaching as a possible career. Needless to say, Howard and I got together frequently during those two months.

Meanwhile Miki, free from encumbering alliances, boldly found herself a job working on the line at a textile mill in Fall River. She was interested in finding out what her fellow workers thought about their lives and their place in the world. They were a varied lot, mostly all women who came from several different countries. In her report about the experience she wrote that she discovered there was no such thing as a workers' point of view because all had different points of view. This adventure later led her into labor mediation.

Miki and I shared more than our big ideas. For instance, admitting our chagrin at being overweight, we decided to take action and go on a diet together. We gave up all deserts except fruit with the pleasing result that we each lost ten or more pounds. She kept her svelte figure all her life, but my excess baggage returned when I had children and stayed with me some forty years.

Although my turmoil over Howard must have been obvious, I did not talk much about it with Miki, but throughout I felt supported by her steadiness and her caring. Edie, my other confidant, was also sympathetic and understanding. Neither passed judgment on Howard when he visited me for a weekend, but it was a different matter with the Joneses. Barbara, who was my advisor that year, did not hesitate to express her disappointment. I had led them to expect a brilliant intellectual, but they found him to be rigid and doctrinaire. She predicted that a marriage to him would end in divorce, but added she thought me strong enough to survive such an outcome. Small comfort! Divorce meant failure to say the least and many people considered it a disgrace. Though I tried to discount her opinion as rejection of Howard's communist beliefs, I was nevertheless shaken.

As the spring term progressed I became more and more distressed. I didn't see how I could keep up the commuting routine for another year. Since the one thing I was clear about was that I intended to finish college, it occurred to me that I would be better off doing so at some far away place. Miki, in consultation with Lewis Jones, her advisor, had already decided to spend the next year at Reed College in Portland, Oregon, since Bennington had expanded the concept of "Junior Year Abroad" to apply to any appropriate off-campus plan. When I proposed to Barbara Jones that I take my senior year elsewhere and confided my real reasons for doing so she readily understood. She thought this way out of my predicament a good one and suggested the University of Wisconsin because it was strong in labor economics, my field of interest. Our official reason for my move was that I would benefit from being in a large co-educational university in contrast to Bennington where I was a big frog in a little puddle. So that is how I came to spend my senior year in Madison, Wisconsin.

Before continuing I should mention Jerry's marriage on April 15, 1935, to Minneola Perry from Montgomery, Alabama. They met in the summer of 1933 at the Farm School on Wheels soon after Jerry's delayed graduation from Amherst. She was one of a group of students whom Olive Stone brought on a field trip to observe farm conditions. At the time of their marriage the school was stationed in Kansas City. As neither Min nor Jerry wanted to return to her home for a formal wedding they were quite content to transact their nuptial agreement at city hall, but not our mother. She wanted to participate! As she had already been planning a train trip with Raymond during his spring vacation to visit Marion at her boarding school in Santa Fe, she simply arranged to return by way of Colorado Springs where Jerry met them in his truck. Ray tells me that on the drive through Kansas he was deeply impressed by the devastation of farmland brought on by the dust storms. At Kansas City he took a train east to get back to school on time while Dad was traveling west to join the wedding party.

Meanwhile, Mother, convinced of the importance of romantic memories, persuaded Jerry and Min to seek out some scenic spot for the ceremony and an attractive place to spend their wedding night. They settled on a small hotel at Excelsior Springs, about an hour's drive south of the city. Incidentally this resort was later made famous by President Truman when he retreated there to sleep undisturbed on election night in 1948. So that is how Jerry and Min came to be wed beside a rushing stream in Missouri by a minister brought in to officiate and with Mother and Dad as witnesses. Somehow Mother managed to secretly festoon the bridal bedroom with flowers and other decorations. She even put rice in the bed, which unfortunately did not endear her to her new daughter-in-law! A snapshot of Jerry and Min in front of a waterfall is the first photograph in the family wedding album, now spanning three generations and faithfully kept up to date by Elex.

That summer Howard and I spent a lot of time together, but the only event that stands out was our visit to his parents in Harrisburg, Pennsylvania. Howard showed me the elegant Victorian houses on Front Street along the Susquehanna and the somewhat less grand ones behind them on First Street. He pointed out the neat sorting of the city's residents by class as the houses became more modest the further away they were from the river. His family home was on Fourth or Fifth Street not far from his father's grocery store. His parents' hospitality to me was topped off by delicious homemade black raspberry ice cream.

The University of Wisconsin

The University of Wisconsin accepted me as a special student with no need to transfer credits because I would be graduating from Bennington. My parents, wanting to be sure I had a safe place to live, consulted their friends, the Dewetters whose daughter, Noelle, had moved to Madison the previous year. Her husband, Henry Sterling, was a graduate student in the Geography Department there. She suggested Ann Emery Hall on Langdon Street, a privately run dormitory for women students. I took a room there for the first semester since none were available for upperclasswomen in the university-run dorms.

It turned out I was surrounded by freshmen, and what a shock that was! They were in the midst of "rush" and could talk of nothing else. Getting accepted by the right sorority was serious business, because, as one explained to me, the best fraternities dated the best sororities. I found little in common with them as they revealed no interest in their classes. Most were majoring in English, but it appeared that the marriage market was their main course of study. I didn't have much luck with my classmates either. For instance, once after a particularly interesting lecture in anthropology by Ralph Linton I spoke to him after class to follow up on some point he had made. When I mentioned this conversation to another student, hoping to continue the discussion, the reply was, "Oh, apple polishing." What a contrast to Bennington!

The Sterlings invited me to dinner soon after I arrived, and later tried to set up a date for doubles tennis with a fellow graduate student of Henry's, but it was canceled because of rain. My partner was to have been Lyle Craine whom I met six years later in August 1941 on a sailboat on the Chesapeake Bay. As that encounter was so fortuitous, I was always glad the tennis date never took place, because neither of us was ready for the other just then. Also at that time I might have thought Lyle was too conventional, and he might have found me too unconventional, a hunch given a boost when I saw his glamorous high school photograph on his parents' piano.

My social life on the Wisconsin campus finally took off when I found a place among the radical students, mostly members of the American Student Union. Ironically nearly all of them were New Yorkers, but my ease with them had less to do with our common hometown than with our shared concerns. Belonging to a mixed group of men and women students was a new pleasure after all my years in segregated girls schools. Furthermore my commitment to Howard freed me to relate to the men as friends rather than as potential dates. Dan Lang in particular was fun to be with as he had a delightful sense of humor and didn't take himself too seriously.

Dan must have given me a new perspective, because when I returned home for Christmas vacation I saw aspects of Howard that I had not noticed before. During a dinner conversation at Duck Island I was shocked and ashamed by his arrogant belittling of one of Dad's mildly expressed opinions. In all the lively discussions that took place in our home with guests of many viewpoints I had never heard anyone show such disrespect toward my father.

Howard, impatient with the long wait till June, suggested we could get married sooner if I took my last semester at Columbia where married students were accepted. In spite of mounting misgivings I promised I'd try to get permission from Bennington to make this transfer. Fortunately Barbara and Lewis Jones were spending the winter break in the city and were glad to see me. After loyally presenting Howard's proposal as convincingly as I could, I confessed that I really didn't want to go through with it, so would they please simply refuse to grant the request. They were more than willing to concur. Since none of this connivance was in writing I was spared embarrassment and given more time to work my way out of my relationship with Howard. I've always been grateful for Lewis and Barbara's understanding support at this difficult crisis in my life.

At mid-term I came home with the intention of breaking off with Howard, but I lacked the nerve because I couldn't bear to hurt his feelings. Instead I wrote him as kind a letter as I could compose soon after I returned. I also naively wrote to the couple who were his closest friends expressing remorse for having to hurt him. As I should have predicted they showed my letter to Howard, which prompted him to write a very angry one to me claiming that I had insulted and humiliated him. Thus my letter to his friends probably served as a more decisive end to our love affair than the "kind" one I had written to him.

Within a year I was glad to learn that Howard had married a faculty colleague who was a year or two older than he. He had once told me about her with the comment that it was too bad such an intelligent and attractive woman should have missed out on marriage because of her age. Our only subsequent encounter was in the summer of 1950 when I chanced to meet him and his twelve year old son at one of the newer public beaches on the south shore of Long Island where I had gone with my children and our extended family group of Ingersolls and Crarys. My main impressions during our brief conversation were his rather prissy manner and how small in stature he was compared to Lyle.

At the end of the first the semester at Wisconsin it was a relief to move out of Ann Emery Hall and into a private home near campus where I shared two small rooms with another woman student. As there were no cooking facilities I took my meals at the Student Union cafeteria usually with Dan. We both had heavy study loads. Although I did well in a labor history class taught by Professor Perlman, successor to John R. Commons, I floundered in a course on the Renaissance given by a renowned authority, who overwhelmed me with an avalanche of allusions to events and concepts of which I was ignorant. But what nearly did me in was advanced statistics, ill-prepared as I was by the introduction received from Andree Emery, the flaky Hungarian. Presumably Dan was taking subjects that he hoped would further his aspirations to become a writer. Later several of his pieces were published in *The New Yorker,* and eventually he became a member of their staff.

Frequently we would join in gloomy discussions with our ASU friends about the rising threat of fascism as we followed the news of Mussolini's conquest of Ethiopia and Hitler's unopposed march into the Rhineland, but our spirits lifted when Spain's popular front won a decisive victory in the February, '36 elections. Although Dan had strong convictions they were tempered by a critical mind. He didn't think he had all the answers or that any one else did either. His sense of humor saved him from that trap. In the spring we enjoyed some lovely walks in the woods and along the lake shore. He and I continued to go together for the next five years. Although I became very fond of Dan I never considered that I was in love with him, but Mario says he was obviously very much in love with me.

In June I returned to Bennington for graduation. There I marched in procession with my fifty-three classmates garbed in royal blue capes and matching skull caps of a sateen fabric that glistened in the sun. Throughout the ceremony on the silo foundation at the corner entrance to the barn, speakers kept reminding us that we were participating in an historic moment—the graduation of Bennington's first class. Predictably the college administration has never let us forget it.

Asho as a young woman; below: camping
in the Smokies and hiking with Mario.

Chapter 5
My First Job

My intention had always been to find a job after graduation, preferably an interesting one that would make a contribution to society, but having no clear goals, specific skills, or previous experience I was ill-equipped for the search. Moreover in 1936 the depression was still severe and work was scarce. I felt uneasy because others needed paid employment far more than I did as my family could continue to support me, but on the other hand I wanted to be independent. I don't recall taking any overt steps toward looking for work that summer, but suppose I must have fallen into the habit of thinking I was on vacation.

Meanwhile Dan had been seeking out possibilities. He learned that the Works Progress Administration (WPA) was hiring statistical clerks in Philadelphia for a national study on unemployment. He applied and was offered a job even though his major had been in English. He was sure that I with two courses in statistics under my hat would qualify also and arranged an interview for me in late September. So I took a train to Philadelphia and showed up for the appointment. In spite of my nervousness I was hired at $27.50 per week ($1440 per annum) a very good entry wage for those times. The study, entitled "Re-employment Opportunities and Recent Changes in Industrial Techniques," was mandated by the act of Congress that established the WPA. Our offices covered two or more upper floors of the city's tallest skyscraper whose top was adorned on all four sides by illuminated red letters—PSFS—standing for *Philadelphia Savings and Fiduciary Society.* I can imagine how shocked the bank's staid Quaker founders would be if they could have seen those red letters blazing forth in the sky as they still do today.

My desk was one of a multitude in an enormous room and far from any windows. I soon found out that I didn't need statistics to do the work that mostly consisted of copying sheets and sheets of long numbers or checking the numbers someone else had copied. Sometimes I multiplied or divided such numbers by entering them into a calculator, a clunky machine with a bank of a hundred keys—ten rows of the ten digits. As a rare treat I'd be sent to the library to copy more numbers from tomes of the *US Census of Manufactures.* Handling the source of all those numbers gave me a little more sense of the relevance of my work to our part of the project. Its purpose was to determine the changes over time of labor productivity by calculating the output per man-hour for various products. The greatest change I discovered was in the manufacture of light bulbs that in just a few years went from being individually hand-crafted to totally machine processed. In sum my job was tedious and boring.

Nor did I find much in the city to cheer me up after work. At my father's suggestion I stayed at first in a women's hotel, a formal and lonely place. Later I moved into a small furnished apartment that, though certainly informal, hardly felt homey. Dan and I spent a lot of our free time together, but he must have been as depressed as I for I don't remember our having much fun. One memory of life in Philadelphia still haunts me. Leaving work at dusk on a cold autumn evening and stepping into the street darkened by tall buildings, I looked up and saw a plume of vivid pink smoke high above me proclaiming a sunset. I was struck by a surge of sorrow for the city's downtrodden, myself included, who were deprived of experiencing its full glory and wished I could capture the thought in a poem. The title would have been "Somewhere a Sunset."[1]*

On occasional Sundays my spirits were lifted by escapes to Swarthmore where Ray was a freshman in the college. He would meet me at the train station, and we would walk through the attractive town to campus. He was glad to show me around and tell me of his new life, while I was happy just to be with him and to drink in his pleasant surroundings. My only specific memory is of hearing a lovely choral concert, but Ray's is of the good dinners we indulged in at Inglenook in the Swarthmore Inn.

Starting in November many of my weekends were devoted to a part-time job as an interviewer for the Gallup Poll. It was then a small start-up company that had just correctly predicted Roosevelt's win of a second term in the 1936 election. Its older and prestigious rival, the Liberty Poll conducted by the ultraconservative Liberty magazine, had assured its readers that the Republican candidate, Alf Landon, would be the next president. When FDR won by a landslide the poll was discredited and the magazine soon folded. Because the Liberty poll was conducted entirely by telephone it failed to reach low income voters who could not afford phones in those days, thus excluding the strongest supporters of the New Deal. Gallup, on the other hand, made an effort to sample a cross section of voters by interviewing them in their homes.

Immediately following the election Gallup, obviously in an expansive mood, flooded the newspapers with ads recruiting college graduates and students. I applied and was readily accepted. I think the whole transaction was done by mail as I don't recall undergoing a job interview or receiving any training. However the instructions were clear and explicit: the interviewer was to select a certain number of high, medium, or low income households, observe the level of affluence of each living room and rank it on a scale of one to five, and ask whether the home was owned or rented and whether there was a telephone. We were to interview only one person per household. There were usually around eight or ten survey questions most asking for yes or no answers with an occasional open ended one.

I did all my door-to-door visits in daylight hours, and traveled to the various neighborhoods by streetcar. Pay was at the rate of twenty minutes per interview, but I always took longer. Probably I was too conscientious in explaining the purpose of the survey and the meaning of the more complicated questions. Also I took a little extra time to be friendly as I thought it rude to rush in and out. Imagine my shock when I ran across some college students also working for the Gallup Poll who boasted that they just went into a local bar and got all their interviews at once. So much for scientific sampling! Nevertheless the experience of meeting poor people in their own homes gave me new insights into poverty. I certainly learned more about the world on that short job than I did at PSFS.

---

[1] * See Three Haiku in the poetry section of this volume.

Chapter 6
Memory Letters to Lyle

I

Douglas Lake, July 1, 1996

Dear Lyle,

Home again for another summer at our well-loved little cabin. Already, after only one night's sleep, I feel the peacefulness of this place penetrating my bones and restoring me to my true self. I'm sitting here at the table looking out at the calm lake through the familiar silhouette of the triple oaks on the ice rampart. As I delight in the morning sunlight sparkling on the not yet trammeled tall grass on the path up the bank, memories of the life we shared here flood over me. At the start of this fourth summer since you died I have a strong urge to capture those memories in writing and have decided to try doing so in terms of letters to you. We'll see if it works.

Mario is with me now for two weeks and there will be other visitors, but I look forward to being alone much of the time. While puttering around the place my actions often remind me of you, especially as I take on some of your chores like carrying the pail of vegetable scraps up to the compost heap by the garden or closing the shed doors at night.

You would be pleased to see how tidy the boat shed is now after being sadly neglected following your stroke eight years ago. You can imagine what a mess the chipmunks and other little creatures made, not to mention the helter-skelter way things got put away by me and friends who came to the cabin for brief stays while you were trapped in the nursing home. I tackled the Herculean task summer before last. There was no way I could lift those bags of organic fertilizer: lime, phosphorus, green stone, and dry manure. Miraculously, various neighbors took them off my hands. I gave some of your garden tools to John Young. He was just a college kid when he laid the shed floor for us, and now he owns a home in Charlevoix with Anna, his doctor wife, and their two small children. A special collection of toxic wastes in Harbor Springs was an incentive to sort through the cupboard and get rid of old paint and insect repellents. I even found some rat poison, which must have been here when we bought the cabin in 1960. But what was I to do about your tools left in open trays on the workbench? Of course I had taken the toolbox with your better ones home to Ann Arbor as we always did, but these were rusted and covered with crud and the pliers wouldn't open. The Cheboygan Hardware manager came to my rescue by advising WD40. Now your restored tools are in a little red plastic box with air vents to keep them from rusting again.

There were other maintenance problems that seemed appalling at first until Betty and Jack Young referred me to a man to paint the cabin and Jeanne Osgood recommended her carpenter who replaced the cover of the electric pump that had rotted off its hinges. I'm so grateful you made arrangements with our plumber to open and close the cabin as it was high time you spared yourself the strain of lifting those heavy shutters. No doubt you were also thinking ahead to the day when I would have to cope alone. You certainly relieved me of a burden, especially when it came time to leave after your hospital stay in Petoskey. Yesterday I found someone to put in and take out the dock and boats so I won't have to impose on the Youngs for that job anymore.

July 9, 1996

Mario and I are having a leisurely and companionable visit. After my yoga stretches and a late breakfast we both spend an hour or so writing. She is composing poetry while I'm just scribbling random thoughts from which I can later select whatever seems to belong in these letters. At noon we walk the mile up the road through the woods and the "avenue of pines" to the mailboxes. There we take the customary pause to look out over Gates Bog before going down the track that cuts through the abandoned orchard. We lunch at the picnic table on the bank, and afterwards settle there in the lounge chairs to read as we used to do. Mario is charmed by our outdoor living room where we watch the late afternoon sunlight strike the soft boughs of the white pines at the end of the hollow behind the ice rampart. So often, wherever I may be outdoors, I find myself noticing the light and thinking how you would have wanted to capture it on film.

We have been reading *Women Who Run with the Wolves*, by Clarisa Pinkola Estés about discovering our essential nature. She advocates "intentional solitude" as a way to go home to one's soul, which I suppose is what meditation did for you. Her concept is less demanding than the Buddhists' as she includes daydreaming, staring into space, and talking to oneself to evoke an inquiry into one's state of being. But sometimes, she says, there are no questions, just rest. That sounds more like "empty mind" to me. How I would love to discuss this topic with you! I wonder if you were able to meditate after your stroke imposed "unintentional" solitude. Probably not, but I believe your previous experience with meditation helped you to accept your loss of speech. I know that the quiet intimacy we enjoyed here after your retirement helped us both communicate without words. Now Mario and I are finding the satisfactions of silent companionship by falling into the same easy rhythm. Remember her earlier visits when she and I would indulge in long talk fests? You would hang in there for a while and then politely excuse yourself. Life is less strenuous now that she and I have outgrown our compulsive need to confide all and have resolved most of our sibling rivalries.

July 15, 1996

The weather has been too chilly for more than a couple of quick dips in the lake, but Mario and I had some lovely canoeing along the wooded shore. Seeing her off at the Pellston airport day before yesterday left me desolate for a while. However puttering at housekeeping tasks has reoriented me to being alone again. I hadn't realized how fatiguing her "leisurely" visit was until I found that I had slept close to eleven hours last night!

Yesterday being Sunday there was no need to walk up for the mail, so instead I made my way through Camp Manitou's overgrown Christmas tree plantation to the row of glacial mounds that border the big field. As I climbed up the highest one, crunching the dry gray moss underfoot, I thought of the many times we had enjoyed that expansive view. We often commented on the subtle colors in the rough field below. Now that the yellow hawkweed is past blooming most of the vegetation is rather dull, but it is enlivened by streaks of the rusty red seed stalks of sheep sorrel and by a patch of tall waving bronze grass.

Steve was the first to love this hilly field where he had played adventure games as an eleven-year old camper at Manitou two years before we bought the cabin. On days too windy to go out on the lake you used to bring the grandchildren here to fly kites. Remember how disappointed little Daniel was when he didn't fly up in the air with the kite like Curious George, the monkey?

The last time we walked here together was a few weeks before your stroke. Suddenly you didn't feel right and had to sit down. The episode passed, but I suggested you wait while I go back for the car. You accepted my offer without protest and I was touched by your excessive gratitude for this small service. You must have been more shaken than I realized. I didn't think it was anything serious even when a few days later you told me that while waiting for me to get the car it occurred to you that if anyone wanted to do something with your ashes this would be the place to scatter them. After your stroke Harold Hart told us that when they visited us you had mentioned having had a couple of blank outs. Perhaps this had been one of the "mini" strokes later revealed by the CAT scan, very small spots where your brain had been damaged and replaced by fluid. Not that there was anything we could have done about them.

July 19, 1996

I had to go to the Laundromat yesterday on my weekly trip to town for groceries, and by the time I returned the day was shot. However I'm proud to report that, thanks to having watched you so often work on electric cords, I managed to install a new switch to the light above the kitchen sink.

Today is Elise's twenty-first birthday. She has become a beautiful and outgoing young woman with Ellen's lovely smile, quite a contrast to the aloof twelve-year-old who was disinclined to participate in walks and other activities the last time she visited us here. Remember the morning Elise refused to come to breakfast, remaining behind in the van der Schalie's cottage where they were staying? After we finished eating I took pity on her and suggested that someone volunteer to take her some food and encourage her to join us. Turning to her little brother I asked, "How about you, Dan?" "Oh no, not me," he replied with a shudder that suggested he knew he would only exacerbate her bad mood. Now they are the best of friends and Elise has become quite a nature lover and back-packer. In fact in her freshman year at Lewis and Clark she and Aaron, her boyfriend from Alaska, took their spring quarter off to drive to Michigan and spend a month at the cabin. It was too early to turn on the water, but they made do with the hand pump and the privy, and Aaron's skill with the ax kept them well supplied with firewood. They love Douglas Lake (and each other!) so much that they returned for another stay this past spring.

Mario phoned last night to thank me for the wonderful visit, which she found truly healing. Though I don't think in terms of healing for myself, I'm greedy to soak up as much of this peaceful place as possible to draw upon when the time comes I can no longer return. I wonder how available your reservoir of memories was to you and if you were able to visualize Douglas Lake when you were confined to the nursing home.

July 24, 1996

With the prospect of Barbara Bach's visit, I finally tackled the parquet floor with a cleaning and waxing fluid I had bought years ago. I started under the table where it was most stained and then moved on, rather unsystematically, to other places that needed attention. The upshot was that I did practically the whole room except under the rugs and the corner behind the rocking chair. Then I realized I had no buffer. Nothing to do but dedicate the old pair of socks I was wearing and buff with my feet. That did the job with more fun and less work, and besides, who wants a buffer cluttering up our small space?

This morning I lay in bed thinking of the newly waxed floor and of the pleasure we had in laying those beautiful oak tiles in the summer of 1983. Our teamwork went smoothly with a minimum of conversation as we were each absorbed in our work and thoughts. I enjoyed fitting the self-stick tiles together and admired the variations in grain and color of the little strips of wood that made up the four squares within each tile. You had the harder job of measuring and cutting the pieces to fit around the edges of the room. We had moved all the furniture, including the pie safe and the Franklin stove, out into the yard. When we were done the sixteen by fourteen foot room seemed like a spacious ballroom. Betty and Jack came by to admire it and give us a hand with returning the furniture. We couldn't wait to show off our beautiful floor to the children who would soon all be coming to celebrate your seventy-fifth birthday.

What a contrast that happy endeavor was to our experience of laying vinyl tile back in the mid-sixties. It was before your retirement so we had to take advantage of a free weekend. Unfortunately cold weather had a stiffening effect both on us and on the tile. We had to warm each one on a heating pad to make it flexible enough to conform to the rough pine flooring, which we didn't know should have first been covered by plywood. You handled the sticky adhesive while I laid the tile. Because I could bend more easily than you, I was stuck in the cooking corner under the sink trying to cut pieces to fit around drainpipe and posts. (It was long before we built the kitchen addition.) I must have been verbalizing my thoughts, as was my tendency, and my chatter got on your nerves. Suddenly you said, "Shut up." I was stunned, but continued to work in aggrieved silence until we finished the job.

I wonder if you realized how deeply you hurt me. We never discussed the incident, but it surely drove the point home that you couldn't stand too much talk. Usually you would simply tune me out, but that hurt my feelings too. I used to take your self-protective silences as rebuffs, for I was slow to comprehend that my enthusiastic bursts of discourse overwhelmed you. Now I can better sympathize with your state of mind because I too find excessive talk fatiguing. Gradually communication between us improved as I learned to hold my tongue and you to loosen yours. After your retirement when you were free from pressures you found it easier to express your feelings in words including how much you loved me, a wonderful gift! How ironic that speech had to be the target of your stroke!

July 26, 1996

Barbara is still asleep. It was after seven when she arrived last evening, loaded with luscious fresh vegetables, and almost midnight when we went to bed. She loves the cabin, as I knew she would. She notices and appreciates every detail, even the handle you carved from a notched stick for the door you made to replace the curtain between the main room and bedrooms. Whatever we do in the next few days is sure to be fun for her enthusiasm peps me up and her readiness to laugh makes me feel quite witty.

Barb and I have known each other for a long time mostly in local Democratic Party affairs. You met her through our neighbor, Alice Whiting, when they were in the group of partners who started the Movable Feast. Subsequently she worked in Lansing on Representative Perry Bullard's staff and later in state economic development services. But we didn't really discover each other until two years ago when, at the age of sixty, she decided to retire and I invited her to join my book review group and Helen Hill's writing class. We share similar outlooks and both enjoy doing things on the spur of the moment like the canoe trip we took last September down the Huron from Hudson Mills to Delhi Rapids. Now we are thinking of canoeing on the Pigeon River after the weekend and seeing something of the Pigeon National Forest.

July 31, 1996

Barb left this morning. As anticipated, I greatly enjoyed her company. Her delighted observation of everything she sees quickens my awareness of the familiar. When we return from a walk she pores over the nature guides to identify the various leaves she has gathered. On a rainy walk in the Manitou woods we found a little balsam fir, which she took home to plant in her back yard, and I dug up a pair of tiny hemlocks. Remember how you intended to transplant a small fir to the area between our back door and the bathhouse where all the trees had been destroyed by the monstrous machine that put in our septic tank? Well, after your stroke, I asked Fred Test to find and plant one for us, which he did the following fall. It was only about eight inches tall, but now that baby is quite plump and taller than I can reach, and the young ash you transplanted is a graceful tree as high as the roof. I placed the little hemlocks closer to the bathhouse where I trust they will someday help further screen the window as we had planned. It is gratifying to see that small patch gradually becoming woodsy again.

Propelled by Barb's strong stroke we got in some good canoeing. The most exciting was in search of the Bald Eagle who has taken up residence on Douglas Lake. After putting our dinner in the oven we set out about two hours before sunset to find a solitary pine on the east end of the lake where the Eddys have seen him perch. We were quietly paddling along our shore toward North Fishtail Bay when suddenly we were startled by a croaky screech. Up flew the eagle, who headed straight for the tree where he obligingly waited for us. At first we could barely make out his silhouette, but as we drew closer his white head, shoulders, and tail gleamed almost golden in the low sun. What dignity!

The rain dismissed all thoughts of the Pigeon River. As I remember, the stretch we tried with Ellen and Steve Fabricant was rather monotonous and the banks were so thick with vegetation that we had a hard time finding a place to beach for lunch. The trip on the Sturgeon with Steve Craine in July of 1987, his last visit here with the two of us, was more exciting. We were not brave enough to take the rapids, but instead put in further upstream at Trowbridge Road and took out at Wolverine. Even so, the narrow stream's frequent bends kept us alert and interested.

August 1, 1996

Recalling these nearby trips has started me thinking back over all the good times we had canoeing. They began with the Au Sable in September 1954 at the end of our first year in Ann Arbor. We had left the children with Mrs. Meyer and taken off for a weekend on Mackinac Island. One day there, sightseeing and biking the road that circled the island, proved to be enough. With unexpected time on our hands, we decided to take a canoe float from one of the liveries in Grayling we had noticed on our drive north. That delightful experience had us hooked. We returned to the Au Sable with the boys three years later, the summer we rented on Otsego Lake. Remember how Tim and I found ourselves balanced on a log? We kept paddling around in futile circles until Tim moved forward to shift the weight. The next year, for your fiftieth birthday present, we bought a seventeen foot aluminum canoe adding a new attraction to our nearby picnics along the Huron. Once you took Tim on an over-night camping trip down the river from Kensington Lake to Ann Arbor. Later Steve had his turn when you had a weekend on the Rifle River with another father-and-son team.

The high spot of our canoeing adventures came in 1962 on the Border Lakes of Minnesota. Tim had finished his freshman year at Oberlin and, with you, had gained valuable experience the previous summer on a canoe/camping trip in Canada under the guidance of Irving Fox. At fifteen, Steve was ready to pull his own weight and twelve year-old Ellen was, as always, eager to keep up with the rest of us. However it was more of an undertaking than I had anticipated, but then, you were always the one to do the worrying.

We set out from the cabin in good spirits, and enjoyed driving and camping along the northern shore of Lake Superior, but by the last day we were all a little tense from being cooped up in the car for so long. When we finally hit the Gunflint Trail out of Grand Marais you became quite anxious about whether we could find our outfitters at the end of the road. I tried to reassure you that the directions were simple and that surely there would be signs. Actually we had no trouble finding the place. The outfitter asked if we preferred big water with the possibility of strong winds or small water with several short portages. We chose the latter, a six-day route going down one chain of small lakes and returning along another. She helped us select food and equipment to supplement what we had brought with us as well as a second canoe. By this time it was getting too dark to pitch our tents so she offered to let us sleep in one of her ramshackle cabins.

It was a miserable night. You couldn't sleep because you were panicked at the thought of risking your family's lives on this foolhardy adventure in the wilds. Among other things you no doubt worried that you might throw your back out again. Our bunks were too narrow for me to crawl into bed with you so I crouched by your side whispering so as not to waken the children. I tried my best to reassure you and eventually you were able to sleep. You later told me how much I helped you that night by my sympathy and understanding. While I welcomed your appreciation of my efforts, it left me feeling a little guilty because at the time I thought your fears were exaggerated and unreasonable. They disturbed me too, because they reminded me of the acute anxiety you experienced during our second year of marriage when you were working for the War Production Board and were caught in the impossible assignment of keeping the allocations of scarce industrial materials fair and honest. Although the month at the sanitarium in Stockbridge put you back on your feet so you could continue to contribute to the war effort and gave you some insight into your fears, anxiety continued to be a problem for you throughout your working life.

Fortunately calm, sunny weather the next morning lifted our spirits. Easy paddling and only one or two short portages took us to our first campsite on a charming little island. At the portages you and Tim started out each carrying a canoe while Steve, Ellen, and I carried some of the duffel. Then we would all return to get the rest of our stuff including the lumpy life jackets. However, your back soon began to bother you, so Tim took to portaging both canoes; a case of the burden literally shifting from the shoulders of the father to those of the son!

All went well until noon of the third day when we reached the end of the first chain of lakes where the map showed we had our longest portage. We were shocked to encounter a steep hill, but with all your study of watersheds we shouldn't have been surprised. We decided it was best to reconnoiter. Tim shouldered a canoe, and leaving the rest of our stuff behind, except for lunch, we climbed the long, steep trail. At the top food took all of our attention before Tim and Steve set off to explore the downward path. They reported it was indeed long and quite rough in places. You and I hesitated to suggest we turn back as we hated to disappoint the children. Then Tim, usually the one most eager to press on, solved our dilemma by declaring he favored retracing our route. We were relieved and pleased that he had the good sense to recognize his limitations. Now he tells me he was thinking of our limitations, not his own!

From that moment on we all relaxed and savored a second view of the beautiful scenery we had hurried past. An extra day made possible a side trip to a small lake lying parallel to our chain. When we emerged from our short portage through the woods and stepped on to the shore of Snipe Lake we sensed that we were among a privileged few to experience this pristine place. A pretty little point on the opposite shore made an ideal campsite where we loafed away the afternoon and you and Ellen did some fishing. I believe you caught a pike though none of us remember eating it. She and I do remember standing at the edge of a little cove and seeing, right there at our feet, a large wounded pike with a lure stuck in it's lip, a distressing sight. That evening we celebrated Ellen's farewell to childhood and welcome to her teens with a cake baked in the reflector oven and adorned with a lighted match for a candle. The next morning, while the rest of us were breaking camp, she decided to take one more try at fishing, though you warned her that you were too busy to help her. She made a good cast and was excited to find she was pulling in a fish. To her dismay it turned out to be that same wounded pike we had seen the day before. She was too revolted to touch it, but you kindly relented, removed it from the hook and tossed the poor fish back into the lake.

Steve had his triumph too. Although all three children willingly did their share of the work, we were impressed by how Steve was always on the spot to help you set up and take down the tents, gather and chop firewood, and load the canoes. We didn't notice that he was especially busy after meals until the end of the trip when he gleefully announced that he never washed a dish!

For both of us the trip fulfilled long-held dreams. I suppose yours started when you were a Boy Scout, but I know mine began with a song I learned as a six year old. I had been sent off to Camp Housatonic in Connecticut while my parents and older brother traveled to northern Maine for a canoe trip down the Allagash River under the care of skilled guides. On their return they taught me the verses they had made up describing their adventure set to the tune of "I've Been Working on the Railroad." That song became one of my childhood's vivid experiences. I sang it with gusto imagining myself "canoeing on the Allagash all the live-long day," cooking by the campfire, shooting down the rapids, and hearing "the loons a-calling."

August 4, 1996

This morning I had just gotten out of bed and glanced out the window when I was astonished to see a small spotted fawn walking slowly toward the lake. Though tempted to step closer to look where it had gone, I remained frozen. A moment later the mother appeared at a deliberate pace. After each step she paused to turn her head first to one side and then the other all the while rotating her incredibly long ears. She too passed beyond my sight but soon reappeared and started up the path toward the Youngs' with her fawn following. They then diverged into the woods heading toward Betty's garden.

Yesterday was a perfect summer day and today is another. Too bad I have to be so preoccupied with food and other arrangements in preparation for Ellen's visit tomorrow, Monday. She, Dan, and Skip arrive in the late afternoon and will stay till Sunday morning, overlapping a day and a half with Tim's family.

Let me tell you about Skip, but first catch you up on events. Although we had known for a long time that Ellen was not happy in her marriage to Steve Fabricant, their decision to divorce came after your stroke and was finalized in the spring of 1991. Three years later Ellen and Skip met at a workshop in northern California and soon fell in love. He is a consultant in planning and marketing conferences for professional and other organizations. Since computers make it possible for him to carry on his business anywhere, he was able to move to Ashland that fall. I first met him when he came with Ellen to the big family party Tim and Leslie gave me for my eightieth birthday and became better acquainted on my annual spring visit to Ashland, but it wasn't until last summer here in the peaceful atmosphere of Douglas Lake that Skip and I came to feel really at ease with each other. Unlike Steve F., who, as you know, usually kept his thoughts to himself and was not inclined to reveal his feelings, Skip is very expressive of his. He certainly lets Ellen know how totally he loves her.

I'm eager to see Dan after nearly a year and a half and to hear about his contrasting experiences in Israel. He spent February and March in an intensive two-month program for American Jewish high school students and the following three months with his father in East

Jerusalem, where Steve was trying to get a public health project with the Palestinians off the ground. It was a frustrating assignment because the recently elected conservative president of Israel had closed the borders. It must have been hard for Dan too as he was alone most of the time and had to keep up his schoolwork. Steve helped him with physics, but his math was pretty much on his own. They both took Hebrew and Arabic classes in the evenings.

I've had fun clearing a few potential sites from which Dan can choose where he'd like to pitch our old tent and for Tim and Leslie to put up the new one they bought last summer for camping on Mt. Rainier. I'll sleep on the couch so Rachel can share my bed with Chelsea who, at three, is still too young for an upper bunk.

Chelsea is our little great granddaughter born six weeks after you died. I doubt if you realized that Rachel had become pregnant at the beginning of her sophomore year of community college. She chose to keep her baby and raise her as a single parent. It was rough going but she has turned out to be a dedicated mother and outstanding student. In the fall following Chelsea's birth Rachel transferred to a program for off-campus students at Smith College, where she majored in biology. You would have been as proud a grandparent as Gerry and Harold and I were when we watched Rachel graduate cum laude last May. She plans to study for her Masters of Arts in Teaching at Central Connecticut State University, where Tim and Leslie both teach now, and has recently moved in with them. They have been wonderfully supportive of Rachel throughout and they thoroughly enjoy Chelsea.

August 14, 1996

Thank goodness it turned out to be a beautiful week of warm sunny days and sparkling clear nights. We all had a lovely time.

You would have been delighted with Daniel. Seventeen and a six-foot beanpole, he is quite grown up but still retains the charm he had as a small boy. In many ways he reminds me of you with his deep-set blue eyes under dark eyebrows arching a narrow face. He has your gentle disposition too. Though not as shy as you no doubt were at his age, he enters easily into adult conversation and is remarkably responsive to whomever he is with. His interests are wide-ranging now that baseball is no longer his consuming passion. He approaches everything with enthusiasm: learning to identify trees, paddling solo and mastering the "J" stroke, browsing through your organic gardening book, which he was pleased to have me give him. That interest took hold when he worked for a while as a volunteer in the Jerusalem Botanical Gardens. Steve wrote Ellen that on a visit there he was reminded of you by the way Dan leaned down to examine a plant. When I asked him what were the highlights of his experience in Israel, he was very clear that it was being with his father.

The first four days drifted along lazily, Dan sleeping in his tent til near noon while Ellen and Skip read or worked on their computer. Skip's favorite spot was sitting in the folding canoe seat on the dock. Ellen kept the most active as she took turns sailing, canoeing, or walking with Dan, Skip, or me. Sailing had to be abandoned when a fitting on the Sunfish became loose and the rudder kept popping out. Ellen had all she could do to maneuver back to shore while stretching to hold down the rudder with one hand and reaching to hold the tiller and sheet with the other. But this mishap did not dampen Dan's spirits for he was shouting joyously as he waded through the water towing her home.

At dinner someone reminded us of the meteor showers so, after challenging each other to a few games of Othello, we all trooped up to the field. The night was sparkling clear and we each had the satisfaction of seeing at least one "shooting star." I remember the many times we used to go star gazing there and the rare occasions when we saw the northern lights. The most spectacular display was early in Ellen and Steve's marriage when they were building the bathhouse or putting in the plumbing. The four of us stood in awe as we watched the aurora's fluctuating rays nearly reach the zenith.

The arrival of Tim's family added more excitement. Immediately Chelsea became the center of our attention. I wish you could have seen the way that little tike would keep running up the path and down again a half a dozen times or more. The big attraction was the huge teepee that Carol Young had made years ago when she and her first husband were living in the Arctic. It is now set up in the clearing on Stony Point where we camped in 1960 when we took Steve to Camp Manitou and Betty's father offered to negotiate the sale of the cabin to us. Chelsea loved swinging in the hammock and of course playing in the water, reminding me of Naomi and Rachel at that age. In fact she looks very much like her aunt Naomi.

Saturday morning Tim settled down at the dining table with Dan to help him understand some math problems that had given him trouble. They used a textbook from the newly published high school series written by Tim and a team of writers he headed. The colorful illustrations and innovative approach so captured Skip's enthusiasm that he spent the afternoon on the dock absorbing mathematical concepts that had baffled him forty years ago. Meanwhile Tim, Leslie, Dan, and Chelsea packed a lunch and canoed to Sedge Point where they played on the beach while Ellen and I lingered at the picnic table with Rachel catching up on her life. In the evening Skip took a solo paddle into the sunset while the rest of us viewed it from the dock.

Early next morning I drove the Oregon contingent to the airport. As always it was hard to say good-bye, but when I returned at 7:30 there was Tim standing outside his tent ready to walk with me while the rest of his family slept. That was just what I needed. We went up the road to the end of the woods then ducked through the Scotch pine plantation to our fields where we emerged upon an enchanting sight. The low morning sunshine was gleaming on a sea of white mist and on the dew-saturated grasses at our feet. We did not climb the little hills this time because our feet were getting wet and the others were no doubt hungry for breakfast. Tim recalled the cold October day nearly three years ago when the four of us came here to scatter your ashes.

The drive up had been through rain showers and the sky was still overcast when we arrived in mid-afternoon. Then, as we walked along the road and looked up through yellow and red leaves, we were heartened to see patches of blue sky. Nevertheless in the open field the wind was sharp and very cold. At the top of the first mound Tim opened the box and, holding it with both hands and swinging his arms across his body, made a neat arc of the white ashes. Then we climbed up the next hill where Ellen swung a similar arc. When Steve made a sweep of the final third at the crest of the last hill, Tim exclaimed, "We didn't leave any for you, Mother!" I assured them I was quite satisfied just to be a witness to the simple carrying out of your wish. At that moment Ellen started to cry. Her beautiful grief-stricken face enveloped in a hood, as in a medieval painting, gave poignant expression to the sorrow we shared.

August 16, 1996

Today is your birthday, and I'm remembering when Ellen came eight years ago to help us celebrate your 80th. You had said you did not want the confusion of a whole family reunion as we had had for your 75th. Now I can better appreciate your mood for I too am finding that I become overwhelmed by a crowd sooner than I used to. Three year-old Naomi had the right idea when, after staying alone with us for a few days, she remarked, "This cabin is just the right size for three people." Perhaps she was anticipating the impending arrival of her parents and demanding baby sister, Rachel.

As it worked out, Tim and Leslie gave you a pre-birthday party on our visit to them early in July. It was the first time we had seen their new home in Windsor, Connecticut, where they had moved the year before to take the jobs at Trinity College. Remember how touched you were by their present of a notebook containing your "Family Letters" neatly typed by Leslie, who had transcribed your hand-written memoirs on to her computer?

Ellen and I wanted her visit to be a surprise, so, on the pretext of meeting a friend of Betty's, I persuaded you to accompany me to the airport. When the plane arrived you told me you would wait there on the bench while I went looking for the stranger. It was a good thing you were sitting down because you were utterly dumbfounded when Ellen appeared out of the blue. There followed a most enjoyable five days. It was so good to have her all to ourselves especially as we hadn't seen her since the previous summer when she came with Steve and the two children.

On your birthday you set up your camera and we took pictures of each other: you standing by the stone chimney, the two of us sitting on a log by the large tree on the edge of the bank, and each of us with Ellen. Later in the day we drove the Crestliner across the lake to the Douglas Lake Bar, where the old dance floor, from which we used to hear the band music blaring on Saturday nights, had recently been taken over by an expanded restaurant. After a delicious dinner of planked whitefish we anticipated a pleasant ride home in the twilight, but instead were faced with a strong wind and threatening rain. You gunned the outboard motor and, bouncing over the waves, you got us home just as the raindrops started to fall.

The following three days slipped by all too quickly and then it was Saturday morning and time to say good-bye to Ellen at her early plane. On our return we had planned to stop for breakfast at Carp Inn in Levering, but, since it hadn't yet opened, we went back to the cabin and I made blueberry pancakes for a treat. I remember we had a particularly happy day reunited as just the two of us once again while still basking in the glow of Ellen's visit. Instead of walking up the road we had a pleasant stroll along the beach to Sedge Point. The afternoon was spent as countless others; lunch at the picnic table followed by reading and snoozing under the trees.

Asho and Lyle

Asho, Lyle, and baby Tim (above); Steve, Asho, and Tim at Virginia cabin (ca. 1949, below left); Asho, Lyle, Ellen, Steve, Tim (ca. 1954, below right)

Family portraits: Tim, Ellen, Lyle, Steve, Asho, ca. 1959 (above); Steve, Ellen, Tim, Steve Fabricant, Elise, Daniel, Leslie, Asho, Lyle, Rachel, Naomi. at Douglas Lake, August 1983 for Lyle's 75th birthday (below).

Asho and Lyle, later years

Next morning, Sunday the 21st, we slept late and lingered a while in bed. I was the first to get up and take a shower. It had turned suddenly cold in the night and I was busy laying a fire when you called from the bedroom for me to come. There, sitting on the edge of the bunk, clad only in your underpants and still damp from your shower, you declared, "Something's wrong. I think I've had a stroke." All I could think to say was "For heaven's sake lie down and get under the covers, it's cold!"

Once you were tucked in I called Howard Eddy. Fortunately the doctor was here for the weekend. He came right away and could tell immediately, by your eyes not focusing to the right and other symptoms including vomiting, that it was a stroke. Together we got you into the car and lying down on the back seat. Somehow I had managed to put on your pajamas and to grab a banana for myself. Howard told me to drive to the Burns Clinic in Petoskey, 35 miles away, at a speed no faster than I felt comfortable with and upon arrival to insist that you be put on a stretcher. I felt strangely calm and detached as I drove along. Once I heard you retching so I stopped the car and held your head while you threw up into the basin I had brought along. It was nearly noon by the time we reached the emergency entrance. Though I tried to tell the attendants to use a stretcher, before I knew it they had you in a wheelchair and were whisking you down the corridor.

In the emergency room various medical personnel worked over you for more than an hour. It was evident to us that you were unable to use your right arm, but you were puzzled and kept rubbing your right hand with your left. You did not answer or ask questions or carry on a conversation, but you made several exclamatory remarks, most of which made no sense to me. Once, however, you clearly said, "This is it!" Finally they wheeled you off for a CAT scan and I sought out the cafeteria for something to eat. Afterwards Dr. Roth, the young neurologist on Sunday duty, confronted me with the grim fact that you had had a severe intra-cerebral hemorrhage resulting in aphasia and right side weakness (i.e. paralysis). Furthermore I would have to give permission for an operation that might be necessary, presumably to save your life. I was so overwhelmed by his blunt statement and manner that I didn't know what to think. Later, when you were settled in the Intensive Care Unit, I met the head neurosurgeon, Dr. Arthur Gindin, an older and kinder man. He told me that no surgery was called for at that time, but we would just have to wait and see. He drew me a rough sketch of your brain showing a large area on the lower left side, which was filled with blood from the burst capillaries, and some small elongated open spaces. The fact that the latter had not shifted was a good sign as well as that you had remained alert.

As the afternoon wore on there seemed no point in staying any longer. The nurses assured me I could call in at any time, so at 4:30 I set out for home. I was still in the same numbed and detached state of mind of the morning as if some one else were telling me what to do. For instance, approaching The Dutch Oven Bakery in Allanson my impulse was to stop and buy some sweet rolls. "No," I told myself, "that is not important," but when the sight of the Marathon station in Levering prompted me to notice that the gas gage registered nearly empty I realized that stopping for a refill was indeed important. I went directly to the Eddys' to report what had transpired. They gave me a welcome drink and the comfort of their concern. Then I dropped in on the Youngs and told them how matters stood. Of course they were ready to do anything to help. They offered to have me stay at their house, but I knew

I would sleep better in my own bed. Back at the cabin I settled down on the couch to phone Mario and each of the children. All the while I was calmly telling them the distressing news, I felt strangely enveloped in an air of unreality accentuated by the incongruous beauty of the moonlit lake.

August 17, 1996

Now that I'm launched on recounting the aftermath of your stroke, I am impelled to keep going. As you might imagine, the scenario has run through my head countless times, but the tale keeps pressing to be told. Fortunately that very first day I jotted down key information and the sequence of events in a three-by-five spiral notebook I carry in my purse. Once started, I kept up the habit little expecting that I would be filling seventeen such notebooks over the course of four and a half years. Don't worry. I do not intend to bore you with all their monotonous details.

Before going to bed that first night and again as soon as I got up next morning I called the hospital. Both times the nurse or doctor in charge of Intensive Care assured me that your condition remained stable and alert, but when I arrived there at 9:30 you certainly didn't fit my idea of "alert." The stroke left you in a sorry state of confusion, and me too for that matter. I was baffled by all those red lights and flashing numbers on the equipment to which you were attached, but didn't even think to ask what they meant. When my attention was not centered on you I was gazing out the window at a beautiful view of Little Traverse Bay, or making a half-hearted attempt at knitting. Reading was out of the question.

Both of us were bewildered by your inability to find words to express your thoughts, irrational though they seemed to be. At one point you said "symbol," and at another you were cross with me for not understanding what you meant by an outpouring of long numbers. You had a way of placing the palm of your left hand, fingers pointing up, on your forehead and then drawing it up over the top of your head, a gesture you repeated frequently in the weeks to come. I wondered if your head hurt or if it was an effort to clear away the fog.

Tuesday morning you seemed a little better. Because you continued to be rather restless, sometimes trying to pull yourself out of bed, you were given sedatives off and on. Donna, the physical therapist, and a nurse helped you sit up for a few minutes with your legs dangling off the side of the bed, and at noon you had your first meal of soup and juice. Dr. Gindin told me I should expect to make a decision in about a week regarding where you would go after discharge from the hospital. All this I took as signs of progress, and that night I slept nine hours. Then on Wednesday, the fourth day, which is predicted to be the worst, I learned your condition had deteriorated. You were less responsive and, although your blood pressure had been brought down to 160, your heart rate was much too high. Dr. Roth, the same young man who conveyed the bad news about your CAT scan, declared that if you didn't improve we'd have to go to surgery to drain the excess fluid from your brain, but Dr. Gindin continued to take a wait and see attitude. In the afternoon Donna showed me how to move your arms and legs, which we did together. Later the speech therapist gave me a handout on aphasia, which explained that it affected the ability to structure speech and to a lesser extent comprehension. Then, just as I was about to leave, another doctor appeared ready to take you for a dye test, a prerequisite to surgery. I had a hard time persuading him that there was no point in subjecting you to the procedure unless we decided to go through with the operation.

Thank goodness Steve would be coming in the morning! Jack and Betty offered to meet his ten o'clock plane and bring him to the hospital so I could go there first thing. I arrived about 8:30 in time to feed you some breakfast of grape juice and cream of wheat. Your nurse, John, showed me how to do this by using a straw for suction. He told me your heart rate had been fluctuating between 150 and 180, which is much too high. Then I talked with Dr. Gindin who was waiting to meet with Steve and me to discuss the question of surgery. He remarked that he had a feeling you were deliberately resisting responding to us. That sounded plausible to me for you always had a way of tuning out unwanted intrusions. Ellen phoned from Oregon to reassure me that although she was worried about your physical condition she felt good about the state of your soul.

You were dozing when Steve arrived, so we soon followed Dr. Gindin to a nearby conference room. A tall man of about sixty, his appearance and thoughtful manner reminded me of you, a resemblance your nurse, John, had also noticed. When he met Steve he was startled and remarked that he saw in him a reflection of his younger self. He described your hemorrhage as an explosion that permanently damaged about one sixth of your brain and the resulting aphasia as a cruel condition, especially for an intellectual person and one that he would want to spare his own father. Although he was carefully non-committal, we sensed his reluctance to undertake the surgery, which, though it might very well prolong your life, could not mitigate the aphasia. Then he left us alone to confer with Tim and Ellen and come to a decision.

First we called Tim. By luck a new telephone system had just been installed in his office so he was able to arrange a three-way conference call with Ellen. After we were connected I turned over the phone to Steve who outlined the situation as laid out by Dr. Gindin. I don't know how much you ever talked with the children about your wishes concerning death, but they certainly were aware that several years earlier we had both signed living wills stating that we did not want our lives prolonged by heroic measures. That made it easier for each one of us to independently reach the same conclusion: no surgery.

August 20, 1996

Yesterday I finished varnishing the threshold and door to the bathhouse that Jim Mummert had put in because the old ones were rotting and peeling. I had only managed to stain them before Barb arrived. All told the job took me nearly two hours, but as usual I was rather inefficient about preparation. At least I facilitated clean up by remembering to wear gloves! The new thin latex ones are much more comfortable than the old stiff rubber kind.

While part of my mind was paying careful attention to my brush strokes, another part was thinking of the impact your stroke had on Steve. Living alone in Portland where he had settled in December, he had no intimate person with whom to share the shock of the news, nor children to divert him from his grief as Tim and Ellen had. He told me that when a fellow worker at Pendleton tried to comfort him by telling of a stroke victim who learned to communicate by pointing to letters on a board, he felt like saying "That would not be good enough for my intellectual father." As you must have realized, Steve was coming to a fuller appreciation of you through your on-going exchange of letters discussing different approaches to the environmental movement. He referred to this correspondence at your memorial service when he said it was so wonderful to relate to his father as a peer.

Unfortunately there was no way he could relate to you on that brief visit in the hospital because you were completely unresponsive. You did grip his hand when he grasped yours so maybe you knew he was there, but when we returned next day your grip had weakened and your general condition had further declined. In fact Dr. Gindin admitted that one could say you were in a coma. Steve felt it was useless to go back to the hospital on Saturday, so instead we stayed around the cabin and went for a long walk along the shore. That respite did us both good, but it was with heavy hearts that we parted at his seven o'clock plane next morning. Steve said later he never expected to see you again.

After leaving Steve I drove on to the hospital and looked in on you briefly. You were resting quietly, but you were still unresponsive. I must have told you I loved you, but what I remember is taking your hand and rubbing it over my face to make your love for me seem more real. It was still early when I left and I felt in a strange state of limbo as I drove down Petoskey's nearly deserted main street. Being in no hurry, when I reached Bay View it occurred to me to explore its side streets, something we had always intended to do. You and I had heard so much about the old summer community from Edna French (Betty Young's mother) who was still attending inspirational lectures there when she was in her mid-eighties. So there I was on a quiet Sunday morning slowly winding my way along streets lined with large Victorian "cottages" with not a person in sight. Soon I found the central portion with a park, church, lecture hall, and another hotel where I later took Mario for dinner. She and I also ate at Bay View's better-known inn on the main highway where you and I had once gone.

Back at the cabin I became caught up in endless telephone calls. Of course I touched base with the immediate family, but I also had calls from other friends and relatives who had kindly waited for a week before contacting me directly. The phone was ringing so constantly that I had a hard time fixing and eating a bit of supper, and it was eight o'clock before I had a chance to phone the hospital. Much to my astonishment, the nurse reported that you had opened your eyes for a moment, had made little grunting sounds and were also moving your left arm more. I was still in a state of shock when Edie Muma called a few moments later, and I told her, as the old expression goes: "You could knock me down with a feather." Here I'd been trying to get used to the idea that you were dying when suddenly I had to make a hundred and eighty degree turn around. I felt so disloyal that I had even been mentally planning a memorial service for you.

Nevertheless you remained in a deep sleep all the time I was with you the next day. After I left they moved you out of Intensive Care into a regular room where Tim and I found you when he arrived late Tuesday morning. Since you were sleeping we went for lunch in the hospital cafeteria, a pleasant room with a long wall of windows overlooking the bay. On our return we were pleased to find your eyes flickering, your breathing less heavy and your mouth making a few little grunting sounds. As we talked to you and hugged you your eyes opened more and your hand gripped Tim's.

The next big decision confronting us was whether you should have a feeding tube. An understanding nurse, knowing our desire to avoid intrusive procedures, held off a younger gung-ho doctor's order to insert one. Again Dr. Gindin did not rush us. He explained that there is a limit to how long one can continue an IV because it will eventually damage the veins, and that although a feeding tube is uncomfortable it is not painful and might not bother you at all. He said, "As long as a patient is improving we tend to want to do what we can to help, but the outcome is still uncertain."

You did not open your eyes for us all the time we were with you on Wednesday, but while Tim was telling me about the book on fractal geometry he was reading he noticed you were moving your arm, an indication, we thought, that you were aware of our voices. That evening we phoned Steve and Ellen and all agreed to go ahead with the tube feeding. Immediately I relayed our decision to the night nurse and when we arrived next morning you were all rigged up with another tube in your nose. You had had one for oxygen right from the start. Actually the feeding tube remained for only three days because you became able to eat regular food. Thus we had sweated out a decision which proved to be no big deal. During Tim's five-day stay he had the satisfaction of watching you take your first sips of water and food and of observing your increased responsiveness as your eyes opened wider, your grip became stronger and your lips tried a tentative smile—all small steps toward survival. What a contrast to Steve's experience!

Ellen arrived Saturday evening. She and Tim enjoyed having a few hours together before he left next morning, especially as they hadn't seen each other since the previous summer. Dr. Gindin kindly took time out of his Sunday to meet with Ellen and tell us he was pleased with your progress. The oxygen tube had been removed so now your nose was free of obstructions. You were decidedly more responsive, staying awake longer and occasionally making exclamations like "Oh" and "Yeah." You even gave me a real kiss, but next day, to my dismay, my kiss elicited a bite! Monday morning Ellen and I had breakfast with the Eddys so it was nearly your lunch time when we got to the hospital. We were pleased to see that when we put a stick, tipped with a water-soaked sponge, in your hand you were able to bring it to your mouth and that you ate most of the lunch I fed you. On Tuesday we watched Donna, the physical therapist, and a helper sitting you up on the edge of the bed as she had done two weeks earlier. They tried to help you stand but your legs wouldn't push. That afternoon we met Mario at the airport. Ellen's departure early the next morning was particularly hard as we recalled that just two and a half weeks earlier you had been with me to see her off after her happy surprise visit.

August 22, 1996

While doing my yoga exercises on the floor this morning, I was fascinated by a triangular patch of sunlight on the Franklin stove streaming through the newly cleaned transom under the peak of the roof, sometimes fading only to reappear again a few moments later in a slightly altered position. It occurred to me that before the sun's rays can enter our window they must first find a window through the thick woods in a direct line with ours and keep finding new openings as the sun shifts until it rises above the treetops and the roof. Now as I sit at the table after breakfast I'm watching the changing patterns of light on the foliage and remember how much you appreciated the spotlighting effect of the low morning and evening sun.

I'm thinking how much we both loved this place, and in particular how fortunate I was to have had it to return to each day of the three weeks you were in the hospital. I'm sure staying at the cabin sustained the children too under those difficult circumstances. A surge of gratitude sweeps over me for the love and support they gave us throughout your long confinement and still continue to give me. Weren't we lucky to have such wonderful children!

We were also lucky to have such a devoted sister, for Mario was certainly the closest to being a sister you ever had. You and she came to a deep appreciation of each other, particularly during the years following Joe's death from a brain tumor in 1971. Remember the many conversations we had sharing insights and speculations over the nature of our world and our fellow humans? She was still at her place on Squam Lake in New Hampshire when she heard the news of your stroke and promptly canceled her plans for a trip in mid-September to the Greek islands. Fortunately her travel agent was able to get her a refund on the grounds of a medical emergency. It was such a comfort to know she could stay to see us through the process of getting back to Ann Arbor.

After I said good-bye to Ellen at the Pellston Airport Wednesday morning I returned to the cabin to have breakfast with Mario. When we arrived at the hospital you were still sleeping, but soon awoke and seemed to enjoy the yogurt I fed you for lunch. You even gave Mario a smile when she said, "See you later, alligator." Then we left for our lunch in the cafeteria where we were joined by Gerry and Harold Hart who were on their way back to Okemos from their place on Beaver Island. That reminds me I forgot to tell you that on the day after your stroke Gerry took the ferry from the island to visit us in the hospital. While we sat on a bench in the sunny courtyard she tried to encourage me with stories of people who made remarkable recoveries from strokes, but I knew yours was of a different kind. When she asked what she could do for me I suggested she find us a restaurant for dinner as I had not had a full-fledged meal in two days. She took me to the familiar Bay View Inn where we had a delicious meal and were introduced to dried tart cherries, which garnished the salad. Since Gerry had to stay overnight to wait for the morning ferry, I accepted her invitation to share her motel room. That barren room fortified my conviction that I was better off driving the 35 miles back and forth each day to the cabin.

Mario and I watched you make some progress during the next few days, the most gratifying being that I could tell by your eyes that you really saw me. You and I cried a little together, but you also smiled and made more effort to talk. Mostly you only said, "yeah," but once you said, "symbol" and then "symbolize" and "I'm sorry." They had you sitting up in a chair too, but couldn't get you to put weight on your feet. When Donna moved your legs in bed she realized your hip hurt. She suspected arthritis and asked for an X-ray. On Thursday Dr. Roth discontinued the IV and ordered discharge planning. He told me you had come as close to death as anyone would want to be.

The first step of the discharge process was a meeting with Dale LaBrie, a very helpful social worker who asked me which nursing homes I preferred. That was easy to answer, thanks to what I had learned through the Gray Panthers' efforts to get better regulations. My first choice was Glacier Hills because of reputation and convenient location, only ten minutes drive from home. The Methodist home in Chelsea was second choice and the Evangelical home in Saline third, but next afternoon Dale reported there were no vacancies in any of these. In fact the only available bed was at Bortz in Ypsilanti, a nursing home with a long history of violations and changing management. What a grim prospect! I could only hope that you would not have to stay there long before a better place opened up. I had of course been keeping Dr. Huff informed, and he promised to work on the problem.

Monday was a downer waiting to hear final confirmation from Bortz and contracting with the ambulance. Throughout I appreciated Dale's practical help and compassionate support. You were asleep most of the day and didn't even wake up while Donna and I moved your limbs. Since you were scheduled to leave Wednesday morning, Mario and I decided to spend Tuesday night in a motel, a much nicer one than where Gerry and I had stayed. We spent the morning packing the car and cleaning and closing up the cabin, so it was mid-afternoon when we arrived at the hospital. There Dale greeted us with the good news that a room was available at Glacier Hills. What a relief!

After Mario and I had dinner and checked into our motel room we decided to take a swim in the pool. It was good that we had it all to ourselves for our accumulation of tension and fatigue was released in the form of silly behavior which we found hilariously funny. Even so we had a hard time getting to sleep. When we realized we were both awake Mario admitted that, worried about my finances, she had been calculating the cost of the nursing home, and I confessed that I had simply been trying to compose a clever message for my new answering machine. The contrast in our preoccupations set us to giggling all over again.

Next morning, September 14, we arrived at the hospital early enough for me to feed you breakfast. Dr. Gindin and Dr. Roth came to say good-bye. Roth told me your CAT scan showed that swelling was still causing pressure on your brain and that the X-ray confirmed arthritis in your hip. Dr Gindin's parting advise was, "Remember, the good days and bad days will zigzag. They zigzag on the way up and zigzag on the way down."

Then it was time to leave. Mario drove our loaded car back to Ann Arbor with no trouble until she came within three blocks of the house when she turned right off Packard onto Brooklyn instead of left, but a passer-by soon set her straight. You and I set off in the ambulance at 9:40. You slept all the way as they had given you Motril to make the trip easier. It was a beautiful day and I especially enjoyed the scenery along U.S. 131, a route I had not traveled. Five hours later we reached Glacier Hills, there to take up a whole new way of life.

August 26, 1996

Summer is winding down and so am I. At this point I'd rather postpone the daunting task of describing the nursing home experience until after my return to Ann Arbor. Actually it may not be for some time because I want first to transcribe these scribbled notes on to my computer and put them in better form for the children and my writing group.

Yesterday we had a real Douglas Lake blow. The wind, roaring in the treetops like an express train, woke me near dawn but didn't keep me from going back to sleep. When I emerged at nine o'clock the sparkling blue lake was covered by whitecaps on waves as big as they come. I was thankful our boats were safely on shore. Remember how you were constantly looking to see if the Crestliner was still there and had not broken loose from its moorings, as indeed it did several times? Once, on a bright windy day like this, we spotted it with binoculars on the eastern shore of the lake. After waiting for the wind to settle down a bit we drove around the end of the lake to the "Bug Camp" and walked a half mile or so up the beach where we found it grounded in the shallow protected water of South Fishtail Bay. I walked back to get the car while you and some boy from the Young household who had come along to help had a rough ride home.

You and I had lots of good times in that aluminum boat: exploring other shores, taking the grandchildren for swimming and picnics at East Point, and giving our guests a spin around the lake, but you never did as much fishing as you had dreamed of. Ever since your stroke the boat has remained upside down on blocks near the hemlock tree, except for one time summer before last when Ellen and Dan were here. Anticipating that Dan, at age fifteen, would get a kick out of running the boat, I took the outboard motor into Johnson's Marina in Cheboygan for a tune-up, a new hose and a fill-up of the five gallon tank with the right mixture of oil and gasoline. A day or two after they arrived, with help from the Youngs, we set out the mooring and carried the boat to the water's edge. To my relief Ellen had no trouble starting the motor. She headed down the lake and soon turned over the tiller to Dan, but on the way back he said he'd rather try rowing. We didn't go out in the boat again. However he did accept an invitation to go fishing with Dennis, Carol Young's husband, and his two children. Dan was pleased to catch his first fish, but watching Dennis clean it so turned his stomach that he declined to eat any for dinner. Perhaps that experience led him to become a vegetarian. This summer Dan's boating was confined to the canoe and his one sail with the misbehaving rudder. He also learned to water ski behind John Young's powerboat. As for the Crestliner, it is too much for me to handle alone and I'm inclined to sell it to the Youngs who have expressed an interest in buying it. I'll talk it over with them tomorrow when they come to dinner.

August 28, 1996

Dinner for Betty and Jack came off well even though my rye rolls were hard from baking too long. It was good to see them relaxed and to have them all to myself. They are as busy as ever with visiting family, church, and sailing, to say nothing of keeping up their sprawling grounds including the garden and the old French cabin. Earlier in the summer the whole family, except for two grandchildren, came to celebrate their fifty-fifth wedding anniversary and Jack's eightieth birthday. He still won't let a strong wind stop him from wind surfing in spite of everyone's concern that he'll become too exhausted. We all worry about Betty, too, who reminds me more and more of her mother for nothing can slow her down or curb her expansive hospitality. She is always urging me to stay for dinner, but I have succumbed only a few times, joining their picnics and singing around the campfire. However I do look in on them every day or so and feel very much a part of their family. I surely cherish their love and support.

How lucky for us that Betty's brother, David, married my good friend Atossa, and was here teaching in the School of Social Work when we arrived in 1953. You once remarked that David was your kind of person, someone whose lack of pretension put you completely at ease. We were sorry to have them move away after five years to take on new challenges leading to service in Thailand, Korea, and Bangladesh. By then we had become acquainted with Betty's family and their parents, Leslie and Edna French.

Your introduction to Douglas Lake was in 1958 when you, your father, and Tim drove Steve up to Camp Manitou. The boys slept in the loft of the Frenches' cabin along with some of their grandsons while you and Grandpa stayed in a motel. I came two years later when we brought Steve back to Manitou and pitched our tent on Stony Point. Given these connections I suppose we shouldn't have been surprised that Reverend French thought we would be suitable neighbors, but remember how astonished we were when he asked if we might be interested in buying the little cabin down the hill? He was distressed to see how neglected it had become, and told us he thought he could persuade Doug Gallery to sell it at a modest price. The timing couldn't have been more perfect as we were weary of camping and jumped at the chance of having a place of our own with a solid roof over our heads. By mid-August we were the delighted owners of seven acres of field and woods bordered by a hundred feet of shore, and a cabin chuck full of junk.

Remember how crowded that fourteen by sixteen foot room seemed, dominated as it was by kitchen stuff with a kerosene stove at one end, a pot-bellied stove at the other and in between a table piled high with battered pots and pans? An old metal glider couch took up one corner and outdoor tools another. What a weeding out process we had, but among the discards we found many useful items including that wonderful thick aluminum pancake griddle. Then, to add to the clutter, there were those corny cartoons and Saturday Evening Post art tacked at random all over the walls. Ellen took charge of removing them, selecting scenes of waterfowl to put above the bunks in the back room and some portraits of Canadian Mounties to adorn the privy.

Your first move was to have electricity installed not only for convenience but for safety. I don't know if you appreciate that your telling us of your childhood experience of watching the neighbors' barn burn to the ground has made us all especially aware of the danger of fire. In fact, just a while ago I bought a new fire extinguisher for the kitchen. Next you contracted with Dan Kewaygeshik, one of the two Indian brothers who had built the French cabin, to put up a shed. He also made some counters to consolidate the kitchen into one corner, which served us well for eighteen years until he built the kitchen addition. Now I don't know how we got along without it.

September 3, 1996

In terms of temperature, July and September seem to have switched places this year. Now swimming has become a pleasant indulgence rather than a daunting challenge. The blackberries are ripening and I wish I could stay to make jam, but it is time to get back to other friends and activities in Ann Arbor. All is in order here for my departure day after tomorrow except for packing and last minute chores such as cleaning out the refrigerator and turning off the hot water heaters and the gas for the stove. It's a satisfaction to know our tidy little cabin, snugly boarded up by Roy Alexander, will be waiting through the winter snows for my return next summer.

II

March 9, 1997

Well, as you might have predicted, it has taken me longer than I intended to transcribe these letters to you. You know from your own experience of writing your family letters how much time is taken up with revising and amplifying, not to mention daydreaming. It's my impression that you didn't let outside activities distract you as much as I do. I find the process to be extremely slow even with the help of my computer, which I bought three years ago when I joined my senior writing group. Then again, slow is the name of the game in just about everything I do these days, so I must be patient with myself.

Slower than slow characterized every aspect of your life at the nursing home. In the first place you were in pretty bad shape when you arrived there. Your recovery was delayed by painful and recurring bladder infections, for which it took some time to find the right antibiotic. Then Dilantin, a medication for seizures, made you so drowsy that it interfered with your physical and speech therapies to say nothing of your responsiveness to people. Thank goodness Dr. Huff took you off of it just in time for you to enjoy Tim's visit in mid-October. That was when, on a beautiful sunny day, he pushed you around the grounds for a refreshing walk, and upon our return you surprised us by exclaiming, "Escapade!"

Within a few weeks it became clear what you could and couldn't do. When you gave us your attention we could tell by the expression in your eyes that you were able to understand us very well. However, the physical therapists were frustrated because you could not "respond on command" nor meet the Medicare requirement of discernible progress week by week. You never did learn to assist in transfer from bed to chair because both your legs would collapse beneath you. Consequently you had to endure that scary procedure of being hoisted in and out of bed in a sling attached to the Hoyer lift. Apparently your brain was simply unable to transmit messages to your limbs, a condition called "apraxia." For instance, your left hand would grab but often could not let go. This and a certain rigidity suggested to your speech therapist that you were suffering from Parkinsonian symptoms in addition to those expected from your stroke. Dr. Huff couldn't give you a firm diagnosis of Parkinson's because it is usually recognized by a peculiar way of walking, but after the first six months, he put you on Sinemet, the common medication for the disease. It relieved your rigidity somewhat but the dosage had to be gradually increased over the next four years until it no longer was effective.

Your therapy consisted of passively moving your limbs; range of motion they called it. After about six weeks it was decided to stop the therapy for a while rather than use up the one hundred days allowed by Medicare in the hopes that you might be reinstated later on. So the assistant therapist taught me how to administer range of motion, a ritual I used to do every afternoon when you were put down for your nap.

You needed assistance with eating. Cookie, the occupational therapist, used to help you with breakfast and I with lunch. When we put a piece of toast or other finger food in your left hand and gave your elbow a nudge you were able to bring the food to your mouth and, once started, continue eating. You could drink from a small glass put in your grasp but not reach for it. I had to feed you your soup because you had difficulty in keeping your spoon level but sometimes you did pretty well with your morning oatmeal. You did better at feeding yourself after we got you the special left-handed spoon and fork with thick handles curved to point into your mouth.

Of course speech was your greatest frustration. From time to time you would surprise us with a spontaneous word or remark, but you were unable to deliberately ask a question and you certainly couldn't sustain a conversation. Your speech therapist, Charlene Zand, worked for a long time trying to get you to say common nouns by asking you to name the objects pictured in a series of cards. You must have been utterly bored because one day, after about a dozen weekly sessions, you told her, "I don't want those cards anymore." That statement was unusual in its directness and because you rarely made a request. Occasionally you would delight us with an appropriate long and abstract word. which seemed to pop out more readily than everyday ones, but it was sad to see you struggle to speak when nothing would come. Then you might swear or give a kind of whistling sigh of resignation. Once I commiserated with you saying, "It must be as if someone had taken your dictionary and mixed up all the pages." You answered, in a tone implying this is what you'd been trying to tell me all along, "You get the point."

March 15, 1997

Looking back I still marvel at your patience and good grace in accepting your confinement, and for that I was indeed grateful. You were never irritable or complaining as were several of the other patients at Glacier Hills, though who knows how much pain they may have been suffering. Your physical discomforts seemed to be largely a result of general stiffness and some arthritis in your hip, but your mental distress could only be imagined. Though I was continually searching for clues to your thoughts and feelings, I couldn't allow my imagination to dwell too much on your predicament because I knew I must keep our spirits up by living as if our lives were normal.

To that end I found spending the middle part of each day with you worked out best, because by evening we were both tired, though I frequently returned for dinner. This schedule gave me time for yoga classes, my Tuesday morning hiking group, and attention to other responsibilities. Your morning routine involved being gotten up (at very irregular hours) and fed breakfast followed on some days by therapy or observing a recreational activity. I would arrive soon after eleven, at the tail end of these events, giving me a chance to inquire of your therapist or the activities director how you were doing. Otherwise you would be waiting for me either in your room, the dining room, or in the hall by the nursing station. My first job, if you had not just come from therapy, would be to search for a nurse assistant to help straighten you up in your chair. Several times I was distressed and angry to find you stretched out, stiff as a board, at a 45 degree angle with your unsupported head hanging off the back of the chair in what must have been a most uncomfortable position. Next I would bring you a cup of water. Only then would we be able to settle down somewhere for a visit while we waited for your lunch. Then I would read you any mail, a short article, or perhaps some nature piece or poem. Your tears told me when you were touched, and your laughter when you were amused, but it was hard to keep thinking of things to hold your attention and you were unable to offer any suggestions. When you closed your eyes I couldn't tell whether you were listening or tuning out for lack of interest or energy. Once when Sukha visited and asked if you would like to hear a brief article on politics you answered with a resounding "Hell no!"

Lunch took us the better part of an hour, because eating was a slow process for you, but you had a good appetite and enjoyed your food. I always brought my own sandwich along with fresh fruit, or homemade applesauce and finger food to share with you. Whenever we had visitors I would invite them to bring their own sandwiches and join us for lunch in the sunroom. Then conversation would flow and you would have something livelier to listen to than my intermittent monologues. Afterwards, whenever the weather was favorable and you were not too tired, we would escape outside for a stroll around the spacious grounds of the retirement center to which our nursing wing was attached. We liked to go down around the pond and in summer we would often eat on the terrace. By one thirty, or two at the latest, you would be ready for a nap, so it was back to the room to wait for your nurse assistant. Sometimes while we waited I trimmed your hair or beard. I'm sure you must have been tired just sitting in one position for so long. For safety's sake two people were required to operate the Hoyer lift, but I soon qualified as the second person. Then, once you were in bed, I held your hand and conversed with the assistant while she changed you. After she departed I gave you your range of motion exercises. There followed our most intimate moments when we were free to express our feelings and cry together if need be. Finally, when you were ready to drop off to sleep, I would tell you I loved you, kiss you good-bye and head home for my own much needed nap.

Privacy was always a problem. Your room was narrow and deep with one bed parallel to the window and the other near the door. You started out by the door, so it was rather gloomy whenever we drew the curtain between the beds. Then after you were promoted to the window position, over a year later, I hated to block out daylight from your succession of roommates (twenty-two all told), yet I always felt self-conscious trying to ignore their presence. But curtains could not obliterate the sound of TV to which some of them were addicted. I don't know how you put up with it! Patients were allowed to bring their own sets from home, but since they could not reach the controls they were completely dependent on others to make adjustments. At least in the new addition, which opened in early 1991, there was a hospital-style TV set and hand-speaker for each bed. The TV was often going full blast in the dining room too, so we couldn't hang out there. That is why we usually sat in a corner of the sunroom at one of the round tables. It was by far the pleasantest place available and very nice for entertaining visitors, but it certainly was not private. Usually two or three other patients also ate lunch there assisted by family members with whom I would exchange some conversation, and, because it was really a corridor, staff persons were always passing by whose greetings had to be acknowledged. I often regretted the intrusions for I'm sure you found them distracting, but at the same time some sociability was probably good for both of us. It was a constant effort to keep a balance.

March 22, 1997

Ever since I moved into this apartment in September 1990, I've been thinking about having it redecorated. Although it was in acceptable condition when I bought it, I did not care for the nondescript shaggy carpet reminding me of a dust mop nor for the beige walls that have since seemed to be yellowing with age. But at the time I had more important things than decor to think about.

The whole point of the move was to have a wheelchair accessible place where, by means of a specially equipped van provided by the city bus system, I could bring you home for brief visits. There was no way I could have gotten you up the stairs to the living room of the Hermitage house. Consequently our only escape from Glacier Hills had been to go to public places, but even with help from visiting family members, they were difficult undertakings.

My worst fear was that the van would not show up at the appointed time and we would be left stranded. (Actually the service was remarkably reliable and the drivers were most considerate.) Since the bus had to be ordered one week in advance, I took a gamble with the weather and was always uncertain as to what wraps to bring. Even so we had several good outings at Gallup Park. The first was in August 1989 when Ellen came with the two children whom we watched navigate a paddleboat. Then in October when Tim's and Steve's visits overlapped they pushed you over the bridges and around the circle for a mile-long bumpy ride that, though probably uncomfortable for you, gave us all a sense of freedom. The last time was the following summer for a birthday picnic with Mario and Steve who by then had moved to Detroit. He escorted us one Sunday afternoon to a delightful concert of chamber music at Rackham Auditorium. Our few attempts at restaurant meals were a strain, though an early bird dinner with Mario at the Gandy Dancer came off well. On my own I managed a trip to the art museum to view some Ansel Adams photographs, which you enjoyed, but my attempt to take you through the labyrinthine halls of the Law School to hear a lecture by Harvey Cox was a disaster. That long story will have to wait for another time. It was evident that what we both needed was our own place where we could relax for a couple of hours, enjoy a meal at our own table and put our visitors at ease.

Thus motivated, it wasn't hard to say good-by to the house on Hermitage. After all, we had enjoyed seventeen happy years there together. I remember a friend questioned whether a split-level with so many stairs was suitable for retirement and your answering that when we could no longer climb stairs we would move. However, during the first months after your stroke I had been too preoccupied with adapting to our new situation to think of such an undertaking, but by spring I began talking with you about the idea. I had already sold some of your photography equipment to a member of the camera club, and in September I started the process of divestment in earnest. I donated a load of artifacts, mostly gifts from Mother acquired on her many travels, to an art bazaar for some worthy cause and sold our silver tableware and some other wedding presents on consignment. As each of the children came to visit they sorted through their boxes of schoolbooks and mementoes as well as stacks of family photos. Tim reclaimed the two Ashanti stools he brought back for us from his Peace Corps service in Ghana, and Steve was glad to have furniture, including your desk and your grandfather's caned captain's chair, for his apartment in Detroit. I was pleased that your niece, Marge, took some of your family portraits and your mother's "Flow Blue" china set, which she said has become quite valuable, but I hung on to your great-grandmother Baker's large blue teapot depicting "Rebecca at the Well." It is now sitting on top of the somewhat battered cherry china cabinet I bought secondhand to take the place of the built-in one at Hermitage.

Mario helped me look for apartments when she came for Christmas. I already had my eye on the high-rise, Riverside Park Place, on Wall Street because Kitty Goddard, who had recently arrived at the nursing home, owned a condo there to which her daughter was able to bring her for a home-cooked meal. A friend of Kay Walker's who lives in the building showed us her apartment, but there were no vacancies, and my real estate agent was unable to find us any other suitable place. So I relied on the grapevine, and by luck a three-bedroom condo with a lovely view of the park and river became available in May just after Mario arrived for another visit. She helped me negotiate directly with the owners who offered it "as is," shaggy carpet and all. Since they wanted to stay through August before returning to Florida I had three months to sell the house. That was harder than I expected because most people found it too unconventional, but at the last minute a young couple fell in love with it, and we signed the sales agreement on the day I made final payment for the condo. They have put oak flooring in the living and dining rooms and turned over your paneled study to their small daughter whose dolls and stuffed animals now adorn your bookshelves.

Throughout I tried to keep you informed of my progress but was never sure how much you realized what was going on. I certainly must have told you what a great help Steve was. For instance he saw me through sorting out piles of your colored slides. We would spread out the contents of a box on the light table, select the ones with recognizable people, and then admire the beautiful scenery in the remainder before tossing them into the wastebasket. It would have been hard for me to have been so ruthless alone, but don't worry, there are plenty left because we kept your first choice selections. Of course I kept all your black and white photographs and the file cabinet with your negatives and contact prints. Later I had videos made for each of us of the movies you took when the children were small.

Moving day came at last and two and a half weeks later your homecoming visit with Steve. It was a tight squeeze getting the three of us and your wheelchair into the elevator, but the apartment seemed quite spacious as I had purposely kept the furniture to a minimum to allow plenty of room for maneuvering your chair. The living room walls were filled with your Japanese prints and the halls and study with your photographs. I don't know how many of our things you recognized, but when I said you hadn't been home in more than two years you cried. When Steve opened the sliding glass door onto the balcony and pointed out the park and the river gleaming through the willows you exclaimed, "Beautiful!"

During the following two and a half years we had many satisfying visits with Steve and out of town visitors. When weather permitted we would walk under the willows along the path by the river, and we always enjoyed eating at our own table. The most special event was our golden wedding anniversary, March 29, 1992, when Tim, Leslie, and Ellen joined us to celebrate with an elegant catered dinner. I was so glad I had enough room and beds for all of them even though I would have grabbed a smaller apartment if it had become available first. In fact once, when Rachel's baby was quite young, I put up seven of us, though Steve had to sleep on the living room floor.

Now that floor is covered by a new close-cropped carpet, and the walls, no longer yellow, are white with a slightly pink glow. I arranged to have the painting done when I went east for postponed Christmas visits and the carpet put in after I returned. Although I am pleased with the new, lighter and pinker tone of the walls and carpet, actually they had not been as dingy a yellow as they had appeared to me. After putting in the redecorating order I had surgery to remove a cataract from one eye. Miraculously not only was my vision no longer blurred, but everything looked brighter. It turns out that my cataract was an amber color through which I had been seeing the world darkly.

March 30, 1997

Recently I read the autobiography of Christopher Nolan, an Irish boy confined to a wheelchair by cerebral palsy unable to speak or use his limbs. He had learned to type by poking typewriter keys with a rod attached to his forehead and by age twelve was receiving prizes for his unique poetry. His vivid feelings of being trapped and his longing to participate in normal life stirred my thoughts of how you must have felt. Of course such a condition must be a far worse thing to endure at the beginning of a life than at the end, but that is small comfort.

Although you were often frustrated by your inability to explain your predicament, I certainly used my imagination as best I could to guess what it must be like for you. However, from time to time you managed to say a few words or phrases that conveyed your feelings quite well. For instance two months after your stroke you said, "locked" and "gates" followed a few days later by "I've got to get into an unlocked status." You made a great effort to talk to Tim when he visited in October, but your distress at not finding the words was painful to watch. Finally you asked him, "Is this an aberration?" He assured you it was, and you calmed down. The following day you had several good snatches of conversation with him including: "I think you don't understand." "Is this a slow day?" "I don't know where I am." At one point you said, "The research is objective," but we had no idea what that referred to. Next morning Tim observed your speech therapy with Charlene Zand during which you succeeded in repeating her name. Afterwards you told him, "These people are very helpful." At Thanksgiving when Steve came you were quite agitated by your futile efforts to talk, and could barely manage to whisper, "gibberish."

You may wonder how I can remember all these remarks. Well, believe me, you were silent so many days that whenever you did say something I would try to hang on to it until I could write it down in my little notebook. Your words took on such significance that I often thought of you as the oracle who speaks! At least, thank goodness, you had other means to express feelings if not specific thoughts. Your tears told me when you were touched as you often were by a letter or something else I might be reading. Laughter was less frequent but a joy to witness. Your nurse assistants took pride in telling me when they had made you laugh and some of our visitors were successful too. I particularly remember the merriment Clayt Miller generated when he and Louise used to drive up from Oberlin to see you every spring and fall. You had a way of raising your eyebrows when something really caught your interest, and whenever your eyes sparkled my spirits lifted for then I knew we were fully connecting.

April 15, 1997

After spending a wonderful week on my annual visit to Ellen, coming home to face a pile of mail and nagging chores is a letdown, but then that's always the way. Now the decks are sufficiently cleared so I can settle down to write this letter.

You would love Ellen and Skip's new home with its expansive view of the mountains across the valley and just enough trees in the foreground to screen the houses below them. It is only a few doors to the west of the old place on Laurel and a little further up the hillside. I was lucky to have arrived last year on the very day they found it so I can appreciate the great remodeling job they have done. The outstanding feature of the original was the windows across the front taking full advantage of the view, a wide one in the living room end and a bay in the dining area. Now all that space is one uncrowded living room made possible by an eight-foot addition providing a new kitchen and a sky-lighted entrance hall. A light and peaceful atmosphere pervades the whole house reflecting not only the pleasing architecture and tastefully arranged interior, but the contentment Ellen and Skip share in starting a new life together in their first home.

Spring was again at its height and the weather was perfect. This time I was glad I could go for long walks every day, unlike last year when I was restricted by an injured foot. The first day Ellen and I walked down to Lithia Park to see the damage done by Ashland Creek in the record flood on New Year's Day. We took the familiar route down Almond Street you and I had walked so often. Along the way front yards offered a feast of colored flowers and in the park the delicate pink and white blossoms of plum, cherry, and magnolia trees were everywhere. But the almond trees were past blooming.

Remember how enchanted I was by the large, apple-like blossoms of the almond trees in Sacramento where we stopped off to see Linda Butler on our first trip to Ashland in 1981, and how delighted I was to find three or four trees in full bloom right along Ellen's side yard on Almond Street? We had enjoyed the adventure of a day-long bus trip through the farmlands of the Sacramento valley past extensive Lake Shasta and up to the little town of Shasta, still in snow. An hour or so later and a few miles over the Oregon border we pulled into the bus stop in downtown Ashland and spotted Ellen and the two children waiting for us. Daniel was then twenty-one months and an eager learner of new words. Remember how he would point to some object and say "no name," (or did he mean "know name"?). Elise, at five and a half, would ask us to boost her up into a certain old almond tree where she would sit on the flat stump of a large branch pruned years before when it was part of an orchard. Ellen always thought of that tree as Elise's until they moved to their little house on High Street in 1990 when she and Steve were getting divorced. Then Dan wrote a paper for his sixth grade English class telling how, although he had moved only two blocks away from his old house, the new one seemed like a different world without his own special "X-Wing Fighter" tree.

We always enjoyed our visits to Ashland, didn't we? Of course the main point was to share in Ellen's life and become acquainted with the children on their own turf, but we were glad to get off by ourselves too. While Ellen was teaching and the children were in school we would walk around the neighborhood and in the park on the lovely wooded trail along the creek. Sometimes we would return to take pictures at some spot Ellen and Steve had shown us. I cherish the memory of our drive to the coast and our stay at the same motel in Bandon overlooking the big rocks where Ann had taken us after your brother Hank died. Ellen and I both have prints of the photographs you took on those occasions. Mine are still in the frames in which you mounted them, but Ellen's were unframed until recently when she had them done by a professional. Her mats in subtle shades of gray are particularly well suited to photos of low contrast such as the ones you took under lowering clouds of the ocean shore and of the old ranch on Dead Indian Trail with its weather-beaten shacks and corral against that bare hill topped by an outcropping of rocks and backed by a snow streaked mountain. The gray mattings also look good on the sharper prints like the scene further up that road of fir trees in spring snow and the one from Mt. Ashland of the perfect cone of Mt. Shasta like a cloud floating in the distance.

April 27, 1997

I've been thinking how bewildering it must have been for you to have so many different people looking after you. The nurses stayed pretty constant, but there was an ever changing array of nurse assistants. Not only were there three shifts of them a day, but every so often they would be rotated to other sections of the floor and not return for several weeks. I suppose that was to protect them from being stuck too long with the most difficult patients, or maybe it was to give each the privilege of a turn with you! After all, didn't Dr. Huff relay reports from the nurses that you were their favorite? Then there was the problem of turnover, as aides would disappear presumably to seek better paying or more compatible jobs, and newcomers would take their places. I had a hard time keeping track of them myself.

The nurse assistants covered a wide range of ability, but fortunately the better ones tended to stay. I learned a lot from them while helping to settle you down for your naps, and soon I was helping to teach the new ones. You know how I kept harping on the importance of giving warning before they did anything to you, such as rolling you over or wiping you with a cold cloth, to say nothing of that scary Hoyer lift procedure. This should have been drilled into them during training which was all too brief. Their caseload was so large that in their rush to get their work done they would rush you too. Looking back I marvel at those who were able to keep calm and unhurried under all that pressure and were relaxed enough to joke with you. Do you remember Michelle, with the long blond hair, who used to call you Santa Claus? She told me one morning that while getting you dressed she rolled you over on your side and you exclaimed, "Hey! Hey!" This prompted her to recite a little ditty:

> Hay, hay, Straw is cheaper, Grass is free.
> Cows can eat it, Why can't we?

to which you replied, "I am not a vegetarian."

You came to know some things about your aides through listening to my conversations with them during the naptime ritual. We learned that several were working their way through college, the first being red-headed Neil, a senior at Concordia, who planned to become a minister. Judging from his kindness to you I'm sure he'll make a good one. Another of the few male attendants, Jean Pierre from one of the French-speaking countries in West Africa, was also a student. He never failed to warn you with a cheerful "Here comes the cold stuff, Lyle." After a few months he left to go home for a visit and we never saw him again. I hope he was able to finish his education. Remember Lori and how proud of her we all were when she achieved her RN and became one of your nurses?

Then there was Abby Marterella, a lively and expressive nineteen-year-old freshman at EMU when she came to Glacier Hills in January of 1992. She says you were her first patient. You might remember her excitement about going off to Key West for spring break with Melena and two other friends. It was fun to hear all about their adventure, but by the next winter her life took a hard turn. I guess it had never been easy, as her parents had divorced when she was quite young. In recent years she had been living with her father and he was paying most of her college expenses to supplement her part-time earnings. Then he married again and told Abby she would have to find some place else to live and that he could no longer give her any financial support. That meant she had to work full-time to cover living expenses. She made a valiant effort to continue with her four courses at Eastern, but the load and emotional turmoil she had been through were too much. Faced with flunking out, she sought the help of an academic advisor who told her she could take an emergency withdrawal, forfeiting the semester's tuition but with the option to return whenever she was able. I felt so sorry for her and encouraged her as best I could.

You must have been somewhat aware of Abby's situation, but I'm sure I spared you the details as all this was happening shortly before you died. Then, not long after you were gone, I had a brainstorm: to set up a scholarship fund for nurse assistants. I consulted some friends at the university's Center for the Education of Women who helped me keep the procedures quite simple. My proposal to Richard Oliver, the director, was that I provide five thousand dollars a year for two years and begin by offering two scholarships. We set up a selection committee consisting of the two of us and Eileen DeLancey, who had been your nurse throughout your stay. Then, hoping to get launched for the fall semester, we distributed and posted the following notice:

THE LYLE CRAINE MEMORIAL SCHOLARSHIP FUND

PURPOSE:
To encourage the academic growth of Certified Nurse Assistants to be provided by Lyle Craine's family in appreciation for the care, respect, and good humor given him throughout his four and a half year stay at Glacier Hills Nursing Center.

IF YOU ARE A CERTIFIED NURSE ASSISTANT:
*Presently employed at Glacier Hills for at least one year
*Working either full-time or part-time
*Enrolled in an accredited college or university in the program of your choice

YOU CAN APPLY FOR SCHOLARSHIP FUNDS:
*Semester funding for tuition, books, and fees (with possibility of extension)
*Monthly stipend for certain living expenses

APPLICATIONS ARE DUE FRIDAY, JUNE 10 TO:
Richard Oliver, RN, Director Health Care Services (516) or
Eileen DeLancey, RN, Clinical Coordinator (527)

Much to our dismay there were no takers. You would have told me to "hold on there" and not be in such a hurry. The delay was probably just as well because vacations would have made it difficult to find times to meet during the summer. So at the end of August we sent out the same notice again with an October 12 deadline for applications for the winter semester. This time we were not disappointed as four applied, Abby among them. The committee's deliberations were made easy by the fact that two were obviously much better qualified than the other two. Abby's qualifications were outstanding. We were impressed by the way she had handled her difficulties and by her determination to become an occupational therapist in order to help stroke patients and others learn how to become self-reliant. When we told her she had been selected she was overwhelmed with relief and joy.

Our other recipient was Donna Tracy, a young black woman whom I had not known because she worked the evening shift on another floor. She had entered a pre-nursing course at Washtenaw Community College in January 1993, bringing 27 credits from a community college in Philadelphia. Her goal was set while still a child when her grandmother, whom she helped take care of, told her she would make a good nurse. I never did get acquainted with her as she seemed rather reticent, but I was pleased she kept plugging away until she completed her associate degree last spring. Starting in the winter term of 1995 we granted scholarships to two more community college students. One was studying how to keep medical records, but soon left for a better job at University Hospital. The other was Renee who had taken care of you from the time you entered the nursing home until your very last day. Unfortunately her high school preparation was inadequate and her personal life too stressful for her to stick it out. I hope that some day, when her little boys are older, things will settle down enough so she can continue her education.

Abby, however, was able to fulfill her dreams. In the spring of 1995 she announced the glad news that she was one of 40 students, from among 150 qualified, to be accepted into EMU's occupational therapy program. She devoted that entire summer to working, and became a full-time student in the fall. Because she was now able to take out loans to cover her tuition, our scholarship went toward living expenses. Throughout, Abby has been very expressive of her appreciation, calling me her angel, and wanting me to be sure to attend her graduation. Finally her big day came last Sunday when I joined her proud family, stepparents included, to sit on the bleachers of the EMU field house and witness the ceremony. In a reversal of roles she gave me a graduation present—a little cut glass angel. Of course I was embarrassed until I thought to tell her that she was sure to become an angel too.

May 7, 1997

Spring has finally arrived in Ann Arbor, fully five weeks later than in Oregon. Yesterday our hiking group saw masses of trillium in a woods just south of town and I saw more this afternoon at the county farm park on a walk with Sukha.

What a generous and devoted friend Sukha was, coming to see you every two weeks the whole time you were in the nursing home! Her gentle chanting must have been soothing to you and perhaps helped you to meditate. She tells me that no matter how unresponsive you were when she arrived, by the end of her half hour she was always rewarded by knowing you were fully aware of her presence. You especially enjoyed the simple Buddhist stories she sometimes read to you.

The staff recognized the importance of stimulating your mind and engaging you in social exchange. That is why I continued your speech therapy with Charlene Zand long past the point where you were actually making progress, and why Mary Ann, the activities director, used to wheel you into the dining room to observe whatever project was going on such as cookie baking, making Easter bonnets, or viewing a film. Do you remember when she got us together with three other couples to form a memory group and tried to lead us in parlor games, like "I pack my bag?" I think you probably found it both too difficult and too stupid. We might have done better on our own, though it certainly takes skill and imagination to engage intelligent but mute adults in meaningful activity. The best session was the last, a "show and tell." I brought your photo taken in Swat of the little laughing girl carrying a chicken, and Arno Mariotti explained how his oboe worked. Surely you remember Carol, a particularly creative young woman who came for a few weeks, under some special grant, to do sedentary play acting. She certainly captured your attention for, after conducting the patients on an imaginary safari in the jungle, you looked up at her, smiled, and exclaimed, "Delightful!" We both enjoyed occasional concerts performed by visiting groups ranging from Sunday school choirs to an instrumental ensemble of University Music School students.

Meanwhile I tried just about everything suggested to entertain you. We listened to some short stories on tape but they were either too long or too complicated to hold your attention all the way through and the same was true of "talking books." You might have learned to set your own pace if only you had been able to turn the switch on and off by yourself. The radio presented the same difficulty. Sometimes I would leave it playing WUOM's afternoon classical music program when I left you for your nap, and, not wanting to disturb either you or your roommate with unwanted gab when the news went on, I would ask him to tell the nurse assistant on the next shift to turn it off.

Of course you enjoyed hearing letters, especially from the children. I'm afraid my reading selections were a rather hit or miss affair—short articles from the newspaper or from the influx of environmental magazines that we never could keep up with. A number of poems about small animals and other creatures in the nature anthology Tim and Leslie sent you often brought tears to your eyes. You were likewise touched by Aldo Leopold's *A Sand County Almanac*, the only book I remember reading all the way to the end. Most of all you liked hearing your own words as I proofread the "Family Letters" Leslie had typed for your birthday. You would laugh at many of the episodes of your childhood you had so amusingly described, but your biggest laugh was for the old family joke, which you must have heard a hundred times, of the man who fell through the ice while ice-fishing. When his friends brought him home severely chilled and in clothes frozen stiff his somewhat batty wife exclaimed, "Did you get your feet wet, dear?"

May 14, 1997

On the whole I think your greatest pleasure came from visitors. Weren't we fortunate to have so many loyal friends and such a devoted family! We would gather by the round table in a corner of the sunroom. Because your eyes did not track to the right nor your head turn to compensate, when we had company I would relinquish my chair on your left side so your visitor could talk directly to you and observe your facial reaction. But only a few were able to break the habit of looking at the person who responds to them verbally, so I would get most of the attention that I had hoped would go to you. However you did seem to enjoy listening to the conversation flow around you.

Although you usually remained silent, sometimes you rewarded your guests with a word or two. For instance, once as our friends the Kornbluhs were leaving you said, "Friends." When Jim Crowfoot came you were very responsive to his telling us about new programs at SNR such as Bill Stapp's work with Detroit high school classes in studying the water quality of the Rouge River and other efforts to get Black kids interested in the environment. You tried hard to talk, but all you could manage was "Thanks," as he said good-bye, but after he left I heard you mumble to yourself, "Not that I don't try." You were able to tell the Harts "I like to see everyone," and when Harold told news of Naomi you opened your eyes wide, smiled, and spoke her name, then added, "Potential." Later when Naomi and Rachel came you said, "application," "expenditure," and "I think you've done it very well," all in reference to Naomi's job and Rachel's school. Then, as they left you said, "Pleasant time."

Among our faithful visitors were our Gray Panther friends—Kay Walker, Harold and Clara Nitzberg, and Bee Green. Kay and the Nitzbergs would help you with your lunch when I took brief trips out of town, and Bee used to drop by frequently after she moved into the retirement center. Another regular, Don Coleman, co-director of Guild House, would usually catch your interest with some timely topic of mutual concern.

Surprise visits from our young relatives, Ruth and John Wood, were always a joy. Remember back in 1986 when they arrived from California as newlyweds eager to start graduate study, Ruth (my nephew Andy's daughter) in physiology and John in a combined program of medicine and engineering? Their high spirits were like a breath of fresh air. We were delighted to have family in town again as they found fun in whatever we did whether a simple picnic by the river or a stay at the cabin. They in turn were happy to have a great aunt and uncle to serve as their family away from home. After your stroke they would breeze in to join us for lunch and brighten our day. Then, near the end of October of the following year they brought four day-old Lyle to show us. We were both touched that they had named him after you. Once when they placed him on the tray of your wheelchair he tugged at your beard, and you said, "Hi there, Fella." From then on you had the pleasure of watching young Lyle grow, and three years later his little brother, Jim. The Woods now live in New Haven and are expecting another baby in September.

May 20, 1997

Yesterday Abby came here for lunch and our first opportunity for a long, unhurried conversation. Following her graduation she has been in an unstructured situation for the first time since she started working at age fourteen, and she finds her new freedom disconcerting. She'll be busy again soon enough when she starts her three-month internship with Community Mental Health in Kalamazoo on the first of June. There she will be helping discharged mental health patients learn to live independently by teaching them how to budget their money, shop, cook, and clean house. Meanwhile she feels quite unsettled, but she has discovered a new calm from yoga, which she started recently. When I asked who taught the class, she said the priest at the Zen Buddhist Temple. Imagine my surprise and hers to learn that your faithful visitor, whom she had thought was our daughter, is her teacher, Sukha. It seems quite miraculous that the four of us are so closely interconnected. Incidentally, Abby tells me that you were the most peaceful patient she ever encountered at Glacier Hills.

May 22, 1997

Larry Gladieux just phoned with the news that his father had died after a long decline. He was ninety years old. A memorial service will be held in Oberlin on June 14, at the Quaker retirement home where Bun had been living for the past several years since Persis died.

June 17, 1997

Yesterday I took two naps! My overnight trip to Oberlin must have been more tiring than I realized, but was thoroughly worth it. By coincidence Tim happened to be attending a conference in Oberlin and was able to go to Bun's memorial service with me and stay for dinner with the family afterwards. We were particularly glad to have some long conversations with Clayt Miller. He, poor man, was in great pain from a recent bike accident and he looked quite frail. All four Gladieux sons expressed appreciation for our coming and for my remarks at the service.

Of course I was speaking for you, as best I could, to tell them of your enduring friendship with their father starting when you were students at Oberlin. I reminded them that Bun was in the class ahead of you and that when you graduated in 1931 you joined him and Persis in Tokyo to teach at the American School. Referring to the countless tales and snapshot albums with which the Gladieux boys grew up, I said they could imagine how much those three years of shared adventures in a strange land had solidified your friendship with their parents. I told them how, after earning your masters in geography at Wisconsin and teaching for a year, you again followed Bun's lead, as Clayt had done earlier, to take up graduate study in public administration at Syracuse University, and that by the time we met in Washington in the summer of 1941 you were working for him in the Bureau of the Budget. I recalled the warm welcome Bun and Persis gave me and their wonderful support when you became stressed out after you moved over to the War Production Board with Bun, and Persis saying he loved you like a brother. My remarks finished with telling how after they moved to New York and we to Ann Arbor we always kept in touch, and how Clayt drove Bun here from Oberlin for a last visit in December 1990.

It has seemed to me that in your relationship to Bun you fell into the role of kid brother even though he was only a year older than you, but I suppose that came naturally as you actually were the kid brother in your family. However, I sensed you were impatient to outgrow your dependence on him (and his on you?). This was especially apparent when you were agonizing over whether to go with him to WPB, though that decision was strongly influenced by the draft breathing down your neck. Anyway, after the war you were both happy to be free to pursue your very different paths. Bun was always more interested in administration per se than you were, so we were not surprised that he become a successful management consultant, whereas your interest in government was as a means to manage and protect our land and water resources. When you took the job of coordinating water programs in the office of the Secretary of the Interior in 1948 we had no idea that within five years you would be returning to academic life. I continue to be grateful to the Eisenhower administration for giving you the "pink slip" which led to your coming to the School of Natural Resources and our good life here in Ann Arbor.

III

September 12, 1997

Well, here I am, back in Ann Arbor after a lovely summer at the cabin. Although cold nights signaled it was time to migrate, I was reluctant to leave our woods and lake, which seemed more beautiful than ever this year. I had been wondering if it was simply old age that had increased my appreciation of nature's beauty. Then one day as I lay on the chaise on our bank and looked up at the high treetops, I discovered that I could easily distinguish the oak leaves from the maple ones, thanks to my new lens implants. My keener eyesight helps me better identify birds too.

This summer I didn't do the writing I had expected as more of my time was devoted to visitors. Mario, Ellen and Skip, and Barbara Bach all stayed a little longer than last year, and additionally Steve came for a week and Naomi for two nights. While I thoroughly enjoyed a special companionship with each one, by the end I was sorry I did not have more days of solitude. Another difference was that last summer my writing of our contented days at the cabin flowed naturally from my being there, but this year trying to continue the story of your stroke seemed like an intrusion on my vacation. So instead of going on with these letters to you, I reread and took notes on most of the little notebooks.

This review reminded me that you continued to make small but significant gains in the first two and a half years. The accumulation of subtle changes impressed returning visitors and gave me a perspective I could not have in the midst of daily ups and downs. For instance, in early April of 1989, Clayt and Louise were delighted to find you much more responsive than four months previously. You joined us in gales of laughter when, in your search for the right word, you came up with "tentage," and then, responding to my remark that I didn't know that word, said, "It's new to me, too." On the other hand, Steve, coming a few days later, saw you as essentially in the same condition as at Thanksgiving though healthier and more content. Leslie returned in early July after eight months. She was pleased with your greater alertness, improved talking, and stronger voice all making you seem like your old self. You were more at ease and agonized less over your failure to express your thoughts. Once when my niece Barby speculated that you must have lots of thoughts which became jumbled because you couldn't get them out, you said, "Sometimes it's easier to let them go by." During a phone call from Louise Wallace just a year after your stroke you told her, "I have more thinking than saying." Her observations were particularly reassuring, both because her long experience as a psychiatric nurse gave her a discerning eye and because she had come to know you so well in recent years. By February 1990 she not only found you healthier and more comfortable, but with a longer attention span and a greater awareness of your surroundings. She reminded me that you have always been an observer and listener with a tendency to test the waters before answering and an ability to tune out whatever doesn't interest you. She also saw that your characteristic sense of humor was helping you to accept your difficulties.

As you became more relaxed so did I, for I too had been trying too hard. Your therapists had told me that stimulation was important, so naturally I tried everything I could think of to capture your interest including "interviewing" your visitors, but I was thwarted by your habit of keeping your eyes closed much of the time. As you became able to sustain longer eye contact I eased up on my efforts and gained more confidence in my intuition. Then I grew bolder in guessing your state of mind, and so our communication, both verbal and non-verbal, improved. Once I remarked that at least you could convey your feelings if not your thoughts, and you answered, "That's pretty fundamental." Another time you laughed heartily at my comment that if the dolphins can communicate without words we too ought to be able to also.

September 29, 1997

Have you ever noticed how often word of a death is promptly followed by news of a birth? Recently I was saddened to learn that Clayt Miller had died, the last of your Oberlin trio to go. Yesterday Tim and I attended a memorial service for him near the Catoctin Mountains in Maryland. Now today I have just heard that your young namesake, Lyle, and his brother Jim have a baby sister named Marion after my mother, as well as my sister, and Ruth's sister. I like the coincidence of the Wood family pattern being like ours—at least so far. I'll never forget your joyous exclamation as you entered my hospital room after Ellen's birth, "Honey, I can't believe our good luck!"

Tim and I met at the Baltimore airport Saturday afternoon, rented a car and drove to a motel in Thurmont. Next morning we had time to walk a couple of short trails in the national park before changing our clothes and getting to the noon service. It was held in an old stone chapel on the edge of the woods a few miles north of Thurmont. Clayt would have been proud of Bob's poise in leading the simple service and of Lani's courage in singing a favorite song of his, "Over the Rainbow." We were touched when Bob guided Louise to an armchair near the altar where, though frail and suffering from Alzheimer's, she read the Twenty-Third Psalm. After Bob and Lani each paid tribute to their father, his friends were invited to make their contributions.

Tim and I had a rough idea of what we might each say if called upon, but I was surprised when he was the second person to volunteer. First he recalled the good times our two families had together while the Millers lived in Ann Arbor when Clayt was working for Ford and they built their house on the banks of the Huron River. Then he referred to his long conversation with Clayt following the service for Bun in June when Clayt told him of his several career disappointments starting with giving up his dream to master the Chinese language and become a Chinese historian. Tim spoke of Clayt's hope of applying his management skills gained in government toward making Ford a more humane corporation, and of his giving up in disillusionment after four years. Tim concluded that in spite of disappointments Clayt never lost his ideals nor his sense of humor.

I followed immediately, grateful to Tim for covering the essentials so well that I was free to be more anecdotal. I started by telling how your friendship went back to Oberlin College days and of your meeting up with Clayt in China the summer after your first year of teaching in Tokyo. Then I jumped ahead to when, on our second date, you took me with Clayt and Louise to climb Old Rag Mountain, a rugged out-cropping of the Blue Ridge. The trail was steep and the heat sweltering, but Clayt showed such an interest in my work with consumers that I was talking a blue streak until I begged him to stop asking questions so I could catch my breath. I reminded Louise that when we finally came down off the mountain I suggested we take off our shoes and socks and cool our feet in the nearby stream. It was almost dark and the guys were anxious to start the two-hour drive back to Washington, so we had to hurry. While I had managed to submerge both my feet, Louise got only one of hers in the water. On the ride home she laughed at how good that one foot felt compared to the other. Finally I ended by telling what a devoted and loyal friend Clayt had always been and how much his and Louise's twice-yearly visits meant to us when you were laid up with your stroke.

The four Gladieux brothers all stood up in a group and took turns telling what an important influence Clayt had on them while they were growing up and how much they appreciated his daily visits to Bun when he moved to Oberlin. The Alumni Office of the college sent a representative to express thanks for the many volunteer hours he had given to their work. After the service we gathered around a picnic table behind the chapel for a light lunch and a chance to visit with the family. It was evident that our coming meant a lot to them, as it did to me, but sharing it with Tim made all the difference in the world.

I feel an inconsolable sorrow for Clayt, not for his death at eighty-eight but for his unfulfilled life: for the cloud of suspicion of disloyalty fabricated by the witch-hunters of the McCarthy era that deprived him of federal employment, for his repeated disillusion in people he worked for, and especially for the great disparity between his and Louise's reality. Remember how we felt she lived in an esoteric spiritual realm unreachable by us humble mortals? I'm sure we sensed that for both of them their laughter covered a lot of pain.

October 6, 1997

It's hard to believe that Tim is fifty-four today. He has had a good year especially since Central Connecticut has granted him tenure and a promotion to associate professor. Although he continues to be as busy as ever, he seems less hectic and more relaxed. I'm sure you would be pleased to find him so content. Leslie too is happy in her work. After the blow of being turned down for tenure at Trinity in 1993 and putting up with unsatisfactory temporary jobs, she has finally found her niche at Central teaching two sections of chemistry and one lab. Tim tells me she likes working only part-time because it suits her slower tempo. Lucky for them she does not keep as fast a pace as he does! They have made extensive improvements to their house, which they have all to themselves now that Rachel has moved to an apartment nearer the university and the school where she will do her practice teaching. Chelsea, now four, continues to be their major recreation and stays with them for part of most weekends.

October 8, 1997

Yesterday I had a leisurely lunch at the Gandy Dancer with Rita Conway and Trudy Huntington, our close friends from Glacier Hills. Rita and I had wanted to get together with Trudy following the death in August of her ninety-four year old mother, Abby Enders. You remember Abby, a Quaker of quiet dignity and simple directness, who epitomized everything we admired about the Friends. I know you and she were drawn to each other soon after her arrival at Glacier Hills in the spring of 1989. She was soft spoken but hard-of-hearing so when her grandson, Caleb, or Trudy sometimes read stories to her after lunch in the sunroom we could not help but overhear their loud voices. Trudy is still carrying on with her research on the Amish, and yesterday I was surprised to learn that she has also been teaching a course on the environment at LS&A. She was interested in learning from me that the School of Natural Resources was originally a school of forestry and thought that might account for the attitude of superiority some of her colleagues had taken toward some of yours.

During those years at the nursing home Trudy, Rita, and I became staunch allies in our efforts to give voice to concerns and suggestions regarding patient care. Our vehicle was the monthly meetings of the perfunctory family council. They were poorly attended probably because most family members had little time or inclination to attend dull meetings and perhaps because they felt isolated and intimidated by the institution. The institution, in turn, seemed to be intimidated by us, judging by the defensive attitude of the social worker who presided and by higher-up officials who sometimes came. It was too bad, because the original idea of family councils, as conceived by our friend Jane Barney, was that they would foster mutual understanding and support between staff and families of patients. I guess that can only happen where the leadership truly wants to permeate the whole organization with a democratic spirit, as the Friends know how to do. However, we hung in there, and yesterday concluded that our efforts had brought about some improvements. At least Trudy established that our minutes be written by a family member rather than by a staff person and that they be submitted to the Board of Directors. Whether that will continue now that she's gone remains to be seen.

We recognized that most of the countless instances of neglect, such as long delays in answering call lights, were due to understaffing. A common cause of falls, we've heard, is when patients who need assistance in going to the toilet become impatient and try to make it on their own. However, we believed that much distress could have been avoided with better training and supervision along with a little imagination and common sense. For instance, it was inexcusable to leave you abandoned in the dining room after breakfast where several times I found you stretched out stiff as a board. All they needed to do was wheel you into the hall by the nursing station where you were visible. I was sorry you were not able to shout for help or, back in your room, to reach for the cord to turn on the call light. Heaven only knows what neglect you may have suffered there, for you could not tell anyone about it. A few of your roommates or their wives would give me feedback, most of it positive, for which I was very grateful. They sometimes would tell me if the aides had trouble with the Hoyer lift or if you were gotten up at an unusually early hour. Once, when I had to leave right after lunch, I was told that nobody ever came to put you down for your nap. What a long, uncomfortable day that must have been for you! Because nursing home regulations require that any accident or serious setback be reported promptly, I learned of the few falls you had and of the time you got your head stuck between the mattress and the side rail. None of these incidents caused injury, but they surely must have frightened you.

An alarming and really serious accident happened to Joe Conway in August 1990. He had been making encouraging progress since suffering a stroke eight months earlier and was able to propel his wheelchair by himself. Cookie, the occupational therapist, was teaching him how he could, with assistance, transfer from his chair to the toilet. That day I was in the sunroom helping you with your lunch when Joe, greatly agitated, came dashing by saying he needed Cookie right away. Then he spotted her through the window at the staff picnic tables. I don't remember whether I spoke to her through the window or ran out to tell her how frantic Joe was, but I relayed her message to him that he'd have to wait a little while until she finished her lunch. Then I returned my attention to you, and Joe disappeared. I was only vaguely aware that he had wheeled down the corridor toward the kitchen and the residential wing where patients were not supposed to go. More important, I did not know that a door to the outside, which is always kept closed and can only be opened by pressing a button high on the wall, had been propped open by someone delivering food to the kitchen. Next thing I knew there was a great commotion. Joe had gone out the door and, ironically, his wheelchair was tilted off balance as he went crosswise over the curb-cut intended for wheelchairs. He crashed, severely injuring his head. It was a permanent setback for he did not fully recover his previous level of functioning, and certainly we never saw him handle his wheelchair by himself again. There followed various inadequate devices for keeping patients from going down that corridor without blocking off necessary traffic by staff and visitors culminating, shortly after you died, in loud alarm bells which would go off unless first deactivated by pressing a button high on the wall. I'm glad you were spared the alarm of those bells, but to this day I feel remorse that I had not been more alert and followed Joe down that corridor.

October 12, 1997

The conversation with Rita and Trudy last week started me thinking about the isolation of the nursing home. It was a little world of its own, wasn't it? I became so immersed in it every day that at times I felt like a member of the staff, but unlike you, we had the outside world to return to. You patients were not only cut off from the outside but many of you were isolated from each other. Some patients never got out of their rooms and those of you who did usually had one disability or another that hampered communication. Most of you depended on others to push you to where you might or might not want to be, and your places at the dining table were more a matter of chance than of choice. Only a few on our floor were able to propel their own wheelchairs. Remember when your roommate, Ralph, achieved that skill? He would take off down the corridor toward the residential wing much to the consternation of the nurses. Once they were afraid that he had wheeled himself onto the elevator, but when the doors opened and you and I stepped off there were exclamations of relief. You wanted to know what all the commotion was about. I explained the situation then remarked that I supposed if you were able to navigate your chair you would want to go places too. "You're darn right I would!" was your emphatic reply.

Of course the primary purpose of my visits to you was to restore our own private world of just the two of us, one that included sharing the interests and concerns we had always cared about. The difference was that I had to be the initiator. I missed the cullings of your reading and ruminations and above all the back and forth of discussion. That is why I was glad to have our many loyal visitors to generate conversation. They stimulated your thinking and reminded you of who you really were in a way that the staff who had not known you before your stroke could never do. For instance, once when Michelle, the aide who used to call you Santa Claus because of your beard, brought you your lunch tray she chided you for not smiling and exhorted you to try to do better. You told her, "Today is not a smiling day." After she left us I commented on her uncalled for admonishment and how hard it must be for you to be subjected to so many people who didn't really know you. I brought it up again when you were in bed saying that at least I knew you and you replied, "You know me and I know you"—a most comforting thought!

As for your isolation from the other patients, some of that was bridged through your listening in as I chatted with them and their families. The Conways became our good friends. Rita and I formed a bond immediately upon their arrival at Glacier Hills. She was at the nursing station anxiously waiting to be called into the dining room for her first "patient care" meeting with staff members when she asked me how long she might have to wait. She explained that her husband had been very upset by the move and she didn't want to leave him alone any longer than necessary. I suggested that she go back to his room and I would alert her when her turn came. Subsequently I helped her learn the ropes and, in effect, became her unofficial advisor as I was for other newcomers. Rita soon assumed that role herself far surpassing me in her outreach. She was a brick always keeping a light touch and a ready laugh no matter how difficult the situation.

It took longer to become acquainted with Joe, because he was still in pretty bad shape when he arrived from the hospital after undergoing by-pass surgery followed by a stroke. Unlike yours, his stroke was on the left side of his brain so he retained his speech and the use of his right hand. However, the section of his brain relating to space and time was affected resulting in some disorientation. For instance, he would become convinced that the roof needed repair or some other urgent matter required immediate action. Rita usually managed to reassure him that all would be attended to, but we often had a hard time knowing where he was coming from. Even so, his kindness and good will showed through the confusion of his thoughts enabling you to establish a meaningful friendship. He once told Mario that he admired your intellect and would like to play checkers with you. Our frequent cheerful exchanges with the Conways did much to raise my spirits, as I'm sure they did yours, because underlying our laughter we knew we shared the same predicament.

October 20, 1997

Among our other friends at Glacier Hills, I cherish the memory of Arno Mariotti the most. His steadfastness and humor sustained us all. Remember how he would entertain us with stories of amusing experiences when he played oboe in various orchestras? The Mariottis were already there when we arrived, and Arno was in constant attendance to Florence whose stroke a year earlier had left her completely mute. She not only never spoke a word, she didn't even smile, but he would jolly her along in an easy and familiar manner as if she were able to respond. They often listened to music on his CD recorder equipped with two sets of earphones. Whenever the weather permitted he took her outdoors to sit under a favorite tree between the parking lot and the vegetable garden. He would get his folding camp chair from his car, put on their earphones and settle down to enjoy his one indulgence, a cigar. You may not have realized that it was Arno who, seeing me struggle to push your wheelchair up the steep section of the path from the pond, told me to go zigzag like mini switchbacks, but you surely remember how readily I would pass along his tip to others.

After a few months I noticed that Florence was beginning to smile, making her a silent participant in our conversations. Then suddenly, more than two years after her stroke, she startled Arno by reading a word she saw in a brightly illustrated magazine he was showing her. Arno was elated! Her speech returned quite rapidly, and she began to respond to his joshing with teasing banter. The new physical therapy crew took her on and soon had her walking between the parallel bars. Though as far as I know she never mastered walking on her own, she did learn to assist in transfer from one chair to another. We all rejoiced with them in these victories. Arno, being strong enough to lift Florence into their car, had been taking her to their home in Ypsilanti for a few hours where she would sit outside and watch him mow the lawn. Now he was emboldened to drive her to their family cottage in Chautauqua, New York, for a week's reunion with their two sons. By arranging for a mid-day rest stop at a motel he was able to make the trip in one day. He reported that everything went off without a hitch and they were happy to be together where they had spent so many summers when he was a member of the Chautauqua Orchestra. During the rest of the year he played in several orchestras around the country and most recently was first chair oboist with the Detroit Symphony as well as a professor in the U. of M.'s School of Music.

Sometime early in 1992 Arno had an operation to remove a cancer on his tongue caused, I presume, by all those cigars he enjoyed so much. He remained upbeat, though he did admit that the loss of saliva from radiation treatments made bread feel like sawdust. Unfortunately he had to undergo a second operation in April and was put on tube feeding, which required that he stay in the nursing home. That is how he became your roommate for a few weeks. As usual he spent all his waking hours with Florence and returned only to sleep and when he had to be hooked up to the feeding apparatus. Lucky for us he was scheduled to be there at the time you went down for your nap giving us a chance to visit with him. Remember his photographs, taken by his son, of some of the elegant Victorian cottages at Chautauqua? They reminded us of the ones at Bay View. Once, when you seemed to have dropped off to sleep and I was talking with him about music, I noticed your eyes were open. Later I asked if you enjoyed listening in on our conversation and you said, "yes."

When Arno left us he was released to more or less resume his usual routine, but after several months he had to become a patient again, this time staying in a room near Florence in the new addition. We used to go down there to visit him. It was sad to see our dear friend, who had so enlivened and enriched our small world, waste away. Our last visit was in February of 1993, when in effect we said good-bye. He died nine days later. There was a memorial service the next day in the "Sunshine Room" that large lounge below the dining room of the retirement hall where we used to escape sometimes for a quiet interlude. I did not take you because I thought it would be too long and tiring, but I'm sorry you missed hearing his two sons talk of their father's career and of their happy life together as a family. Beforehand Florence had been afraid she couldn't keep from crying, but as soon as her boys started to speak she was smiling in rapt attention. She has since been transferred to a nursing home nearer the son who is the schoolteacher in Royal Oak. When last I heard she was doing well.

November 5, 1997

Much as we were both frustrated by your inability to express your thoughts, at least we understood the cause, namely that your stroke had done permanent damage to the part of your brain that organizes speech. We knew there was nothing we could do but learn to live with the situation. I tried to find out what I could about strokes in general and aphasia in particular and even attended a support group for families of stroke victims for a while, though it didn't help me much as their cases were not as severe as yours. More worrisome for me were the discomforts you were suffering because of your rigidity, presumably related to Parkinson's disease. Had you actually been diagnosed as having it, I might have joined a Parkinson's support group, but as it was I felt I was groping in the dark with no guide.

My first concern after you arrived at Glacier Hills centered around getting you a comfortable wheelchair. It took more than two years before we bought one that really fit you. The physical therapy department was supposed to provide each patient with a wheelchair, but their supply was inadequate and the staff of two part-time therapists seemed indifferent to your problems. To be sure they tried out different kinds of chairs, but the high-backed Gerry chair was too stiff, others were too small and the shafts of their footrests too short and all were jarring over rough pavement. Nothing worked well because of your tendency to stretch out straight. Your left foot would keep slipping off the small footrest and tripping you up. Noticing that another patient had a broad footrest made of wood, I went home and improvised one at your work bench, which helped some. Then, after you had been at Glacier Hills for about six months they finally got a salesman to come. I would have been glad to pay for a new chair for you, but he gave me no satisfactory idea of what he had to offer that would be any better, so I simply bought a seat cushion and some wider footrests with straps to hold your feet in place.

A year later, the PT crew left, one for a full-time job with The Word of God where she had already been working part-time. They were replaced by a larger, more competent and committed staff, who took you back for therapy and in due course addressed the wheelchair issue. They removed the tray, which was placed across your armrests to help keep you upright because it was not very effective and was in fact making your shoulders hunch. Then they brought in a representative of a different wheelchair firm who was much more responsive to your needs. Through him Joe Conway bought an extra large sized chair with balloon tires. When we saw how much more comfortable he was I ordered one for you. It made a big difference and gave you such a smooth ride that you no longer cried out when I pushed you over bumps in the sidewalk.

Your return to physical therapy relieved me greatly. Up to then I had been the only person who was doing anything to keep your joints limber. I felt that the range of motion exercises I gave you at naptime were most inadequate and that I needed more instruction, but whenever I would protest the staff told me I was doing just fine. Nancy, the new PT director, was willing to take you on even though you didn't meet Medicare's requirements as long as we covered the cost. She had you reaching and pulling, lifting your foot, and leaning forward. Mostly you seemed challenged by the exercises and proud of your small accomplishments, but sometimes she was over zealous. Once I was appalled to find you angrily shouting, "No! No! No!" and shaking your finger at Nancy. She was trying to teach you to propel your chair by "walking" your feet while she nudged the chair forward, but was probably pushing it too fast. I was shocked that she did not stop when you were so obviously distressed, for I felt it was a violation of your autonomy. I managed to calm both of us down, but found the whole episode depressing. However, after that Nancy took a less aggressive approach. She was amused a few months later when she asked if you knew who she was and you replied, "My damned side-kick." Eventually she turned you over to a new member of the staff, Robin, a gentle young woman with a delightful sense of humor. Remember how I used to come in on Tuesday mornings toward the end of your PT session? You might be on the tilt-table in a nearly upright position, and as you "stood" there I would tell you both where my hiking group had gone that morning. Robin was particularly interested because she and her husband were new to our area. Then I would ask about Aaron, her toddler, and she would gladly tell us of his latest antics. She became very fond of you and we of her. Now, whenever I return to the nursing center, we greet each other with heartfelt hugs.

Regrettably the kind of guidance and support I would have appreciated from our doctor was not forthcoming. While I fully trusted his competency in medicine, there were times when I felt that Dr. Huff didn't care enough about your comfort. Since you couldn't articulate your complaints, he had to depend on me and the nursing staff to bring problems to his attention. He would make his monthly rounds early in the morning when you were usually still in bed and not fully awake. When your rigidity became extreme I persuaded him to come at noon so he could see for himself. It was then that he prescribed Sinemet but offered no sympathy for what you were going through. In November of '92, when I was in his office for an annual physical, he told me how good you looked sitting up so straight in your chair. I suppose he was trying to cheer me up, but my reaction was that he of all people should know that your ramrod posture was due to your being stiff as a board.

That triggered my anger and I sputtered, "You just don't know what he is suffering!"

"Only Lyle knows that," he replied.

"Granted," I thought to myself, "but couldn't he use his imagination?"

No doubt Dr. Huff was just as much in the dark as I was but it would have helped if he had shared his bafflement with me.

A few days later I told Janice Locke, the special nurse in charge of infectious control, about your increased rigidity. She suggested we consult a neurologist and Dr. Huff readily gave his consent. The neurologist ordered a CAT scan which revealed that your paratonia was not primarily caused by Parkinson's after all but more likely by two enlarged ventricles whose fluid was putting pressure on your frontal lobes. He suggested the possibility of a shunt to drain off the fluid, but later told Dr. Huff that he had a gut feeling it wouldn't work. Whether it would have done any good to have had the CAT scan sooner I will never know.

November 30, 1997

Tuesday the hiking group started out in my front yard here at Riverside Park. We followed the river upstream past the canoe livery at Argo Dam and along the base of the wooded bank below Long Shore Drive. You and I had walked parts of the trail before your stroke, but since moving into this building seven years ago I have covered the ground many times. On your visits to the apartment I was always so happy when weather conditions made it possible for you to enjoy a ride along the paved path in the park. I have some fine pictures of you beside a bench with Mario and me taken by Steve in the summer of 1991 and some she took of him with us.

Many good conversations have emerged walking along that path by the river. One I shall never forget was with Tim on the morning of Saturday, April 17, 1993, the day you died. Originally I had intended to visit the Hannums in Washington that weekend. I remember showing you the photograph I had had framed to give to Erwin which you took of desert grasses on our trip with them in the southwest. But when I realized that your swallowing problem was becoming worse I cancelled my trip, and Tim decided to move his planned visit up a week. I met him at the airport Friday morning and we arrived at Glacier Hills in time for lunch with you. You half opened your eyes for him and squeezed his hand, but did not say anything. He could see for himself that you were not eating and that you had lost a lot of weight. When we left you at nap time he and I probably stopped for a walk at Gallup Park, and I reviewed what I had told him a few days earlier by phone about your increasing difficulty with swallowing, and the decreasing effectiveness of your Parkinson's medication. I also must have reported on my conversation with you the previous Monday when we enjoyed the spring sunshine sitting behind the carports, which partly sheltered us from a cool breeze. There I told you that Dr. Huff could no longer increase the dosage of your medicine without serious side effects, and that before long the only way for you to receive nourishment would be through a feeding tube. I asked if you would want that and you responded with an emphatic "No!" Your sparkling eyes told that you were very much with me and I felt we both knew the end might be near. However the closest I came to acknowledging it was to say that talking about sad things was easier outdoors than inside where everyone tries to be so cheerful.

By the time Tim and I stepped out the door for our walk to Argo Dam that Saturday morning we had reached the point where there was nothing more we could say to each other about your condition. So I asked Tim about his job prospects for I knew he had resigned as director of the Math Center at Trinity College because they had offered him only a short-term contract. He explained his dilemma was whether to accept a position that did not challenge him, or wait in the hope that the job he really wanted at Central Connecticut State University would receive funding. It was a difficult time for both of them because Leslie had just been turned down for tenure at Trinity and would have only one more year there. Finally I asked him how he might manage if he gambled on the Central job and it fell through. Immediately his optimistic nature prevailed, and he started brainstorming possibilities including even going back to high school teaching if necessary. Later he told me that our conversation had clarified his thinking so he could go ahead and take the risk of waiting for Central. Happily the job came through, and last spring he received his promotion to associate professor.

After our walk we went back to Glacier Hills and were distressed to find you looking worse than I had ever seen you. Your lips were dry and almost purple and your breath was very rapid and wheezy. However, you opened your eyes for us a couple of times and you reached out your hand toward Tim who took and held it. Most of the water I offered you just dribbled down your chin. The only thing I was able to do for you was wipe off some of your unswallowed breakfast that had stuck to your teeth and request that you be put back to bed. While we were waiting, I put on the tape of American Buddhist songs sung by the young people of the Zen Buddhist Temple whom you and I heard at the Kerrytown Concert House the end of February. I particularly wanted Tim to hear the song that so amused you about tossing out the junk mail that clutters up our heads. Renee, your nurse assistant, came soon with the Hoyer lift and together we got you into bed. She did some further cleaning of your mouth and called for the nurse who found your lungs still sounding all right but some congestion at the back of your throat. When they left we listened to one more song whose refrain happened to be "Let go, let go, let go." Then, with the promise to return after your nap, we left you to sleep.

Back at the apartment I was too tired to do anything but take a nap myself while Tim turned to grading papers. I was just waking up when nurse Mary Beth called to say that you had a fever which could not be brought down by Tylenol and that your breathing was labored. That seemed strange because your forehead had been cool when we left you two and a half hours earlier, but I wasn't alarmed because you had had plenty of fevers off and on before. I even took time for a cup of tea before returning to the nursing home. When we got there Mary Beth, who was just leaving, stopped to talk with us. She explained that your shortness of breath meant that you were not getting enough oxygen so your blood was being withdrawn from your head and extremities, which was why your head was cool and your lips and hands were purple.

When Tim and I entered your room you appeared to be staring at the ceiling, but I doubt if you saw anything because your eyes were clouded over. Your mouth too was wide open and your breathing heavy. Mia, a black afternoon nurse whom I had never met before, was taking your blood pressure. I was astonished when she told me it had fallen to 40/20. As soon as she was finished I took her place on one side of the bed while Tim stood at the other and held your hand. Then Mia surprised me by asking if you were saved. It was a question that required a positive answer, so I boldly stated, "Yes, he's saved!" I don't know whether you heard or comprehended, but if you did surely you understood that I knew you were at peace. After that I just kept repeating, "Sweetheart, sweetheart!" as I stroked your head. Within only a few minutes you stopped breathing with a gasp, then came another and finally your jaw dropped wide open as you gave a long third exhalation. The timing was so close I really believe you waited till we came. I also believe it was easier for you to "let go" knowing that Tim was there to help me.

December 17, 1997

Last weekend I was in Prescott, my third return since we were there twenty years ago with the Hannums on our camping trip through northern Arizona and New Mexico. Remember the torrential downpour we were caught in at Casa Grande on our first day out from Tucson in our two rented RVs? We took refuge in the visitors' center hoping the rain would let up, but when reports came that flooding had closed the bridges into Phoenix the park ranger let us stay in the parking lot overnight. Next day the bridge we wanted was open and we happily headed for Prescott to visit our mutual friends, Betto and Jerry Everall, in their charming retirement home at the foot of Granite Mountain. Their warm hospitality was most welcome as the rain had started up again and at five thousand feet altitude it was very cold. I remember

Betto thought we were crazy to start our trip on the first of March, but Cynth, intent on avoiding crowds, had planned to hit the national parks as soon as they opened for the season. You and I had been more than willing to let the Hannums make all the arrangements so we had nothing to say when they would not believe the Everalls' prediction that the road to Havasu Canyon would be impassable at that time of year. After a rough hundred-mile drive we found out the road was indeed closed. Fortunately the Indians were able to switch our reservations to the end of the month when we were blessed with perfect spring weather. While the horseback ride down into the canyon to the village of Havasu was sheer delight for me, it was an ordeal for you though you were compensated by the rock formations along the way. When we finally reached the bottom we were rewarded by lush green vegetation. I shall always cherish the memory of the day we wandered off by ourselves in that enchanted valley discovering and photographing lovely spring flowers and following the stream to where a slender waterfall spilled into a large turquoise pool. We all agreed that our stay in the Indian village of Havasu was the climax of our trip. A few days later we were able to tell Betto and Jerry all about our adventures as we rendezvoused for a picnic at Montezuma's Castle. We saw them once more in January 1988 at our casita in Green Valley where they came for lunch after one of Jerry's swim meets in Tucson.

Then, after you died and I felt an urge to reconnect with old friends, I paid the Everalls a visit that fall. This time the sun was shining and Granite Mountain was no longer shrouded in clouds. Betto and I enjoyed taking her dog on some long walks, doing a little sightseeing and most of all laughing over our escapades when we were twelve-year old roommates in boarding school. Of course I promised to come again sometime, but I had no idea that in two years I would have a double reason to return, because by then Elise had transferred to Prescott College after her sophomore year at Lewis and Clark. Without delay I flew out in October and had a delightful visit dividing my time between them. Elise was bubbling with enthusiasm over her new college and right then invited me to her graduation.

So that is how I came to be in Prescott last weekend. How I wish you could have been there too. Remember what a volatile little girl Elise was: sunny one moment and stormy the next? Later she became a moody teenager. She was wearing braces when they all came for your birthday the first year after your stroke and you exclaimed, "Silver teeth." You certainly would be glad to see what a beautiful and poised young woman she has become!

The graduation was a happy occasion for a Fabricant family reunion, the first time I had been with all four of them since they visited at the cabin in 1987. We arrived at various times on Thursday. Steve had just returned from an assignment in Kenya and fortunately Dan had finished his classes at Evergreen, where he is now a freshman. They took separate shuttle flights from Phoenix, but Ellen and I, scheduled our arrivals at Phoenix close enough so we could rent a car and enjoy the two-hour drive together. She and I had more good visiting throughout the weekend as we also shared a room at the old hotel on the town square.

However, Elise was far too rushed for anyone to have more than a few snatches of conversation with her, and these were mostly at our group meals in noisy restaurants. She spent most of Thursday night and much of the next day setting up her art show for the opening that evening. Of course she wouldn't let any of us help her, so while the others went for a hike

I had a chance to visit Betto. She had suffered a stroke two months earlier so I didn't know what to expect. I was sorry to find her quite frail, but at least she can walk cautiously with the aid of a cane. Jerry's attentive support and her courage and sense of humor are sustaining her through a rigorous and fatiguing regimen of therapies.

The high spot of the weekend was indeed the display of Elise's quilts. She titled the exhibit "Uncoverings: Introspection through Creative Quilting." She had made three small squares representing different periods in the history of quilting and personalized them by placing in the center of each a photograph transferred to cloth of her mother, her grandmother, and her great grandmother taken when they were approximately her age. On the labels she described a few things about our lives at the time and the characteristics of the quilts. She made a crazy quilt with stitches of embroidery for my mother who was twenty-two in 1902, a more conventional one in pastels for my depression era coming of age, and a freestyle early seventies one for Ellen. We were impressed by her painstaking work and imaginative touches, but it was in her other three hangings that her creativity really took off. They were truly works of art and also, as she explained in the label, an expression of her own growth. The first, representing hibernation and introspection, had a drawing of a bear above a kneeling woman in a dark center mounted on some brown handmade paper and surrounded by midnight blue cloth with drawings of wolves and stars. The second was of a snake coiled around the figure of a woman beside its discarded skin with scales made of starch-stiffened cheesecloth. Elise's final piece, a magnificent red bird with a cascade of flowing tail feathers topped by a nude woman with outstretched arms holding up the wings, was labeled "Rising from the Ashes." On second thought maybe those red feathers were supposed to be flames. Either way it was a spectacular piece of art.

In the three and a half days we were there I gained a greater appreciation of Elise and of her college experience. She loved Prescott's freedom and informality and its dedication to the environment. Even though her concentration was in art and most of her other subjects were in human development, she learned a lot about the wilderness, especially on her three one-month courses conducted while camping in the desert. She has emerged as an accomplished and self-confident young artist.

The graduation ceremony revealed the individualized curriculum and personal attention given each student. Judging by the program, which listed the forty-five graduates with their areas of breadth and competence, fully half concentrated in some form of environmental studies. You would have been interested in the wide range of topics including such fields as Outdoor Adventure Education and Therapeutic Use of Wilderness. Graduates were presented their diplomas by a faculty member of their choice along with a one-minute tribute to which they responded with gratitude to everyone who had contributed to their education. I was quite moved, as I know you would have been too, especially by the caring and admiring remarks of Rose Ann, Elise's art teacher, and by Elise's heartfelt thanks.

January 8, 1998

My joy this holiday season was being with each of our children. In addition to my good visit with Ellen in Prescott, I had Steve's company here for five days over Christmas and Tim and Leslie's for two at New Year's. I'm so glad to see that they are all happy, especially Steve who has taken a big turn in his life. You probably sensed his discontent during the three years he was living in Detroit though I never spoke of it to you. Mostly he told you about amusing incidents at Lear Seating, one of his more satisfying jobs where he got along well with his coworkers. However he would confide in me that he was having problems with his fellow socialists, which he attributed to personality incompatibilities. Finally, two months before you died, he took action by moving to Pittsburgh and a year or so later to Morgantown, but in both places he ran into the same difficulties and became increasingly unhappy.

Tim, too, was worried about him and in early 1996 encouraged him to move to Boston so they could see more of each other. There he found an apartment in East Boston and a job nearby in a garment factory that employed mostly immigrants from Guatemala. That May I saw Steve at Rachel's graduation from Smith and again at the end of the week after visiting Ray and Elex. By good luck my flight home from Islip was routed through Boston so I was able to take a 24-hour stopover. The first afternoon we had a pleasant walk through the arboretum followed by dinner at a Vietnamese restaurant in South Boston. Afterwards he drove me around the harbor before returning to his small apartment in a narrow little house on Princeton Street. There I slept in his bed while he took to the floor.

Next morning, instead of going to some art gallery as he had earlier suggested, we lingered in his tiny living room. The conversation wandered until he revealed his troubles with the announcement that he was considering resignation from the Socialist Workers Party. Of course I was surprised that after nearly twenty-five years of dedication to the cause he would leave the party. He explained it was not a matter of change in his political thinking but in how he thought about his role in the world. He had gradually come to realize that essentially he was an intellectual. That insight, plus the margin of economic security you had provided for him in your will, led to the recognition that the gulf between himself and factory workers would always be a difficult one to bridge. Moreover he was bored and hungry for intellectual challenge, but unsure of what he would do. He spoke of his growing interest in the environment and the possibility of breaking into the publishing field. Remember how much he enjoyed being copy editor for his socialist international news magazine and before that his work on the Oberlin Review?

Well, it was another six weeks before he took the plunge and resigned from the party. Then he signed up with a temporary employment agency that placed him in a series of proofreading jobs, and on his own has found intermittent work with Harvard Press. Suddenly he had lots of time on his hands now that he was free from political obligations. He took advantage of his new leisure to join the community sailing club on the Charles River, attend some lectures and to audit a Harvard extension course in ecology. In the winter term he took a class in human evolution for credit, and by this past fall he had made up his mind to prepare himself for graduate study in biology. To that end he has just finished a course in cell biology and another in genetics at the Boston branch of the University of Massachusetts, doing very well in both. He is confident that two more undergraduate courses this coming semester will qualify him for graduate school. Presently he is looking into which schools in the area have biology departments with good environmental programs.

Biology seems a most appropriate field for him because he has always been a keen observer of his natural surroundings. Remember once when he was quite small and we returned from a walk he asked, "Where have you been? I see stick tights on your pants"? He was the family collector of nature specimens. We certainly found him, at seventeen, to be a delightful traveling companion on your sabbatical for he would point out interesting details we might not have noticed.

You can imagine how heartwarming it has been to watch Steve's old sparkle return. He is overflowing with enthusiasm not only for his studies but for his genetics professor, as well. By coincidence she graduated from Oberlin, but they missed meeting there, as she is five years younger. Although he was attracted to Rachel right away, he confined his conversations with her strictly to genetics knowing that any social contact would have to wait until he was no longer her student. Now that she has turned in the grades they have started to date. Prospects look promising!

January 25, 1998

Writing about Steve has rekindled my gratitude for his coming to Detroit to give us his support during the last three years you were in Glacier Hills. His very presence was reassuring and raised our spirits. He had an easy way of falling into our routines that reminded me of how smoothly and silently you and he used to work together on chores like breaking camp and packing the car, a wordless relationship going back to his infancy. He was a contented and undemanding baby in contrast to Tim who suffered from colic and Ellen who seemed to be perpetually hungry. I can picture the two of you playing on our big bed for that quiet interlude between my nursing him and our turning in for the night. Once I told Natalie Deyrup, our pediatrician, that Steve taught me patience, and her response was we'd probably learn something from our seventeenth child if we had that many.

Believe me he needed his patience on his weekly visits to you because many times you were unable to respond to him as you surely would have wanted to. However, he learned that by waiting you out sooner or later he would find you alert and in a sociable mood.

I always felt more confident about taking you on the AATA bus when Steve was with us. Do you remember the delightful chamber concert the three of us attended at Rackham one beautiful Sunday afternoon in April? You seemed to enjoy the music and the several people who spoke to us at intermission, but I hoped you didn't notice when a colleague of yours averted his eyes as he walked up the aisle right past you. I was hurt and unforgiving, although in retrospect I suppose seeing you in a wheelchair put the poor man into a state of shock. After Steve helped me move out of the house we would take you home to the apartment about once a month, especially when we had out-of-town visitors. And wasn't it nice to have him share in entertaining them? While I would be busy getting the food on the table he would quietly take charge of helping you with your meal. Once after he had lunched with us when Mario was visiting she remarked, "Steve's a good egg." to which you added, "Good heart!"

He provided me with welcome recreation too when sometimes, after stopping for a short visit with you and help with your supper, we would go out to dinner or to a movie. Of course we took walks whenever time and weather conditions allowed, and at least once a summer we went up to the cabin for a long weekend. Upon our return your evident enjoyment of his vivid accounts of our activities made us feel better about having left you.

Steve was also a great comfort in times of discouragement, the worst one being when you came down with pneumonia in February 1991. I had been very depressed by the Gulf War and both of us had come down with colds. Just as I thought you were recovering, the long awaited time came for you and Joe Conway to move to a new room in the recently completed wing of the nursing home. It was a pleasant room with a window for each bed, but, except for the one over-worked supervising nurse, all the staff was new. You were probably even more uneasy than I was to be at the mercy of strangers who were not acquainted with your abilities and needs. Both Rita and I found the move tiring.

Four days later, on a Sunday morning, you greeted me with "My God, My God!" You were very uncomfortable and so rigid that the aide and I couldn't straighten you in your chair. Although you calmed down for lunch, afterwards you were trembling uncontrollably. The nurse said she would keep track and call Dr. Huff if necessary, but when I phoned her first thing next morning she said you seemed all right. However your eyes were closed throughout my visit and during lunch you kept mouthing your food without swallowing it. Cookie said you had been coughing up a lot of sputum at OT. She told me that Parkinsonian symptoms are often worse with viral infections. Before I left the nurse reached Dr. Huff who prescribed an antibiotic.

The next ten days were a nightmare! You were zonked out much of the time, your temperature and pulse were rising and your breathing had become rapid and shallow. Dr. Huff examined you on Friday and phoned me next morning to say you had a touch of pneumonia and that we should push liquids. When I reminded him of your difficulty in swallowing he suggested sherbet, which I added to my offerings of thick liquids. Since you ate better for me than anyone else I tried to be there for most of your meals, but it was slow going. The various nurses had different ideas as to treatment. One would think it best for you to rest in bed and another would insist on getting you up in your chair. The upshot was that I felt abandoned. Meanwhile my cold was getting worse and I felt like a wreck.

On Tuesday I pointed out to the day nurse that your hands were swollen and again to the evening one. Upon coming in at 8:30 next morning I happened to run into Janice Locke and told her about your swollen hands. She came right up and decided to call Dr. Huff who ordered an IV. Then he asked to speak to me. He told me he was pessimistic and gave you a 30% to 40% chance of pulling through. I felt more desolate than ever. Since IVs could only be given in the skilled care section you were moved back to the old wing right after lunch. It was like coming home and such a relief to have nurse Eileen take over! You can imagine how ready I was to sink into sleep when I returned to the apartment.

The next day you seemed better, but by afternoon your fever flared up and purple blotches appeared on your knees. I would see this same kind of mottling again two years later on the day you died. In fact, though of course I didn't realize it at the time, this illness with your difficulty in swallowing was a forerunner of your final days. On Saturday Dr. Huff found you to be better than he had expected so he discontinued the IV with instructions to get two liters of liquid into you a day. My spirits rose when you said, "Good-bye Honey"—your first words, other than yes and no, in two weeks—and they soared a few days later when you looked directly at me with a real sparkle in your eyes.

Then you began the long slow haul toward regaining your vitality and strength, a process that took four months or more. During this period I particularly needed and appreciated Steve's steady support. He could see progress week by week while I was often discouraged by daily demands. So much of my energy went into trying to give you more liquids and urging the nurse assistants to make a greater effort to do so. How fortunate we were to have Steve to cheer us up and bring us his fresh perspective.

February 15, 1998

Remember how satisfied we were with the Quaker-style memorial service we had for mother under the big maple tree at Duck Island in June of '72? The informal sharing of memories was very personal and gave a sense of intimacy to the gathering. My minister-cousin, Steve Crary, started it off with a simple blessing, and, as planned, my brother, Ray, gave him the nod when he thought it was time for the benediction. His assignment was made easy by Mary Ingraham, a true Quaker and mother's oldest friend, who waited to make her remarks until she sensed that everyone had sufficient opportunity to speak. There was never any doubt in my mind, and I think in yours too, that this was the sort of service we would want to have when our time came.

So on a Sunday morning a week after you died about sixty family members and friends gathered in your memory in the Sunshine Room at Glacier Hills. The children had rearranged the chairs in two arcs facing each other leaving a wide, open space in the center where people in wheelchairs, including Joe Conway and Abby Enders, could have front row seating. We the family sat at the joining of the arcs in front of the windows. Tim took the lead in welcoming our guests and inviting them to share a brief memory of you. Having no Mary Ingraham to guide us we gave her role to my sister, Mario. We planned that my remarks would follow hers and that Tim would close the meeting.

Everyone was moved by the spontaneous expressions of love and appreciation for you. No one seemed rushed, yet twenty people spoke and several letters were read all within an hour. My five nieces and nephews came—the first time all the cousins were together since the Ingersoll family Christmas in the Bahamas in 1956. One theme ran through their comments, namely that they remembered you at Duck Island as a tall, quiet presence in the background. Their memories triggered mine of how overwhelmed you were by all the talk and commotion of those family reunions when the children were small.

Among our Ann Arbor friends who spoke were three younger colleagues who had joined the Conservation Department about the time you retired in 1973. Jim Crowfoot and Bunyon Bryant told of how generous you were in offering them welcome and support, and Jonathon Bulkley praised your significant contribution to the National Water Commission's report, *Water Policies for the Future*. He said that in the twenty years since publication it has been widely used as a basic reference and that many of its 285 recommendations have been implemented. Rick Fox read a letter from his father, Irving, telling of how much he valued working with you on the Program Staff to the Secretary of Interior, and Tim read Joe Conway's letter he had written to you on the computer at Occupational Therapy. Twice poor Clayt was too overcome with emotion to read a message that Bun had sent with him from Oberlin, so John Wood volunteered to read it for him. Clayt appreciated Steve's compassion in seeking him out afterwards.

I was touched most of all by our children's recollections. Each had selected some incident that represented a special gift from you. Tim went first by telling about your taking him camping in the Blue Ridge when he was eight years old. You had pitched your tent at Big Meadows Campground off the Skyline Drive and decided to take a hike before cooking supper. Your goal was a nearby mountaintop, but at a fork in the trail you found some delicious wild strawberries. After picking a few you posed the question, "Should we press on to the summit as planned, or take the other trail up a smaller hill so we can have time to enjoy some more strawberries?" Tim chose the alternate plan. He concluded his story by saying that this episode taught him that we do better not to stay locked into a goal when life presents us with strawberries. After several others had spoken, Ellen introduced herself and recalled your send-off upon her departure for college. She said that because she thought of you as rather serious and was a little in awe of you she expected you to admonish her to study hard. Instead you told her to have fun, a liberating and wonderful gift! When Steve stood up he spoke about your long-running correspondence concerning your different philosophical approaches to ecology. In fact you had written him a long letter just one week before your stroke. He finished by saying it was so wonderful to relate to his father as a peer.

Naomi, the only grandchild to speak, remembered you at the cabin, and said that whenever she felt stressed out she thought of the peacefulness of the lake. Mario told us how much you have meant to her over the years and how much she learned from you even while you were laid up with your stroke. Finally it was my turn. I reminded everybody that your limited speech meant you rarely got out a complete sentence, but that once you told a nurse assistant, "I appreciate everything you do for me," and added that surely you must have often had the same thought about your many caregivers. I also expressed my gratitude to the staff for their considerate care and to our friends for their steadfast support. Then Tim thanked everyone for coming and invited them to stay for refreshments and to look at a poster display of photos spanning your life.

Following the services family members and the few friends from out of town relaxed at lunch in the community room of my building. Regrettably Ray's foot, injured by an aneurysm, kept him from coming. We ended on a celebratory note with a cake in honor of Mario on her seventy-third birthday. Throughout, I felt I was floating—supported by the outpouring of love that surrounded me—and a deep sense of gratitude swept over me.

March 4, 1998

Because it was simply out of the question, I never told you how often I wished I could have cared for you at home. If you had been able to put weight on even one foot to help in transferring from bed to chair we might have managed, but there was no way I could handle that Hoyer lift alone. I witnessed enough mishaps to be nearly as scared of the contraption as you were. We would have needed round-the-clock help, but even so it would have been a difficult undertaking. I can imagine that my preoccupation with responsibilities and details of your care would have constantly infringed on our companionship. As it was we had enough of such distractions at the nursing home.

Just this past week I had an experience that reaffirmed this conclusion. Mario and I were halfway through what was supposed to be a relaxing and carefree vacation in the Yucatan when, not noticing a stone step in the sun's glare, she fell and broke her foot. We were staying at The Blue Parrot Inn on the north edge of the town of Playa del Carmen right on the beach looking out across the blue-green Caribbean to the island of Cozumel in the distance. The inn's several small thatched-roofed buildings were in various stages of repair, and for the first three nights we stayed in the most decrepit one. Dark and shabby, our room barely had space for two double beds, a small table and one chair. Quantities of sand blew under the ill-fitted door while more sifted on to our beds through the screen of the unglazed window. Mario was more shocked than I, for, judging from the low rates, I had suspected that the place would be on the seedy side. Nevertheless we enjoyed some delicious swims in the surf, barefoot walks along the shore, and strolls down the main avenue of the town lined with colorful shops where at night pedestrians swarm into the middle of the street. On the third day we were moved to a bright and spacious bungalow complete with a combination sitting room/kitchen and verandah where, once settled, we felt our vacation had really begun. Next morning we relished our breakfast of instant oatmeal and raisins brought from home. Afterwards I enjoyed a solitary walk far up the beach beyond the last buildings and another great swim with Mario. We were looking forward to devoting the following day to the extensive Mayan ruins of Chichen-Itza and our last three to leisurely companionship, though we were tempted to go parasailing if the wind was calm enough. Just as Daniel had wished when he was three, I wanted to soar like Curious George on his kite.

So much for our dreams of an idyllic vacation! Mario's fall that afternoon suddenly changed the whole picture. The management of the inn gave her prompt attention and whisked us off in a cab to their doctor's clinic. Three hours later we were back at the Blue Parrot with a green cast on Mario's foot and stitches in her elbow. It took three men to carry her in her wheelchair over the soft sand to our bungalow where she was confined for the next two days. There we each faced problems of coping: she with learning to maneuver in and out of a wheelchair and to hop her way on overlong crutches through the narrow bathroom door, and I with helping her, foraging for food and attending to various tasks involved in rescheduling our return home. In spite of frustration and exhaustion we tried hard to be good sports and not dwell on our disappointment. However, even though I found time for a walk the second morning, I didn't go far because my heart had gone out of it. Neither had I the spirit to brave the surf alone.

We planned our day of departure with ample time to return the wheelchair and crutches to the clinic and reach the Cancun airport by noon. After the eager helpers who carried Mario to the waiting taxi succeeded in fitting the chair and our four bags into the trunk, we took off through the barren back streets of Playa del Carmen whose cinder block buildings glared white in the bright sun. We reached the clinic in less than ten minutes only to discover that the crutches were missing. Nothing to do but race back to the inn hoping that someone had turned them in at the front desk. Our driver wisely returned to the spot where he had picked us up and there, to our great relief, stood our crutches leaning against a small tree! One more trip to the clinic and we hit the road north and even arrived at the airport as planned, two hours ahead of our plane's scheduled departure. In spite of our worries someone found us a wheelchair all right, but it took Mario only to the door of the plane where she had to hop her way inside until she reached the seats and could brace herself on the arms on either side of the aisle.

We didn't relax until we sank into a pair of first class seats relinquished by a kind passenger sitting alone in the last row who took pity on Mario's plight. Those comfortable seats provided our most companionable moments as we snuggled under cozy blankets offered by an attentive steward. I was sad to leave Mario in St. Louis where we took separate planes though I knew she would be met by Dick and Happy Fernandez in Philadelphia and would be well cared for in her retirement home. As it turned out her doctor took off the cast because they now believe her kind of break heals better by bearing weight. She tells me she is making good progress with walking in spite of some mild pain. Needless to say we were both sorry that our long anticipated trip had such a disappointing ending, and it has taken us both some time to regain our spirits.

However my three days stint of care giving made me aware of my limitations both in terms of stamina and anxiety. Of course ten years ago when you were stricken I had more energy than I do now, but worry and being rushed has always made me feel harried and irritable, a mood certainly not conducive to intimate communication. Looking back now I think the nursing home was not only a practical necessity in your circumstances, but an opportunity for more peaceful interludes together than we might have had at home.

There was an advantage to my coming to you each day with fresh anticipation. I was always glad to see you and felt a special lift when you greeted me with sparkling eyes. A few times early on you surprised me by saying, "There you are," and once in your last year you exclaimed, "Hey, there's my girl!" In my eagerness to reconnect with you I often found myself annoyed at things that needed attention before we could settle down to enjoy each others' company. How I might have handled that difficulty if you had lived at home I do not know. I do know that your attitude of acceptance had a calming affect on me. You were able to articulate it one time when I was fretting over some wheelchair problem that O.T. had not yet resolved and you wisely advised, "We'll let them take their time." Once we were alone, I would tell you the news of the day including whatever had given me pleasure as I felt a strong need to enjoy life for both of us.

Most of all I cherished our intimate moments when I lingered after you had been put down for your nap. Then I would indulge in some sweet talk and remind you of the countless times you used to tell me you loved me. On rare occasions you echoed my declarations by saying, "I love you too." Sometimes, when you were crying, I might try to express what I suspected was making you sad at that moment or, if I missed the mark, we'd cry together about your whole predicament. I marvel that we seemed to be on the same wavelength so much of the time. I guess that's what half a century of living together does for two people who love each other.

Though I still grieve that you had to suffer those long years of confinement I want you to know how grateful I am for what you gave me. You taught me to be patient, to accept ambiguity and to trust my intuition. You helped me discover levels of understanding that don't require words. Above all, the gifts of your peaceful and courageous spirit and your love sustain me now and surely will help me face whatever the future may bring.

Did I ever tell you of the dream I had about my wedding ring? It came to me in the first year or two after your stroke and I think it sums up what I'm trying to tell you now. I dreamt that while I was staring at my hand my gold wedding ring transformed itself into delicate filigree. Then I showed it to someone, it was not clear who, and said, "You see this ring is my marriage. There are holes in it because much has been taken away. But it is still beautiful!"

With Mario (above); in nursing home (below left); 50th wedding anniversary, March 29, 1992 (below right)

Appendices
1. Something about Asho Ingersoll Craine

My life has been both blessed and burdened with a social conscience fostered by my reform-minded parents. I was born in 1915 in Brooklyn, New York, where in 1933 my father was elected borough president on the fusion ticket with Fiorello LaGuardia. Previously he served as the first industrial arbitrator of the cloak and suit industry. My mother, a woman of many enthusiasms, was an early supporter and friend of Margaret Sanger. Both parents were followers of John Dewey's theories of progressive education, which led to my entering the opening class of Bennington college.

In the summer of 1934 I traveled with the first student group to enter Russia after F.D.R. recognized the Soviet Union. There I was all too ready to believe that they were building a more just society than ours. After graduation in 1936 my most interesting job was with the Milk Consumers Protective Committee associated with a consumer-farmer milk cooperative. This led to a job in Washington in June of 1941 with the Consumers' Counsel Division of the Department of Agriculture. I soon met my future husband, Lyle Craine, who was working in the Bureau of the Budget, and we married in March. He spent the war years at the War Production Board while I started raising our family—two sons followed by a daughter.

After the war Lyle headed a small staff in the office of the Secretary of the Interior that coordinated the department's programs in several major river basins. Following the abolition of his job by the Eisenhower Administration, we came to the University of Michigan where Lyle obtained his Ph.D. and taught in the School of Natural Resources. We never regretted the move to lively Ann Arbor where we enjoyed forty years together.

Because I found family life so fulfilling and was financially secure, I lacked sufficient determination to pursue a career. Instead I became a volunteer and community activist primarily through the League of Women Voters and the Gray Panthers, and once ran for school board. I still feel a passionate urge to right the wrongs of this sorry world, but alas, while its injustices continue to mount my energy dwindles. My hope lies in my children, five grandchildren and two great-grands, who, in their individual ways, will surely carry on their heritage.

Written for the Nation *cruise, December 2000*

2. The Making of a Social Activist

My intention is to focus on three influences that led me to become a social activist: my parents, Bennington College, and problems and disasters of the wider world.

First let me give you the basic facts. I was born in 1915 in Brooklyn, New York, where my philosopher/lawyer father, Raymond Vail Ingersoll, was active in the politics of social reform. My mother, Marion Crary Ingersoll, was an early supporter and friend of Margaret Sanger and an enthusiastic parader for women's suffrage. I came between two brothers, one older by nearly four years, the other nearly four years younger. My sister, my junior by five and a quarter years, and I are the survivors. In 1933 when Fiorello LaGuardia was elected mayor of New York City, my father was elected borough president of Brooklyn on the same Fusion ticket. He died in office in 1940 at age 65 from an overdose of sulfa, the miracle drug of that time.

Both my parents fostered my concern for the needs of others, my father by his dedication to the betterment of society and Mother by her generous hospitality, especially to refugees. Their temperaments were complementary. Dad's was calm, compassionate, and consistent; Mother's was spontaneous, adventurous, and unpredictable. When her passions collided with mine, Dad would listen to my grievances and then help me gain perspective. He always elevated my self-respect by taking my ideas seriously.

As for religion, the four of us children did not attend Sunday school because Dad, a free thinker, believed religion required mature minds. Nevertheless some of his mother's Quaker beliefs seeped down to us.

Perhaps he was right about mature minds because when I turned forty I started taking Bible classes from Dr. Leroy Waterman, a biblical scholar and historian at the University of Michigan. Over the next five years I attended eight evening courses of eight weeks each. I even taught Sunday school!

Now it's off to the exhilaration of being in the first class of Bennington College! Up to that point school had never been a comfortable place for me. The exception was in seventh and eighth grades in a small boarding school in New Hope, Pennsylvania where my roommate became my first best friend. Mother, assuming that my unhappiness was the schools' fault rather than my shyness as a newcomer, would transfer me to a new school every two years. All were private, and only Friends included boys. Finally in the Fall of 1928 it was back to stuffy old Packer where I was stuck for the full four years of high school.

An embarrassing mistake was wearing a donkey pin to show support for Governor Al Smith, the Democrat running for president against Republican Herbert Hoover. My classmates jumped on me with "How can you be for that 'wet'? The Pope would run the country." "Who would want Mrs. Smith in the White House?" "He says *ra-adio* instead of *radio*." My feeble protests that my father had worked with Governor Smith to get good things like health and safety laws for tenement homes fell on death ears. As for the Pope, I was ignorant of his powers, but I knew he had no authority over our government. I am sorry to say I did not have the courage to wear that donkey pin to school again.

Gradually I found friends among others on the fringes, but satisfaction came mainly from conscientious study. I did well in most subjects, and some of the teachers were excellent. In my senior year when it became time for applications, I sent mine to Smith and Vassar, but without enthusiasm.

Reports of a new progressive college to be started in Bennington, Vermont, that fall of 1932 aroused my interest. It sounded exciting. Dad was impressed that its Board of Trustees was headed by Dr. William Kilpatrick, President of Columbia's Teacher's College and a former student and colleague of John Dewey. Dad had great admiration for Dewey, with whom he had participated in a discussion club for several years before World War I.

By the time I was taking the College Boards, I knew I wanted to go to Bennington. When Smith and Vassar sent acceptances, I requested a year's postponement just in case Bennington did not meet my expectations. In fact, it far exceeded them.

An air of high energy greeted the eighty-three pioneers. Even the setting on an open hilltop was invigorating. The mostly young faculty were also pioneers and must have been just as excited as we were. Right from the start our education became a collaborative undertaking. With the guidance of a faculty member of our chosen area of concentration, we designed our own curriculum.

Choosing a trial major was a challenge. Many talented students were attracted to Bennington because it gave full credit to the arts. While I would have enjoyed drama and dance, I had no ambition to become a professional performer. I was too slow a reader to undertake literature and had no aptitude for art or music. My abilities could have led me to math and science, but my conscience compelled me to choose social studies.

My advisor was Louis Jones, who taught an introduction to economics. He and his British wife Barbara, also an economist, had met at the London School of Economics a few years earlier. Together they were the backbone of the Social Studies Division. New faculty were added each year until our class graduated in 1936. Louis was just right for me that first year, for his enthusiasm encouraged me to speak up and express my opinions. Two years later when Barbara became my advisor, her more rigorous approach was what I needed as she would not let met get away with unsubstantiated generalizations. She saw me through the turmoil of falling in and out of love with a man a dozen years my senior.

In his economics class, Louis was good at relating his teaching to current events. In the fall term the Great Depression gave purpose to studying such concepts as the business cycle, inflation and deflation, supply and demand, etc. I was disappointed that these did not address the big question of why we had "poverty in the midst of plenty." In the spring Louis abandoned the textbook and divided us into teams to study the new agencies (disparaged as the "alphabet soup") that Roosevelt, the president-elect, had proposed to Congress as the foundation of his "New Deal." A girl from Nebraska and I took on the AAA, the Agricultural

Adjustment Act. We reported to the rest of the class that family farms had been in a depression since before we entered the World War and were rapidly being foreclosed. (This rings a bell with me now because when my husband, Lyle Craine, was a ten-year-old in 1918 a severe hailstorm was the final calamity that drove his father off their small dairy farm near Geneva, Ohio, a small town 40 miles east of Cleveland and 10 miles south of Lake Erie.)

John Dewey saw education as a process that continues throughout life and advocated learning by doing. His social philosophy embraced community as being necessary for democracy. In line with these doctrines, Bennington advocated joint student, faculty, and staff decision making whenever possible.

At our first community meeting after our arrival in early September, President Leigh challenged us to hammer out some standards as guides to conduct—nobody liked the word "rules." We thought we were making progress those first two weeks until the start-up of Williams College, fifteen miles south of us. Then a horde of young men invaded the campus. Their curiosity had been spurred by illustrated news stories showing liberated Bennington girls attending classes in shorts. Immediately the college had a crisis on its hands. This was not time to dally with community decision-making! President Leigh acted promptly. Next evening a heavy chain stretched across the entrance road, and soon a booth and telephone were installed for a night watchman. The policy became that every visitor must be an invited guest whose host would be held responsible for his behavior. That was accepted as fair enough despite its undemocratic enactment. An unforeseen consequence was a scramble for blind dates. I wasn't involved, but I heard plenty of rumors. Fortunately the situation soon calmed down. This episode reminds me of modern day controversies over how to deal with immigration while still preserving democracy.

My first two jobs out of college were tedious, one as a statistical clerk in a huge government study concerning technological unemployment, the other handling membership dues in the three-person office of the National Consumers League.

I hit my stride when I became the staff person for the Milk Consumers Protective Committee. I was associated with a thriving Consumer-Farmer Milk Cooperative that sold milk through local stores throughout New York City at much lower prices than home-delivered, when cartons were beginning to replace glass bottles. I produced a newsletter, spoke to various groups, and testified at government hearings about setting milk prices farmers receive. This experience led to a job in Washington with the Consumer Council Division of the Department of Agriculture in June of 1941.

In August an officemate invited me to go sailing on the Chesapeake Bay with a friend of his, Lyle Craine. It was love at first sight. He at 33 and I at 26½ were ready for marriage. The wedding took place the following March. Lyle was working for the Bureau of the Budget but soon was transferred to the War Production Board. Meanwhile I was busy raising our three children: Tim born in 1943, Steve in 1946, and Ellen in 1949.

After the war Lyle headed a small staff in the Secretary of Interior's office coordinating its programs in several major river basins. When his job was abolished by the Eisenhower administration, we came to the University of Michigan where he earned a Ph.D. in Conservation in the School of Natural Resources. He subsequently taught resource policy, particularly in regard to water.

When Ellen started kindergarten, I joined the League of Women Voters and gained a valuable education in effective citizenship. Although I appreciated the League's thorough study of each issue, some things happened that cried out for immediate action. For instance:

1. Atmospheric testing of nuclear weapons (late 1950s). My first vigil was in response to a letter in the *Ann Arbor News* from Elisa Boulding, a well-respected Quaker. She invited everyone opposed to the testing of nuclear weapons in the air to join her on the steps of Hill Auditorium. Later I took part in the Sane/Freeze campaign by going door-to-door with petitions urging U.S. support of a test ban treaty.

2. Desegregation (mid 1960s). As a first step toward desegregation, our school board adopted a plan to close the only all-Black elementary school and bus its students to a scattering of other schools. In preparation for this move the superintendent called for volunteer tutors, and I readily enlisted. The Black community considered the plan unfair as it put the whole burden on their children. So three years later when faced with adjusting the balance in an already racially mixed school, the board decided to bus some white students in from outlying neighborhoods. This evoked cries of "don't bus my child," and my decision to run for school board. As the only woman candidate perhaps I was perceived as too radical and/or not tough enough. Although I lost, the next year four women ran and two were elected.

3. The War in Vietnam (1960s). Opposition to the Vietnam war and the draft was strong in Ann Arbor. Teach-ins initiated by some professors in response to a student strike spread to other campuses. While Lyle and I were attending countless meetings, Tim and Steve took part in actions at Oberlin College. In 1969, soon after Nixon's inaugural, a group of us traveled to an antiwar protest in Washington.

   That fall Lyle and I moved to Washington where he had a year's leave of absence from the University to serve on the National Water Commission. With no family responsibilities, I was free to look up old friends, volunteer as a teacher's aide in an all-Black elementary school, and attend two huge peace mobilizations on the Mall. Finding myself merged with thousands of demonstrators who shared my hopes and fears was an extraordinary experience.

4. The Gray Panthers (1979-2004). My introduction to Maggie Kuhn, the charismatic founder of the Gray Panthers, occurred at an intergenerational conference on aging, co-sponsored by the University of Michigan's Institute of Gerontology, two of whose students had come with me. Impressed by Maggie's talk we decided to form a Gray Panther network in Ann Arbor. It turned out that the process had already been started by Ann Bonar, an eighty-five-year-old retired social worker who had recently moved to town from Pittsburgh. She welcomed our help in recruiting members and drawing up by-laws. Ann became chair, and I became assistant chair.

During meetings, Ann would often become diverted from the agreed-upon agenda. She loved to tell stories of how her father, a socialist, would take her to union meetings of steelworkers held in a cave to hide from company goons. She loved poetry and would often remind us of the human need for beauty. My role was to keep our actions on track.

On the national level the Gray Panthers had evolved over the previous decade into an effective organization. Spurred on by Maggie Kuhn's boundless energy they achieved better nursing home regulations, a ban on compulsory retirement, and other legislation to prevent age discrimination in employment. Subsequently they have been strong supporters of universal health care.

On the local level we were free to take up any issue that fell within the goals of peace and justice for all. Consequently we attracted a diverse membership and speakers crusading for various causes. In the fall of 1980 when I was elected convener, I found it a challenge to handle discussions that sometimes became quite heated. However, during the four years I served I had the satisfaction of seeing our group settle down after a few fanatics dropped out. I continued to be an active Gray Panther until I left town.

5. The War in Iraq (1990s ff). It seems to me we were protesting U.S. aggression against Iraq for a dozen years before the current war was launched in 2003. During the build up to that disastrous mistake I joined other peace activists in the vigils we held every Tuesday noon at the downtown Post Office. I also participated in peace meetings, marches, and rallies.

In January 2004 it was hard to leave so many friends and fifty years of good life in Ann Arbor to move to Seabury. Only after the fall election when "In Support of Democracy" was launched did I discover fellow social activists who made me feel I really belong here.

Presented October 27, 2007, to "The Story Tellers"—a monthly program of women for women and by women at the Seabury Retirement Community, Bloomfield, Connecticut

3. A Pivotal Moment in My Life

A pivotal event in my life was my husband's stroke that deprived him of speech and confined him in a nursing home for nearly five years. The moment of revelation when I realized how this event had changed my approach to life came much later.

Throughout our long marriage, Lyle and I strove to bridge the differences in temperaments and backgrounds. He was cautious and reserved while I was impulsive and expressive. He thought I talked too much and was over-demanding of his attention. I wished he would be more responsive and interpreted his withdrawals as rejection. When retirement relieved him of the stresses and anxieties of work and we were no longer distracted by the commotion of growing children, he became more open in expressing his feelings while I became more comfortable with silences. We enjoyed fifteen years of companionship and felt we were truly equal partners.

Then came the stroke that unbalanced everything. Lyle's inability to speak more than an occasional word or phrase left us both frustrated and groping in the dark. It was a cruel irony that having found his voice, he was deprived of using it. I had to operate by guesswork and make decisions without the benefit of his advice, though most of the time I felt I had his consent. There was no doubt he understood what was said to him. When his eyes sparkled, I knew he was with me.

It took the perspective of five years after Lyle's death for me to focus on the particular ways his illness had changed me. In writing about the experience in imaginary letters to him, I thanked him for teaching me to be patient, to live with ambiguity, and to trust my intuition.

March 25, 2004

Asho with Leslie at antiwar demonstration, ca. 1982 (above); with Ray and Mario (right); Elex, Asho, Ray, Mario (May 1999—Elex's 80th birthday) (below)

Tim and Asho (above); Steve and Asho at Douglas Lake cabin (below)

Ellen and Asho (above); Steve, Ellen, Asho, Rachel Skvirsky, and Ilana (below)

FAMILY AND FRIENDS

My Father in Law, Earl Craine

Lyle and I were a little apprehensive that day in early February 1942, as we drove from Washington to visit his parents in the small town of Geneva, Ohio, forty miles east of Cleveland. They had not approved of any of his former girl friends and now, with our wedding date already set for the end of March, he was about to introduce them to their future daughter-in-law. Moreover, I had the impression that his two older brothers' wives had never felt fully accepted by them. Of course Lyle had filled me in on some of the family history. His father, Earl Craine, was born in 1872 in Perry, Ohio, the middle of three sons of Franklin Craine, a harness maker and trainer of horses. After completing eight grades of school he took on full-time farm work. In his mid-twenties he came to work as the hired hand on the Eggleston farm near Geneva since Mr. Eggleston and his son were spending most of their time at some business in Cleveland. In effect Earl ran the farm for Mrs. Eggleston and in due time he married her only daughter, Belle, a schoolteacher. She was devoted to her church and strongly disapproved of drink and tobacco. They had four sons born between 1900 and 1908: Capron, Henry, one spoken of only as "baby" who died in infancy of whopping cough, and Lyle. As with so many small farms in the World War I era it became harder and harder to make ends meet, so when a devastating hail storm in 1918 ruined their crops the family decided to sell the farm and move into town. There Earl worked for the dairy to which he used to sell milk and later for a bakery. When I met him he was about to retire from managing a gas station a couple of blocks down Main Street from their house.

My anxiety mounted as we pulled up to 407 West Main Street, old route 20, where Lyle had lived since the family moved to town. The graceful, though unpretentious, Victorian white frame house (or was it Queen Anne?) sat on a large lot stretching almost to the N. Y. Central Railroad tracks with ample room for a vegetable garden. Earl and Belle greeted us at the door with restrained pleasure and led us to the living room behind the front parlor. To my relief they were not at all formidable, but simply gentle and modest old folks. Right away I could see family resemblances. Earl was tall and handsome with a strong jaw and kind, blue eyes. He was more heavy-set and an inch or two shorter than Lyle whose more slender features must have come from Belle. Her small stature was accentuated by a stoop and she seemed rather frail and withdrawn. During the course of dinner our mutual shyness began to wear off and conversation became easier.

Later, when they told Lyle that they liked me because I wasn't "all painted up," we knew I had passed muster. We were pleased with the visit and hoped it had prepared Lyle's parents for the wedding, but colds and the complexities of travel kept them from coming after all. Probably it was just as well because I'm sure they would have been overwhelmed by my mother and her large house on Duck Island. Even though I had managed to hold her to fifty guests, (a small number compared to the two hundred at my sister's wedding the following July), they would have felt surrounded by strangers.

In preparation for our next trip to Geneva over the Labor Day weekend we saved up enough precious gas coupons to get us to Ohio and home again. Since in those early months of gas rationing only the Eastern seaboard was covered, once we reached Ohio we could fill the tank freely. The need for careful planning added zest to our adventure, especially as Lyle had arranged to take his parents for an overnight stay in Cook Forest in western Pennsylvania on our return trip. They rarely went anywhere because Belle was a reluctant traveler, so this would be a treat for Earl upon his retirement from the gas station.

Sunday morning we attended the small Christian Church where Lyle, as a twelve-year-old, had been baptized by immersion. There I was pleased to see how his mother brightened as she introduced me to her friends. Lyle also drove me three miles north of town to Lake Erie and a colony of summer cottages, Geneva-on-the-Lake, where he used to work during summer vacations developing snap-shots in a photography shop. On the way we passed his old farm overgrown with brush, and further on the site of his two-room schoolhouse. The high spot of our visit was a great picnic on the beach hosted by Earl's younger brother, Max, at his truck farm near Painesville that bordered on the lake. It was the height of the melon season and uncle Max took delight in making sure I tasted his best. With a flourish of his sharp knife he would slice open a melon, take a taste of its juicy yellow flesh, then toss it aside as not good enough. Finally, after several tries, he presented me with one he thought would do. It was indeed the most luscious melon I ever ate. I was surprised by his flare for showing off, so different from Earl's quiet modesty.

Next morning, well provisioned with food, we set out in our two cars for Ashtabula, ten miles to the east where Earl parked his car at the railroad station. Then Lyle drove the four of us to Cook Forest, about thirty miles south of Warren, where we found the little cabin he had reserved among the ancient trees. After we had eaten our picnic lunch, Belle preferred to remain in her rocking chair on the porch while the three of us walked a trail in the woods. The tall pines were indeed impressive, and delighted Earl even more than we had anticipated. Every time we came upon an especially big one he would exclaim, "Isn't that a dandy tree!" Perhaps he was thinking of the stories his father, Franklin, used to tell of the winters he spent logging in Michigan when he would rent out his team of farm horses to a crew and hire on as cook. What we did the rest of our stay in Cook Forest I don't remember, but I'm sure it was early to bed and early to rise. After dropping Lyle's parents off at a railroad station somewhere, probably, Oil City, to make connections to Ashtabula we headed for the Pennsylvania Turnpike and home to Washington.

Soon afterwards they sold the house on Main Street and bought a smaller one in a quiet neighborhood away from the noise of trains and traffic. They had hardly settled into their retirement home when Earl responded to the call for war workers and took a job at American Fork and Hoe making radio antennas in the department that used to manufacture fishing rods. I still use the small foxhole shovel he gave us, a reject from another section of the plant. The job required standing all day and was hard on Earl's varicose veins.

A year and a half slipped by before our next reunion when they again took a train, this time to Washington, to see their six-month-old grandson, Tim. I don't recall how they stood the trip because the only clear memory I have of that visit is one reinforced by a photo of all three on the sofa-bed in our apartment where Tim is perched on his grandma's lap reaching for the gold watch grandpa is dangling from its chain. Nine months later we found out for ourselves about the rigors of wartime travel when we went to spend Christmas in Geneva on trains jam-packed with GIs and civilians. The only relief from the overheated coaches was to stand at the coupling between cars in a freezing draft. Somewhere we changed trains to the Nickel Plate line, exposing us to more extremes of temperature. Lyle and Tim survived this better than I, for after we returned home I came down with pneumonia, but fortunately we all stayed well during the visit. Together Earl and Belle prepared a fine Christmas dinner for us. Tim responded with sufficient interest in his presents and the lights on the tree to please the assembled adults, but he was more fascinated by trying to catch his grandpa's fingers as he poked them through the holes in his cane rocking chair. Later Earl attached a cardboard carton to a sled for Tim's first ride in the snow.

Finally with the war over we were able to fit in a leisurely stay in Geneva in September 1946, two months before our next child was expected. Tim, who was almost three, was happy to "help" grandpa in the garden while I became better acquainted with Belle. Once as I watched her ironing one of Earl's shirts I remarked, "With three sons you must have ironed a great many shirts in your life."

"Yes," she replied, "And they sent their laundry home from college too. I suppose Lyle would have sent his from 'Jap-an' if it hadn't been so far."

No wonder she habitually ended her letters with "Work is waiting."

I noticed that Earl was doing most of the cooking. Lyle had told me that his grandmother took charge of the kitchen until her final illness when he was a teen-ager. As a consequence Belle was relegated to house cleaning and laundry so she never gained confidence as a cook. I found it rather sad that she was deprived of watching her family enjoy food prepared by her own hands. I was also sorry she missed out on some of the satisfactions of mothering because Lyle found his grandmother more accessible and used to seek her out when he needed comforting. In a letter after we returned home Earl wrote, "Mother hopes the baby will be a girl. She was always looking for girls."

On November tenth I gave birth to another boy, Steve, and we had to wait nearly three more years for our girl, Ellen. I regret that Belle never saw either of them.

That winter, for the first time in years, Lyle decided to attend the annual meeting of geographers right after Christmas. The fact that it was held in Ohio gave him the opportunity to go to Geneva afterwards. Although he was away for only a week, it seemed much longer, and I was very glad to welcome him home one early evening. As we played with the baby on our big bed he told me about his trip. He found the meetings worthwhile, but was especially glad that his visit with his parents pleased them so much. I told him about what our two little boys had been up to and how I had managed without him. We had just gone to bed when the phone rang. It was a telegram from his father reporting that Belle had died of a heart attack.

Lyle and I were incredulous at the news and spooked by the timing of his impulsive decision to pay that visit. He returned to Geneva the next day where he was joined by his brothers, Hank from Mt. Vernon, New York, and Cape from Akron. Following the service Uncle Max, who had flown up from Florida, invited his brother to return with him, and in a few days they set out in Earl's car for St. Petersburg. On the way they visited Max's daughter, Thelma, in Gastonia, N.C. Although Earl had never taken to Ruby, Max's second wife, I guess she was adequately hospitable, and certainly Max did his best to give him a good time. They played shuffleboard at the senior center and he was pleased by his developing skill at the game. It was evident from his letters that he was taking in all the sights and enjoying his new freedom. Early in the spring he drove north, again stopping off at Thelma's, and then to us at our house in Bethesda, Maryland.

So began Grandpa's seasonal sojourns of anywhere between a week and a month during the next six years as he migrated between Florida and Ohio. Well schooled in promptness, he invariably arrived long before the time he had told us to expect him, so I was usually not quite ready to receive him. At the end of summer he would appear with a load of fresh farm produce and before I knew it would take over my small kitchen and start canning tomatoes or peaches. Somewhat disconcerted at first, I soon learned to work around his operations and would lend a hand as the demands of the children and household allowed. He in turn would often dry the dishes for me. While working together he would tell me stories about the improvements he made on the farm, a marginal one at best, which was quite run-down when he came to work for Mrs. Eggleston. He was proudest of his rigging up a windmill to pump water up from the stream into a trough in the farmyard so the cows would not have to be driven down to the stream in winter weather.

Grandpa seemed to enjoy observing the children, although he seldom became involved in actually playing with them. No doubt he found their chatter hard to understand. The only time I remember his taking disciplinary action was with Steve who was not yet two years old. We had been watching him play quietly on the living room floor with some blocks until he decided it would be more fun to throw them about the room. Though told emphatically to stop, he kept right on with his new game. Then, without a word, Grandpa picked him up, sat him on the couch and, firmly pinning his upper arms against the back of the couch, held him immobilized for what seemed like several minutes. I was aghast, but said nothing. When Grandpa finally released him with instructions to pick up the blocks, Steve went at the job with dispatch, handling each block as though it were a hot potato.

During Earl's first winter in St. Petersburg he lined up a small apartment for the following fall and invited "Aunt" Lilly, his father's cousin, to come and keep house for him. Evidently she required little persuasion and that September they set out together for Florida. On his way to us Dad dropped her off at her granddaughter's in Baltimore where she spent a week sewing curtains for her new house. Then she came to us for the last day or two of his visit. I liked Aunt Lilly right away, a spry old lady in her mid to late eighties with a sharp wit. I was delighted with her twist on old sayings such as "The proof of the pudding is in chewing the string." She explained that in the old days a pudding was tied up in a cloth before being boiled in a kettle of water, so a taste of the string could test it for doneness without untying the whole bag. She also told me the story of Franklin Craine, Earl's father, who injured his leg when he was a young man and had to have it amputated because it became gangrenous, and how he used to say, "It was a choice of a wooden leg or a wooden overcoat."

Lyle and I gathered from his father's letters that his and Aunt Lilly's ménage was working out well, but on his return visit in May he shyly confided in me that he had become friends with a neighbor woman named Annie who lived in his building. She always greeted him with a smile whenever they passed in the hall. As they became acquainted he learned that she came from a large Irish Catholic family in Massachusetts and, starting at age fifteen, had worked in a textile mill for many years. She had never married because she was the one family member left at home to care for her parents. After they died she traveled to Miami where she got a job as a chambermaid and eventually worked her way up to becoming head housekeeper of an elegant hotel. He told me she was four years older than he but was so lively you'd never know it. How Aunt Lilly reacted to Earl's interest in Annie I do not know, but I imagine it was hard for her especially if, as I vaguely remember, she returned to keep house for him the following year. In any case during that winter the romance flourished with or without Aunt Lilly's blessing.

I don't recall first meeting Annie, but I have a vivid memory of her visit in September 1949. It was not the most convenient time for us as Ellen was barely three weeks old and a demanding baby constantly needing to be fed, but we wouldn't have dreamed of asking Lyle's father to change his plans. Moreover, they were looking forward to getting married during their stay with us. As luck would have it, on the day of their arrival the cleaning woman I had counted on to help me put the house in order didn't show up. I was in a quandary as to what to tackle first the unwashed dishes or the unmade guest bed. I chose the later, ordinarily a small job, but I found it fatiguing. Before I could get to the dishes Ellen was hungry again, and then it was time to prepare lunch for Tim so he could catch the noon bus for his half-day session of first grade. I was sitting at the table nursing the baby while the boys ate when the phone rang. Mistaking the caller's voice for that of our close friend, Persis Gladieux, I poured out my tale of woe. Then to my embarrassment I realized it was a friend of hers whom I did not know well, but it was too late to back off. In reply to her question about my father-in-law's time of arrival, I wailed, "Two o'clock, but he always comes sooner than expected!"

"I'm going to call Persis right away," she said firmly.

Within twenty minutes the two of them appeared and went straight to work on my kitchen. They were still there when Dad and Annie arrived. To my dismay, poor Annie was suffering from a bad case of shingles spread over her body. Sitting in the car had been so painful that all she wanted to do was crawl into bed. I was thankful that I had decided to make her bed first and grateful to my generous friends for coming to my rescue.

Annie's shingles improved sufficiently over the next two weeks or so for her to feel able to continue the journey south. On the afternoon of the day before their departure Earl and Annie were married in our living room. Persis had arranged for her minister to perform the ceremony, and she and Louise Miller joined Lyle and me as witnesses. Afterwards Annie gave the minister a brief account of her life and concluded by saying, "You see, I've had a good life and now this is such a happy ending!"

Sometime earlier Lyle and his brothers had helped their father clean out his house in preparation for selling it. We persuaded him to keep the proceeds to supplement his small savings and let us buy him a house in St. Petersburg as an investment. They found a little, four-room house on a big enough lot for a small vegetable garden and a workshop where Dad used to cane chairs. (We still have some of the family heirlooms he re-caned including the rocking chair at the cabin.) Glad to be able to grow things again, he planted a variety of flowering shrubs to supplement those already there. And grow they did! In just about every letter he would report on the number of blossoms on his hibiscus bushes. Earl and Annie enjoyed several happy years together in that little house. She taught him to play games including Chinese checkers with long jumps that became a favorite of our family. Their summers were divided between her relatives in Massachusetts, his in Ohio, and us. They liked spending part of their time in the Blue Ridge mountains at an old cabin of squared off logs we had bought the spring before they were married. During the week they would have the place to themselves, and we would join them for the weekends. Lyle and I gave them our cots on either side of the fireplace while we slept in the attic with the children. The main room was only about ten by fifteen feet with some space taken out for the stairs, and the lean-to kitchen at the rear was less than half its size. A screened-in back porch was just big enough to accommodate a refrigerator and a beat-up glider. Such small quarters provided little privacy for seven people, but a play-tent Lyle had rigged up with a tarp gave the boys their own domain—that is until one day Tim came to us complaining that grandpa was taking a nap in his tent!

One summer Earl's older brother, Page, showed up at our cabin towing his battered house trailer. He was much smaller than Dad, but even in his eighties he was still proud of his reputation as the black sheep of the family. At an early age he had taken off on wild adventures in the Yukon, and for many years had lived openly with a woman to whom he was not married. His main claim to fame was that he had his own small Alaskan exhibit at the 1889 Colombian Centennial Exhibition in Chicago. Subsequently he took it on the road as a traveling show that included a team of sled dogs and a young Eskimo boy. Sadly, within a few years, the poor boy died of tuberculosis. Uncle Page struck me as rather pathetic in his childish efforts to impress me that he was really a bad character, but I can certainly imagine how shocked Lyle's parents, especially Belle, must have been by his risqué language and life-style! As a child Earl suffered from Page's relentless bullying until, in his early teens, he had grown considerably bigger than Page and in one last fight emerged as the undisputed victor. I wonder now if Page's bad-boy behavior cast Earl as the good boy, a role accentuated by Belle's piety. In any case Max, the younger brother, seemed to be the freest and most self-confident of the three.

In the summer of 1953, shortly before we moved to Ann Arbor, we took our first big family car trip to visit Grandpa and Annie. On the way I was glad to finally meet Thelma when we, too, spent a night at her home in North Carolina. Lyle and she had become fast friends when he was about fourteen and she lived with them to finish her senior year in high school after Max and her step-mother moved to Florida. She used to ride the interurban streetcar for the eighteen mile trip to school in Painesville. Thelma told me how much Belle's kindness meant to her that year. Her mother's death had been a great loss to Belle too for, as Earl used to say, they had been as close as sisters.

Our stay in St. Petersburg was a happy time for all of us. At first I was taken aback by Grandpa's remarking on how much Tim had "improved," for I had always thought my son was pretty good in the first place, but he probably just meant that Tim, at nearly ten, had grown up a lot. Dad and Annie enjoyed watching the children feed pelicans on the pier and play in the sand and water at the beach. And of course we all played Chinese checkers.

Our return, three and a half years later, was a different story. Since my mother had invited her four children and their families to spend Christmas week with her in the Bahamas, we naturally wanted to take in a side trip to visit Dad and Annie. We divided forces by my taking Ellen out of school two days early so she and I flew to St. Petersburg first, and Lyle and the boys went there on the return trip. Ellen and I walked into a crisis caused by Annie's irrational jealousy of the woman who lived next door. Deafness prevented her from hearing the exchange of conventional greetings between Earl and the neighbor, but their smiles were proof enough for her that they were flirting or worse. In fact she accused him of breaking the seventh commandment. Poor Dad was completely defeated in his efforts to convince her of his innocence. Her crazy shouting scared Ellen while I was at a loss to help. By the time Lyle and the boys came the following week the situation had deteriorated further. He encouraged his father to seek out a psychiatrist to evaluate Annie's condition and to communicate with her nephew in Massachusetts. She had been increasingly homesick and often expressed the wish to die among her people, so it was a great relief when her nephew took responsibility for her care. He found a nursing home in his vicinity where she stayed until her death a few years later.

Earl was on his own again, though he did hire a housekeeper to help out. He managed to come to Ann Arbor almost every summer for the next five years, but now he flew instead of driving. They had flown on Annie's last visit, her first ride in an airplane at age eighty-seven duly reported in the St. Petersburg paper. During this final period of Dad's life I came to know him best, and the children did too. We enjoyed his stories about his father's ingenious ways of training horses. One was about a horse which, once harnessed would simply lie down and refuse to get up. Nothing would make him budge. Then one day, in desperation, Franklin grabbed some heavy planks from a nearby stack and piled them on top of the horse. The horse lay there quite a while without moving until, with a great heave and a wild snort, he rose up scattering lumber in all directions. He never lay down in his harness again. Somehow that story reminds me of how Grandpa cured Steve of throwing blocks.

My best conversations with Dad were while working together in the kitchen. Once, after visiting Cape and Bea in Akron, he arrived when the ground under an old apple tree in our yard was strewn with fallen apples, early transparents in sad condition because we had never sprayed the tree. Seeing them as potential applesauce not to be wasted, he set to work patiently cutting out all the bad spots. I was pleased with the applesauce, but distressed to have him thank me for letting him make it. He explained that Bea wouldn't hear of his going to the bother of cutting up her windfalls, but it seemed evident to me that he liked to feel useful and preferred working to idleness.

Dad particularly liked to talk about his life as a farmer, though he told me a lot about his work in the bakery where he reached the point of running the whole establishment for the two sisters who owned it. When I asked him once of all the jobs he had held, what was his favorite, without hesitation he answered, "farming." That, of course, did not include his youthful hoeing onions for twenty-five cents a day, but getting the job on the Eggleston farm was his big break. Mrs. Eggleston developed full confidence in him and he greatly admired her. I wonder how much his marriage to Belle was more for attachment to his place on the farm than for love of her. But he had not been without sentiment for her. He told me how he used to ask Belle to walk down the lane with him in the spring when the flowers were so pretty, but she always preferred to stay near the house. He didn't say whether this was before or after they were married, but there was ample evidence that she was fearful of leaving home. Certainly she never liked to travel. It's possible she was near-sighted without knowing it. That thought came to us when, much to our surprise, Ellen told us she had "flunked" an eye test in fifth grade, because as far as we knew all the Craines and Ingersolls were far-sighted.

During Dad's last visit with us in August 1962 he suffered a mild stroke, but apparently made a quick and good recovery. As usual he enjoyed drives in the country and a family picnic or two, taking particular interest in the passing farms and the condition of their crops. He was in good spirits when we celebrated his ninetieth birthday on September second before he flew back to St. Petersburg. However, that fall he had a variety health problems and two or three brief hospital stays. At some point Lyle went down there to check out the situation, encourage his father and give assurance to his housekeeper. Unfortunately he was himself undergoing a gall bladder operation at the time of Earl's death at the end of December. Our whole family attended the funeral in Geneva in early January. The service was held at a funeral parlor that was formerly the gracious home of Lyle's best friend from high school, Bur Martin.

These reflections have deepened my appreciation of Earl and of how much he and Lyle loved each other. I'm grateful for the insights he gave me into Lyle's childhood and a foretaste of his old age.

February 1999

My Brother Ray

To Ray on His Eightieth

Now that you've joined me as an octogenarian, Ray, I trust you won't mind if your big sister indulges in some sentimental memories, because I've always been very fond of you. You were a sweet little boy even though you did your best to live down the angelic image projected by your big blue eyes and golden curls.

Stubbornness was your main defense, especially with Mother. As we were growing up I envied you your strength and independence in resisting her insistent demands. You were only twelve when you would frequently not show up for dinner having gone to the movies after school and stayed through the feature twice. No amount of scolding cured you, so finally your wayward ways were accepted. I knew I could never have gotten away with such behavior. I always assumed that Mother considered your stubbornness to be a grievous fault until near the end of her life when her nurse relayed a remark about you. Mother had been trying to persuade you to do something against your better judgment, but you calmly held your ground. After you left she turned to the nurse and said, "Stubborn, isn't he? But I admire him for it!"

You had a flair for the comic and your sense of humor delighted us all, Dad in particular. He always had a soft spot in his heart for you. I remember how he would pace the upstairs hall at Duck Island with you when you were a little fellow so covered by mosquito bites you couldn't sleep. He declared that you were a pair of peripatetic philosophers. Perhaps it was then that you began to acquire his philosophical outlook on life.

The time you and your friend, Jenks, drew colored chalk cartoons all over the plaster walls of your room aroused my admiration for your boldness and artistic talent along with alarm at how our unpredictable mother might react. Fortunately, upon her return she found your murals amusing, and even had them sprayed with a preservative for the enjoyment of posterity.

Remember our private talks after you had gone to bed when you were about twelve or thirteen? They were a welcome break from homework for me and a chance for you to confide what was on your mind. Those conversations solidified our friendship. I was often reminded of them in later years as I shared similar going-to-bed rituals with my children.

You in turn, have given me loving support throughout my life by your steady good judgment, your quiet courage, and your uncritical acceptance. You summed up our feelings for each other in a note for my 75th birthday album. Referring to sorting through early family photos you wrote

The picture of you and Jerry and me on the porch at Centerport probably is the beginning of my awareness of it all and the start of our loving growth and expansion of all our lives. As growing children, young adults, and now "seniors" we have related to each other in our special diferent (sic) ways. It has been so important to our generation and our youngers to have this relationship to continue and carry on. I'd better stop here. (No appologies (sic) for spelling, not from me)

Love,
Ray.

I am so grateful, Ray, that we have lasted this long so we can all be here together to celebrate your eighty years!

October 1998

Remembering Ray

As his big sister I am the only one who knew Ray all his life. He was a comical little fellow and sweet too. I was very fond of him. Grown-ups used to make a fuss over his blue eyes and mass of curly blond hair, but, as you can imagine, he fought against the angelic image. His preferred way of asserting himself was passive resistance that gained him the reputation for being stubborn. It also gave him considerable freedom to do as he pleased.

In a family of talkers he kept his own counsel and quietly pursued his interest in the tangible world of nature and hands-on construction. No wonder that he chose to become an engineer. I remember how amused our father was when Ray would pipe up at the dinner table with some odd fact. When asked where he learned that he would invariably answer, "I read it in The Book of Knowledge," a multivolume encyclopedia for young people handed down from our brother Jerry.

Ray had sufficient confidence in his own judgment that attempts to persuade him to change his mind were futile. The capsizing incident when we were teenagers that Mario described earlier illustrates the folly of not respecting his good sense. When he bluntly refused to take us sailing because the wind was too strong we thought he just didn't want to go. It didn't look strong to us. Feeling rejected we defiantly decided to go by ourselves. We soon found out he was right. The wind was strong. By the time we got the sails up it was very strong. I was scared as I gripped the tiller and so anxious to avoid jibing that I headed too close into the wind. Before we knew it the mast snapped and we capsized! As Mario told you, she had the presence of mind to toss the anchor overboard only to discover its rope was not fastened to the boat. Fortunately we were near enough to shore for a quick rescue by the Crarys' motorboat. I'm ashamed to say that I never had the courage to skipper again.

Since that long ago day Ray taught sailing, skiing, and other skills to many youngsters with wisdom and encouragement. Just as he used to share his discoveries found in The Book of Knowledge he continued to delight in telling all of us about many wonders of nature, ingenious inventions, and elegant structures gleaned from extensive reading of science, history, and biography and devoted attention to the *New York Times*.

He was indeed a sweet man and I loved him dearly.

Remarks at Memorial Service on October 2, 2005
(with revisions including Mario's extemporaneous remarks, October 7, 2005)

For Elex in Celebration of Her 75th Birthday

The prospect of this party started Mario and me thinking about how our sisterly bonds with you, Elex, have grown over the years. Their strength has come from many scattered episodes some of which we'll try to recall tonight. We hope you'll add your embellishments later.

It all began when we realized that Ray was getting serious about a certain redhead in the class below him at Swarthmore. Naturally we were curious but he didn't tell us much beyond the fact that you were interested in drama. We had to wait till the summer of '39 when he brought you to Duck Island to meet the family. Then we quickly found out you were smart, witty, and full of ginger. That was the only time you met Dad, wasn't it?

We didn't see much of you for the next two years as you had transferred to the University of North Carolina to major in theater. We gathered that Ray was a frequent visitor, especially after he graduated and was working at Wright Aeronautical. Then he told us of the joys of flying his Piper Cub to Chapel Hill and to Manteo where you performed in a summer pageant dramatizing the lost colony. We're sorry we never got to see the production.

The dramatic production we did attend was your wedding in Cambridge in September 1941. You were a beautiful bride in your elegant wedding gown and our brother was obviously a happy man. We had fun at the party with your Swarthmore friends. Six months later came my wedding followed by Mario's in July. Remember the photos of you helping to adjust our wedding veils? There were many more undocumented attentions you gave us. I know Mamo could always count on your help. She took to you right away.

Mario and I saw little of you those early years as we lived in separate cities tied down by war jobs and gas rationing. But remember when you and Ray and Lyle and I set out on Memorial Day weekend in '44 to climb Mt. Graylock and camp out overnight? We were ill equipped and had misjudged the weather. It was frigid! You must have thought we were crazy as indeed we were.

Usually when we did get together it was at Duck Island in the summer. These were the days when the grandchildren were arriving one or two a year. I marvel at how we put up with the commotion and our diverse parenting styles, but Mamo's attitude was the more the merrier. Remember how determined she was to corral the whole gang to take group pictures? Now you are the custodian of those much-cherished photographs and can always dig up appropriate ones for special occasions. You and Ray were smart to build your own house at Duck Island. It not only provided privacy for your little family, but was a welcome retreat for the rest of us. Now of course it has become the house we come home to knowing we can always count on your warm hospitality.

Mario tells of when you both were needing to escape the harassment of small children and took off for a weekend in Atlantic City. She was crushed to find your room was at the back of the hotel but you boldly phoned the manager and insisted on being moved to a room with a view of the ocean. He promptly complied. Mario was greatly impressed by your assertiveness and that was long before anyone had heard of assertiveness training!

Your concerns for our welfare were usually expressed in concrete practical terms. For instance, after Lyle and I had moved from our apartment in Washington to a small house in nearby Bethesda, you were shocked to learn that we had no washing machine. I explained we got along fine sending most things to the commercial laundry and washing out the delicate items by hand. Besides we couldn't maneuver a machine through the narrow space between a pantry closet in our kitchen and the top of the basement stairs. "Well then," you said "get rid of the closet." "But where would I keep our food supplies?" I protested. Come spring we had a stairwell excavated, an outside door cut into the basement and a tile floor laid. Then a fine new washing machine was installed and now I don't see how we ever got along without one.

Forty some years later the same scenario was repeated when you walked into my kitchen and exclaimed "What, no microwave!" "Where could I put one?" I asked defensively. "Right here in this corner." "But that would block out too much of the window." "Well, get a small one then." A little later you suggested we drop into an appliance store just to look. Sure enough there was a small microwave at a moderate price so I bought it just to make you happy. It quickly became indispensable and continues to be a daily reminder of you.

Your determination and persistence paid off in other ways. Mario and I admired the way you earned your masters degree while handling two small children and then pursued a 25-year teaching career. You didn't stop with retirement either. You were always working for the things you believed in, on the school board and school elections, in village government and for several important environmental committees. You are a powerful player, Elex, in whatever arena including the tennis court and the ball field.

But you also have a tenderness that we especially appreciated in your attentions to Mamo. Of course you needed your toughness too in dealing with her—quite a balancing act. We have often laughed over how you helped her plant tulip bulbs. She would always order an unreasonably huge quantity and then feel overwhelmed by the task. One fall the two of you set out in her golf cart to the garden with a large carton of bulbs. First you dug holes where she directed. Then while she was busily filling them you would surreptitiously toss handfuls of bulbs under the shrubbery. You then moved on to the next location till by the time you were both ready to call it quits the box was empty. Mamo was so pleased at her accomplishment and the vision of all those lovely tulips that would adorn her garden in the spring. Now you are continuing to cultivate her garden, on a less grand scale to be sure, but with her spirit.

There are other ways you have kept our memories of Mamo alive such as rescuing many of her unclaimed things from the big house and thereby becoming custodian of Ingersoll memorabilia. You're our genealogist too. You have welcomed each new member of the family with baby gifts and loans of cribs and highchairs. Above all you have carried on Mamo's generous hospitality. Lyle and I were touched that you braved the crowds and confusion of Kennedy International Airport to meet us on our return from Afghanistan and again from Syria.

Finally, Mario and I have come to realize at long last that when you're fussing and fretting or even scolding us you're just expressing your love by doing our worrying for us. So here's to you, Elex, with sisterly love and heartfelt wishes for less worrisome years ahead.

May 1994

Jubilee for Mario

You've come a long way, baby sister; from the cute five-year-old who listened to the Wizard of Oz to the wise woman you are today. Back then at South Oxford Street, when we were engrossed in Dorothy and Toto's adventures, there was much talk of a severe earthquake in California. You asked Mother which she would rather have, an earthquake or a cyclone. Preferring neither, she turned the question back to you, to which you replied brightly, "A cyclone, because it takes you someplace!" And you were determined to go places! You were a spunky and often sassy little kid in your struggle to catch up to your three older siblings.

Once, in your eagerness to be a good catcher, you stood too close to home plate so when Jerry took a swing of his bat it hit you right across your eyebrow. I was horrified by the stream of blood and the possibility that you might become blind in that eye. I guess you still have the scar to show for it.

Try as we might, the more than five-year gap in our ages kept us from finding common ground. You once accused me of using big words just to show off, yet you would have been very quick to think I was talking down to you if I had tried to simplify my language. We did share in bringing up Pokey, our lively little Boston bull terrier, and in teaching her to play ball and other tricks. In fact she became the baby of the family, helping you to graduate from that role. Later your mastery of the guitar put you in the center of our family's attempts at song. Remember how you knew just which tearjerkers would get me to cry?

But it was backpacking in the Smoky Mountains the summer after Dad died that really put us on an equal footing. At twenty you had become a fellow adult, and we discovered a new companionship. Already in some respects you were more experienced than I, at least when it came to judging meat. We had assembled a stringently planned supply of dry food plus one orange a day for our three-day trek, but decided to treat ourselves to steak for our first dinner. It had to be purchased the night before as we were setting out early in the morning. After swinging along the Appalachian Trail for ten miles with thirty-pound packs on our backs and finally getting our campfire blazing, we were hungry for that steak. To our dismay it had turned an unattractive gray. You were sure it was not safe to eat, while I thought we could take a chance. When you asked me whether I had had any experience with spoiled meat, I admitted that I had none, and meekly deferred to your superior knowledge recently gained through an encounter at work camp. That left us with such a skimpy meal we had to dip into the next day's rations.

By the time we hit the highway at the end of the three days and our wakeful night in a cow pasture, we were starved and nearly broke, for we had underestimated our car's appetite as well as our own. On the look out for an inexpensive place to eat, we saw a sign "Truck

Stop," and immediately remembered that in The Grapes of Wrath truck stops provided the best cheap meals. As soon as we were seated we were each presented with a stack of four slices of bread. In our weakened condition this struck us as very funny, but we really cracked up when we found that even before the rest of our food arrived we had wolfed down all eight slices.

Two years later came our weddings, Lyle's and mine in a spring blizzard and yours and Joe's on the hottest day of summer. During the early years of marriage and child rearing we were more aware of our differences than of our underlying similarities, particularly in the chaos and confusion of family gatherings at Duck Island. We had some conflicting notions about how best to bring up our kids, complicated by our mother's strong opinions. It took three year-old Tim to put this problem into perspective for me. You wanted Jon to have a full-fledged dinner at noon while Tim was used to having a light lunch. I told him I'd fix him a peanut butter sandwich if he asked me quietly so as not to distract Jon from eating his dinner. His reassuring reply was "I know, different families do things different ways."

Although memories of our annual reunions at Duck Island tend to merge, certain visits to each other stand out vividly. The year Joe was in France, you, with Aunt Grace and our toddlers, Tim and Jon, shared Christmas with us in our new house in Bethesda. In 1955 while Lyle was writing his dissertation, the three children and I took a train to New Hampshire for our first visit to Squam. Like everyone else, I was enchanted by its beauty. Joe gave us a great boat ride to Yard Island for a swim and picnic, and hiked us up Rattlesnake Mountain. Ten years later we introduced you to our summer cabin on Douglas Lake. That visit, no longer distracted by young children, gave you and Lyle time to really get to know each other. You and I found a new intimacy when I came to keep house while you recuperated from an operation. "Love me love my dog"—the height of sisterly devotion was your offer to take care of Gypsy for the year we spent in Washington.

Unfortunately, preoccupation with Mamo's stroke kept me from staying with you after the services for Joe. Our visits with her were staggered throughout the long winter until we finally came together over the Memorial Day weekend. That was a tender time, softened by the beauty of dogwood blossoms, when we shared our grief and our last visit with Mother.

We were grateful that you had the support of close friends, and were proud of you for undertaking a new career at Temple. You surely found your calling, and earned the recognition you received as an outstanding and much loved teacher. You also had the courage to start again on a new topic for a Ph.D. dissertation. Lyle and I were always glad to have you stop off in Ann Arbor on your way from conferences or from visiting Jon or Pete.

All too soon came the devastating news of Pete's death. Sorrow again brought us closer and deepened our understanding. Lyle, too, appreciated your insights, and the three of us shared many meaningful conversations. After his stroke your frequent visits and phone calls sustained me during those four and a half years.

Since then we have entered a new phase of companionship and fun. Right now we are anticipating a canoe trip in the wilds of Canada in September. We may be cold, but surely Elderhostel won't let us go hungry. Who knows what adventures await us after that?

It's high time to end this with congratulations, Mario, on your seventy-five years of becoming the wonderful person we all cherish. It is a privilege and a joy to be your sister!

April 1995

Ilana Marta's Arrival

Who would have thought that at fifty-two my son, Steve, would become a father and I, already with four grown grandchildren and two great-grands, would become grandmother to a six-and-a-half month old baby girl from Guatemala!

Ilana's arrival is the third life-changing event for Steve in as many years. The first was his decision to make a career change soon after he moved to Boston in the spring of 1996. He had become increasingly discontented in his affiliation with the Socialist Workers Party because, although he still was convinced that capitalism would eventually collapse, he could no longer believe that socialism would inevitably follow. This realization made him feel out of place and depressed. No wonder he had lost his zeal for engaging fellow factory workers in political discussions as he had tried to do on many different jobs in various parts of the country. So, after twenty-five years of dedicated service to his cause, Steve finally resigned from the party.

Encouraged by his previous brief experience as copy editor of their international news magazine he thought he would like to get into publishing in the environmental field. His first step was to sign up with a temporary employment agency that placed him in a series of proofreading jobs. On his own he found work with the Harvard Press and continues to be one of their favored proofreaders. In the fall he enjoyed auditing a Harvard extension course in ecology, and the next term he took one for credit in human evolution. We, his family, were delighted to see the return of his characteristic sparkle and humor. With his confidence as a student restored he decided to embark on qualifying himself for graduate work somewhere in an environmental program, since as a history major he had had no biology in college. So in September 1997 he enrolled in two undergraduate courses in biology at the Boston branch of the University of Massachusetts.

One of these, a class in genetics, presented Steve his second life change, as he promptly fell in love with his professor, Rachel Skvirsky. He confided in me that he didn't see how he could hold out for the whole semester. Nevertheless he furthered their acquaintance after class by way of frequent conversations strictly confined to the subject of genetics. Not until Steve returned from visiting me at Christmas and Rachel had turned in all the grades did they have their first date. Much of their courtship was spent painting the first floor of an old two-story house in Brookline where Rachel had moved in November. Steve reported they worked well together, a good sign. He told me she had bought the apartment because of Brookline's excellent school system, and that was important because she had embarked on the long process of adopting a baby from Guatemala. In fact numerous delays had already caused her to postpone her sabbatical, but that was probably just as well since redecorating, even with Steve's help, took far longer than she had anticipated.

Meanwhile they had more time to come to know each other and for him to meet her family and friends all of whom took to him at once, especially when assured that he welcomed the idea of adopting a baby. By coincidence Rachel had graduated from Oberlin five years after Steve, but neither had been back to the campus. So when a classmate persuaded her to attend her twenty-fifth reunion he went along for his thirtieth and they had a wonderful time.

The first members of our family to meet Rachel were his brother and sister-in-law, Tim and Leslie. They liked her right away, Leslie describing her as "bright, petite, and lovely." My happiness for Steve led me to love Rachel long before I visited them in June. Yet my joy in meeting her was dampened by sorrow. Just two days before I departed for Boston, Steve called with the sad news that the mother of the baby girl whom they expected would come to them in the fall had changed her mind and was going to keep her. Rachel had received a picture of the infant taken at the time of her birth in April, so she had become a real person to them. Their loss seemed like that of a miscarriage.

Of course I had expressed my sympathy to Steve over the phone, which he passed on to Rachel, but I felt constrained from mentioning the baby when I first arrived. Instead I admired the apartment with its handsome woodwork and the beautiful furniture she had inherited from a dear, elderly cousin. Conversation started to warm up during dinner, but tension lingered until Rachel invited me to share her grief by showing me the picture of the baby she had thought would be hers. Then she moved on to pictures of her family and we were launched on the process of becoming close friends. I could see so many ways in which Rachel and Steve are well suited to each other. He is perked up by her vivacity, and she appreciates his subtle though sometimes corny sense of humor. They seem completely at ease with each other and obviously very much in love.

We next met over the Labor Day weekend in Windsor, Connecticut, at Tim and Leslie's family reunion in celebration of the marriage of their older daughter, Naomi, to Dean Hazlewood. There Steve was happy to introduce Rachel to his sister, Ellen, and her children, Elise and Daniel, and a month later to his Ingersoll relatives at my brother's eightieth birthday party on Long Island. Once again U. Mass postponed the sabbatical, and Rachel returned to her teaching and research. Steve took two more courses at Tufts where he had enrolled the previous winter hoping to qualify for their graduate program. He has recently been accepted for next fall and offered a teaching stipend.

In October Rachel was assigned a baby girl named Marta Maria born on September first in the same Mayan town where a friend's adopted baby boy came from three years ago. As with all the adoptees she had been placed with a foster mother in Guatemala City and again a tiny birth photo was sent. Later, when some more discernible snapshots came, Rachel and Steve could see she looked healthy and happy. They were charmed by the baby's dark wondering eyes, chubby cheeks, and cute little mouth. A few scattered reports on her health and progress with the paperwork added to their sense of her reality. They knew that the usual waiting period was about six months and that the earliest possible date they could expect to get her would be the first of February when she would be five months old. That hope was dashed when they learned that an error in the recording of her birthdate meant that the documents had to be sent to another agency for correction, and there they sat for the entire month of January.

Meanwhile Steve and Rachel put up bookshelves to accommodate their two libraries and worked on finishing touches to the decorating. Her younger brother, Mark, and his wife Mary, who also live in Brookline gave them a baby shower in January. With the new semester Steve resumed classes at Tufts and Rachel's sabbatical began so she was free of teaching responsibilities. However she is still supervising graduate students in her research project so that and other academic chores took up some of her waiting time. In February she learned that she was officially the adoptive mother and by the end of the month all that remained was for the Guatemalan government to issue the baby a passport and for our embassy to approve a visa.

In early March the adoption agency told Rachel she would soon be receiving one week's notice to come and pick up the baby. Then on Wednesday, March tenth, President Clinton's visit closed down the embassy for three days, which they expected would further prolong their waiting. So Rachel was surprised when her agent called at five-thirty Monday evening to say that the pick-up date at the embassy would be either on Thursday, the eighteenth, or the following Monday and that she would phone at the same time next day to tell her which. Wouldn't you know, after all that waiting they learned Tuesday evening that they were to catch a two o'clock plane the next afternoon. What a lot of scurrying around and excited telephone calls followed!

Shortly before noon on Wednesday, with a minimum of baggage that included necessary items for the baby, Steve and Rachel set off for the subway to Logan Airport. They had arranged for Mark and Mary to pick up their car with newly installed baby-seat and meet them at 4:00 PM on Friday. The flight went smoothly arriving in Guatemala City late in the evening. As soon as they got to their hotel they went right to bed, but were too excited to sleep. At seven-thirty in the morning the lawyer met them in the lobby to take them to the embassy. He escorted them to his car, and, to their surprise, there on the back seat was the foster mother, her fifteen year-old daughter, and the baby! Rachel climbed in beside them, and not being able to speak Spanish, communicated with smiles mostly directed at the baby. Steve sat in front with the lawyer who of course spoke English but was disinclined to act as interpreter between them and the foster mother. Their arrival at the embassy, only a short drive away, was followed by a long wait, but when their turn came the lawyer had all the papers in order and their business was quickly dispatched. All that was left to do was for Steve to return to the Embassy in the late afternoon to pick up the baby's passport properly stamped with a U.S. visa. They spent the rest of the day in their hotel room admiring their little daughter except for a stroll to a nearby shop to find some souvenirs. Steve carried the baby while Rachel did the shopping. Through all this the baby was remarkably good and seemed quite content. She only woke up once in the night, but again Steve and Rachel were too excited to sleep much. Besides they had to get up at five-thirty to catch their flight home. Miraculously, after hardly more than forty-eight hours, there they were back in Logan Airport proudly showing off their beautiful baby daughter to her welcoming relatives.

There followed a flurry of phone calls proclaiming Ilana's safe arrival. Now that she was actually theirs they started calling her Ilana, the Hebrew name Rachel had chosen for her. They are keeping Marta as her middle name. Over the weekend a stream of visitors came to hold and admire her. Fortunately the following week was spring break so the new parents could give their full attention to Ilana and to figuring out her needs. Steve called me nearly every day to tell me of their discoveries and perplexities, but mostly to exclaim over how cute she was. She seemed remarkably content during the day, but night was a different story when her frequent waking kept Rachel and Steve hopping. A checkup with their pediatrician and nurse practitioner found Ilana to be in good health, though she was bothered by sores on her feet. These turned out to be scabies and easily treatable. However there was no such simple cure for her nighttime wakefulness and her parents' sleep deprivation.

My first impression upon meeting Ilana in mid-April was of penetrating dark eyes studying the world. An air of tranquility suffuses her broad face made rounder by her fat cheeks and topped by abundant black silky hair. She seems wise beyond her seven and a half months. I call her my little pumpkin. We fell into a game where she would stare at me with solemn intensity while I returned her gaze until quite unexpectedly her tiny puckered lips would stretch wide into a joyous smile and so did mine. Then we would resume our sober stares until she chose to break into another smile. She would keep this up for quite a long time. Ilana's powers of concentration showed in other ways too as when examining her fingers or a toy. We all agreed she appears to have a placid temperament.

Before my four-day visit with Ilana I stayed with Tim and Leslie for two nights spending one rainy afternoon in West Hartford with my granddaughter Rachel and her baby, Emily. A month younger than Ilana, she is fully four pounds lighter with more delicate features. She has her sister's same alert, pixie look. Rachel and I had a good chance to talk until time to put Emily in the stroller and walk down the block to meet the kindergarten bus. When it arrived Chelsea jumped off and ran toward me with open arms. Then we piled into the car to go to her skating class. Chelsea's achievement was in only falling down once. When I complimented her on her skating she corrected me by saying she was not gliding, she was marching. Afterwards we drove over to Tim and Leslie's and I treated everybody to dinner at a nearby Italian restaurant. The little girls were happy and well behaved. They are obviously very fond of each other.

Since Tim and Leslie had offered to drive me to Boston Saturday morning I had told Steve that I would love to stop off in Springfield to call on Miriam Skvirsky, if Rachel thought her mother would like to see me. Miriam responded by inviting us to come for coffee at 9:30. We hit it off right away and, as I had anticipated, enjoyed sharing our mutual delight over our children having found each other and over Ilana's arrival. Leslie snapped a very nice picture of us two grandmothers for Ilana's baby book. I was glad we took this opportunity to meet, as I didn't know when another would present itself. Rachel's brother Mark came by to help Miriam shop for a new car. I met him again the next day in Brookline when he and his eleven-year-old daughter, Sarah, dropped in with her friend to see Ilana and I joined the three of them in taking the baby for a ride in her stroller. My four-day visit with Steve and Rachel went by all too quickly, absorbed as we were with the baby. On the last evening they announced their big news: they had decided to get married! I was delighted, but not surprised.

* * *

In keeping with the unconventional sequence of events in their life together, Rachel and Steve's honeymoon preceded their marriage. Ever since they started dating in January 1998 Steve had been eager to bring Rachel to our cabin on Douglas Lake in northern Michigan where he had spent many happy days since childhood. At last, after setting the twenty-eighth of August as the wedding date, they decided they could fit in a visit during the third week of the month. Most of the essential arrangements were in place by the thirteenth when they took off on an early flight from Boston with Ilana, their eleven-and-a-half-month-old adopted daughter, encumbered by all her equipment: car seat, stroller, back pack, and life jacket. A long delay in getting their rental car at Detroit Metro put off their arrival at the cabin until after seven, but the baby held up quite well. In terms of time it was a longer trip than when her new parents flew her from Guatemala five months earlier.

Rachel was as delighted with our little cabin and its setting in the woods as Steve was in showing it to her. Chilly and windy weather the first few days confined our activities to walking, but it soon warmed up enough to go swimming. We had one glorious day picnicking and walking on Lake Michigan's beach by the sand dunes on Sturgeon Bay with Ilana riding on Steve's back. Another time, when the wind died down, all four of us took a canoe paddle along our lake's wooded shore to North Fishtail Bay, Steve and Rachel taking turns sitting in the middle holding the baby. I was sorry I could not take care of her so they could go sailing or canoeing together, but they were afraid that at twenty pounds she would be too heavy for me to lift. So my services were confined to meal preparation. Once when I remarked that it was too bad they would not have time for a honeymoon before going back to work after the wedding, Rachel exclaimed, "This is our honeymoon with all your gourmet dinners!"

The night before their last day Ellen and Skip flew in from Oregon so she could meet her new niece and become better acquainted with Rachel whom she had seen only at the marriage celebration of my eldest grandchild, Naomi. They all made the most of a perfect day, swimming, boating, and lounging in the hammock. Steve was happy for the chance to take Rachel for a sail while Ellen and Skip played with the baby. Once while we were sitting around on the dock Rachel took off alone in the Kayak. When she reappeared in view Ilana, trembling with excitement to see her mother, shouted, "Dada, dada, da!" the greeting she applied to everyone. At dinner Steve mocked a fierce face at Ilana with the same tense tremble she had displayed that afternoon. She responded to the joke by turning down the corners of her mouth and tensing her jaw with a little shudder while she glanced up at him to see his reaction. The incongruity of such a fierce expression and mischievous eyes in her chubby baby face set us off into gales of laughter. Naturally she repeated her act with glee, but when she pulled her stunt the next day on the man who shared their seat on the airplane and again at day-care her parents decided they had to turn a cold shoulder to her clowning. Luckily she dropped the scary pose in time to avoid alarming their wedding guests.

Ellen and Skip's visit was all too short, but I was grateful for their help with countless chores in closing the cabin and with the drive back to Ann Arbor. Next morning the three of us flew to Logan Airport where we met Mario, who had just arrived from Philadelphia. Both our flights had been delayed for an hour before takeoff because Boston was closed down by fog and rain. That put us at the height of rush hour traffic through which Skip maneuvered our rental car. We were well over an hour late in reaching the restaurant where Tim's family had been patiently waiting in the private dining room for the party in celebration of Ellen's fiftieth birthday. The delay was probably hardest on my great-granddaughters, six-year-old Chelsea and eleven-month-old Emily, or perhaps on their mother, Rachel Craine, but they all held up very well.

I was glad that Rachel Skvirsky's mother, Miriam, and her friend, Dorothy Goldman, joined our happy family reunion so we mothers could exchange exclamations of joy in our children's marriage. The high spot of the evening was Tim and Leslie's presentation to each of us of a book, *Family Letters* by Lyle Craine, hot off the press. It was a project long in the making. Lyle had started the letters in 1983 in response to a seventy-fifth birthday gift from Ellen of a blank book with her request that he jot down what he had done before she knew him. Setting the blank book aside, over the next three years Lyle hand-wrote fifteen letters covering memories of his childhood and his life up until we moved to Ann Arbor in 1953. These he photocopied and sent out in installments to family members and a few friends. Later Leslie transcribed them all on her computer and, in honor of his up-coming eightieth birthday, presented him with a binder of the typed letters. A month later he suffered a severe stroke. Subsequently I found that it gave us both much pleasure when I would read his letters aloud to him, a few pages at a time. Recently Leslie typed up two additional pieces Lyle called "Ponderings" and a chronology of major events, which, along with some well-selected photographs, she and Tim turned over to a printer. Having the copies of the book in our hands with Lyle's smiling face on the cover made us feel he was celebrating Steve and Rachel's union with us.

The wedding was scheduled for one o'clock on Saturday in South Dartmouth, a little over an hour's drive from Boston, at the summer cottage of one of Rachel's colleagues, Judy Clark. Skip and Ellen planned to meet Mario and me at our motel on Beacon Street in Brookline in ample time for Ellen to rehearse the recorder duets she and Rachel's best friend, Robin, were to play for the wedding. However they were delayed in getting started and also had difficulty finding their way through unfamiliar streets in Cambridge where they were staying in an apartment offered by another friend of Rachel's. Once they picked us up it seemed to take forever to get out of the city and on to the open highway where we were further delayed by a long back up. With mounting anxiety we divided our attention between the clock and spatters of rain on the windshield. Near New Bedford patches of blue sky lifted our spirits, and when we finally arrived, on the dot of one, we were greeted by full sunshine. But it was as we walked through the shady back yard filled with several round tables prettily set with white tablecloths and garden flowers that I felt the enchantment of wedding festivities envelop me.

Much to our relief there were several others later than we. A relaxed and unhurried atmosphere pervaded that pleasant house whose double doors opened wide to a verandah overlooking the water. In fact Rachel had not yet changed into her wedding gown, but she soon went upstairs and reappeared looking lovely in a simple lavender shift. Steve was more dressed up than I've ever seen him. He had on a handsome new navy blue jacket with brass buttons, a mostly blue silk tie with a glint of lavender to match Rachel's dress, and gray slacks which seemed excessively long. As we waited for the ceremony to begin I whispered to Mario, "What a shame Steve didn't have the tailor shorten his trousers."

"Oh, that's the style now," she replied. "Look at the other men."

Sure enough all their pants were hanging over their heels and dragging in the dust.

Meanwhile, Jim, who was going to perform the service, was standing around taking notes in a small leather notebook. He is an un-ordained liberal rabbi married to a Protestant minister both of whom became justices of the peace in order to conduct interfaith marriages. The house was filling up with more people and after a while recorder music summoned us to the chairs set up on the front lawn. We were a company of twenty-five adults, six children ranging in age from fifteen down to six and two infants. Sitting there in the warm sunshine looking out upon the water we were united in a glow of happiness for Rachel and Steve.

When the music ended Ellen stepped forward to hold one of the bamboo poles of the chuppah while Tim and Rachel's brothers, Burt and Marc, held the other three. The fabric, an orange-red weaving Rachel had found in Guatemala years ago and used as a wall hanging, waved in the breeze. Its undulating motion was enhanced by the elastic cloth covered hair-bands, which Steve had sewn at each corner to tie to the poles. At the start of the service Jim explained the symbolism of the chuppah as being open to the sky and thus to God in nature. Rather than standing with their backs to us, Rachel and Steve faced each other letting us see their faces and observe how Ilana quietly amused herself while Steve held her on his left arm throughout the ceremony. She examined his brass buttons, pulled a stay out of his collar, and even found in his inside pocket the marriage certificate, which he gently retrieved and transferred to his hip pocket. Best of all, at a musical interlude, Ilana gaily kicked her legs in time with the recorders.

Jim included Ilana in his remarks about her parents' marriage and their future life as a family, showing an unusually personal appreciation of them. He said that Steve and Rachel came together as more fully formed persons than most couples whom he had married and therefore had a deeper understanding of the meaning of their commitment. Mary, Marc's wife, read a thoughtful piece about what marriage entails, and Mario read a beautiful Apache love song. A flute solo by twelve-year-old Sara was thwarted by the wind blowing her breath away from the keys until she stepped back into a more sheltered spot. After Jim interpreted the drinking of the wine and the breaking of the glass, Rachel and Steve each took a sip, Jim carefully wrapped the glass in a cloth and Steve stepped on it. Then Steve and Rachel recited a modified version of the traditional Christian marriage vows. At a signal Rachel's two teenage nephews, Eric and Jared, Burt's sons, stepped forward from the audience with the wedding rings. The one Rachel put on Steve's finger had been Lyle's. Then they embraced.

After the ceremony champagne was passed around, and Tim made the following toast to Rachel and Steve:

To Oberlin College, their common alma mater:
Leslie and I can attest that relationships between Oberlinians (whether they meet in their sophomore year or 25 years later) are strong and solid;

To the University of Massachusetts, the venue where Steve and Rachel met:
(and we congratulate them for not taking the University's sexual harassment policy too seriously);

To Miriam and Asho:
for waiting patiently until their second born found a suitable partner;

To Ilana:
for having chosen such wonderful parents;

To Steve and Rachel:
as your love has blossomed you have spread joy to members of both your families. We wish you and Ilana great happiness in the years to come.

Then Mario sang the following verses she had composed to the tune of "Ruben, Ruben, I've been thinking."

> Rachel, Rachel, I've been thinking
> What a grand life it will be:
> To have found a sturdy daughter,
> and a husband like our Steve.
>
> 'Lana, 'Lana, I've been thinking
> what a marvelous family:
> To have Rachel for a Mama
> and for Papa to have Steve.
>
> Stephen, Stephen, I've been thinking
> of a life I'd hoped for thee.
> Wife and daughter all together:
> New Beginnings for all three!

As Steve and I waited to be called to the buffet he remarked on how the wedding served as a nice joining of the two families. In the dining room our plates were piled with delicious grilled vegetables and chicken, which we carried out to the tables in the back yard. There in the refreshing shade, welcomed after our hour in the sun, we reunited with our own families and mingled with our new relatives as we shared our mutual joy in Rachel and Steve's marriage. In due time the bride and groom cut the wedding cake, and eventually each of us was served a piece—a delectable pound cake one layer spread with raspberry and the other with lemon filling. No sooner had the impatient youngsters devoured theirs than they took off for the waterfront where they played on the dock or shore waiting turns to ride in the rowboat. The rest of us wandered about while I found a comfortable wicker chair on the front porch and watched the two Rachels give their babies freedom to crawl on the grass. They quickly discovered that skirts are a hazard to crawling and grass is tempting fodder to one-year olds, so off came the party dresses and thereafter bare-skinned Emily and Ilana played happily on the porch floor. While others came and went throughout that golden afternoon, I was content to linger in my chair floating on a cloud of happiness.

Actually our carload was the last to leave. We tailgated Steve and Rachel back to their home in Brookline where the out-of-towners helped them eat up leftovers of the day's feast. We were joined by Rachel's cousin Alan and his wife, Anexora, who had not been able to attend the wedding. The celebration continued Sunday morning with Marc and Mary who gave us a delicious brunch of their own making on the day of their departure for a week's vacation in Tennessee. Their daughter Sara had made blueberry muffins and her older sister, Anna, helped serve. I was glad to further strengthen my ties with the Skvirsky family, especially Miriam. The climax of the party was an early celebration of Ilana's birthday coming up on September first. Since Emily's birthday is on September twenty-ninth, Ellen had brought a gift for her and some paper dolls for Chelsea. Both babies enjoyed playing with the wrapping paper as much as with the presents. However, the birthday cake made no impression on Ilana until Rachel guided her hand to touch the icing. Then her fingers flew straight to her mouth conveying the delicious discovery of the taste of sugar.

As soon as the party was over Marc's family left for their vacation while the rest of us cleaned up the kitchen. Within the next hour or two Miriam and Dorothy drove off to Springfield, Tim's vanload headed toward Hartford, and Mario, Skip, and Ellen drove to the airport. Since I was staying over with Rachel and Steve until Tuesday, I went back to the apartment with them and Marlene, Burt's wife.

Though still in a state of subdued euphoria, by now we knew we were very tired and needed to relax. As we sat in the living room Rachel commented that Ilana felt hot and passed her to Marlene who confirmed her suspicion and helped her take the baby's temperature. It turned out to be 102—her first fever. Rachel called her pediatrician's office and was told by the nurse to administer Tylenol and watch for symptoms. None had appeared by the time she talked with the doctor on Monday, but he set up an appointment for the next day. Meanwhile Ilana didn't seem to me to be very sick as she acted like her usual self, so I presumed that it was just a virus that would soon run its course. Nevertheless after our joy had soared so high Ilana's illness brought us down to earth with a thud.

When I phoned from home Tuesday evening Rachel told me Ilana's white blood cell count was up, as was to be expected, but more serious her red cell count was below normal. It continued to drop during the week and on Monday evening she was admitted to Children's Hospital. There she stayed for the next two and a half weeks with her parents by her side while she was administered countless tests. These gradually ruled out some of their worst fears such as TB and leukemia, but it was an anxious and stressful time for all of them. Ilana was so freaked out by the hospital scene with its many strangers poking and prodding her that she screamed whenever put in the crib and would sleep only in her parents' arms or snuggled beside one of them on the bed. By the second week she was sleeping better, so Steve and Rachel took turns going home for the night, and were able to go home together on the last weekend when Mary volunteered a two nights' vigil. A group of Rachel's women friends took turns bringing them home-cooked dinners. Meanwhile Ilana, in spite of her weakened condition, was winning the hearts of the hospital staff. One doctor called her his miracle baby. Finally a biopsy of a swollen lymph node in her neck indicated a tentative diagnosis: histiocytosis, a rare disorder of a group of white blood cells that attack various parts of the body. Although not a cancer, it is treated with chemotherapy. Rachel and Steve were relieved to have a diagnosis, even though a scary one, so now they could leave the hospital and take up a semblance of normal living. On Thursday evening the twenty-third, after Ilana had a port inserted in her chest and had been fortified by a blood transfusion, she was taken home to familiar surroundings where at last she was allowed to crawl on the floor.

The next day I flew to Hartford to spend the weekend with Tim and Leslie. On Saturday we drove to Springfield where Miriam took us and Marc out to lunch. We shared our concern over Ilana's illness and our relief that she was home at last and getting the treatment she needed. In the evening we had a party for Rachel Craine's twenty-sixth birthday. Then on Sunday Tim drove me into Brookline for a four-hour visit. I was sad to see Ilana looking pale and listless, such a contrast to her high spirits of only four weeks ago. Although she occasionally gave us a small smile and played peek-a-boo with her cousin Sara, who dropped by, she certainly didn't have the energy to crawl that day. Before I set out on this trip east I had told Steve and Rachel I needed to come just to give them big hugs. The visit served that purpose, and I was able to convey my love and support, but I left with a heavy heart. I couldn't help worrying about how Ilana was going to respond to the weekly chemotherapy treatments, and whether her parents would find a competent caregiver so they could get on with their careers.

Reports from Rachel and Steve this past week have been cautiously optimistic, although so far the medical tests remain inconclusive. Then last night I had a most heartwarming conversation with Rachel that has lifted my spirits. She says Ilana has really perked up and seems like her old self. She is vocalizing new sounds and is learning the meaning of new words. For instance, when crawling caused her pants leg to slip down over her foot and Steve asked, "Where's Ilana's foot?" she pulled back the fabric to reveal it to him. She has also become more assertive in asking for what she wants. From Steve's attempt to teach her to follow the direction of his finger when he points at some object she has grasped the idea of pointing, only her way is to point her finger into the air with an imperious gesture whenever she wants something. She even made one of the doctors at the ontology clinic crack up with laughter when, in response to his clowning, she gave a little shiver and turned on her fierce face for him.

October 1999

Visits to Family, May 2001

During the month of May I had the pleasure of touching base with every member of my family except my eldest granddaughter, Naomi, who lives in North Carolina, and my sister, Mario, but she will be coming to Ann Arbor the end of June and will drive up to the cabin with me for a two-week visit.

First I flew east to LaGuardia on Saturday May 5 and spent a leisurely week with my brother, Ray, and his wife, Elex, on Duck Island. As always I was glad to be back in their comfortable little house overlooking Northport Bay and to roam my childhood terrain. Sunshine and fresh spring foliage and flowers enhanced its beauty. Everyone was pleased that a pair of ospreys have settled on the high nesting platform Ray and a neighbor recently installed near the entrance of the causeway.

Elex showed me around my mother's old garden where I helped her tie up the climbing roses on a long lattice and a rickety arch. For the first time in nearly thirty years I stepped inside the big house, thanks to the hospitality of its new owner who is much more compatible than his several predecessors. He has kept the essentials pretty much the same but is making necessary repairs including replacing the rusted casement windows with new ones that keep the old look.

One day Ray and Elex drove me out to Riverhead at the eastern end of Long Island to visit my long-time friend, Edie Muma. While Elex claimed she needed a nap and Ray settled down with his *New York Times*, Edie and I, taking advantage of their tactful retreat, spent nearly an hour on her porch reminiscing about our childhood and our respective mothers. Then she served us a delicious salad lunch under the shade of a big maple. We all enjoyed the afternoon immensely.

On Friday their daughter, Carolyn, drove down from her home in Danbury, Connecticut especially for the purpose of driving me back there the next day and on up to Tim's in Windsor, just north of Hartford. Of course I was grateful to her for providing transportation, but I was also glad to have such a good opportunity to visit with my niece along the way and to see her charming little house and lovely garden where we stopped for a leisurely lunch. No sooner were we back in the car than it started to pour. Heavy rain continued almost all the rest of the way, but stopped just before we arrived. I wondered if Tim and Leslie would have to hold their picnic indoors, but there, under the carport, all decked out with red checked clothes were two card tables and a small picnic table for the younger children.

After hugs all around it was evident that my granddaughter Rachel's little girls, Chelsea almost eight and Emily two and a half, were impatiently awaiting Ilana's arrival. When Steve and his Rachel drove in a few minutes later, Emily immediately grabbed Ilana, who is only a month older but considerably larger, and insisted that she sit beside her at the little table. The eight of us adults promptly found our places so the party could get under way. Chelsea presided by giving a formal little speech of welcome to the celebration of Mother's Day and handed me a great grandmother's card. Then she presented all five women with corsages, which she and Tim had bought that afternoon. It was a jolly gathering, and I was glad to get a little better acquainted with Erik, Rachel Craine's young man. All too soon it was time to depart for Boston, but even such a short visit with Tim and his family had its satisfactions.

The special feature of my visit with Steve and Rachel was staying in their new house on Blake Street in Newtonville [Massachusetts]. I had seen it empty last Christmas, but now I could better appreciate how well it fits their needs and tastes. It is light and airy with a window on the north wall lighting the side staircase and both the downstairs and upstairs halls. The living room is spacious, big enough to take the oversized Afghan carpet Ellen sent them with room to spare. Steve and Rachel's bedroom above is nearly as large. Their bed faces two large front windows while Rachel's desk fits between the smaller ones at the south end, quite a contrast to the cramped quarters they put up with in their former place. Ilana was proud to show me her room on the southwest corner and her grown-up bed. The smaller third bedroom will be for the new baby they are hoping to adopt. It is now a guest room where Rachel's mother, Miriam, has been staying while courageously undergoing chemotherapy and radiation following an operation last December. I slept on the single foldaway bed in Steve's little study behind the kitchen. The dining room is a comfortable size and the kitchen easily accommodates a table large enough for the four of us adults and Ilana. A full basement provides lots of work, play, and storage space.

Steve and Rachel have been delighted with all the nice flowers and shrubs in their yard, and the former owner is equally pleased to pass on her gardening lore to them. Although the yard is small, there is a large playground half a block down the hill at the elementary school that Ilana will attend in three years. A block or so further up Blake Street is an extensive woods where Steve and I had quite a long walk.

I was amazed to see how big and strong Ilana has become. She now weighs thirty-five pounds and has boundless energy and determination. She runs with a little galloping skip, turns somersaults, and tries to climb everything, A walk around a sculpture garden on Sunday kept us all hopping. She loves to go to the playground and play with the other children. Although she knows that if she hits she will be taken home, she still strikes out when her desires are thwarted. Her parents worry that she is too aggressive, but I try to assure them that she will become civilized in due time. She still has her happy disposition sparkling with fun and curiosity and has acquired an impressive vocabulary. Dogs are especially appealing to her. Still confused about pronouns she will ask their owners, "Can you meet your dog?"

You can see by the above that much of my attention centered on Ilana and the new house, but I did have some time alone with Steve. Most rewarding was a drive to the Cape on Monday to see the four Coastal Plain Ponds where he has been doing his research for his Masters degree from Tufts under a grant from the Massachusetts Nature Conservancy. The shores of these ponds and some seventy-five others are habitat for some of the rarest plants and animals in the state. The ponds are kettles formed by blocks of ice left by the glaciers and have no inlet or outflow, but instead get their water from the underground aquifer. Although Steve's ponds and several others are protected nature preserves, they are affected by the draw down of ground water by wells that serve the ever increasing population in the surrounding areas. Steve is working on the problem of how the propagation of pitch pine, an invasive species, is affected by various degrees of flooding. He has cultivated hundreds of pine seedlings in the greenhouse and has planted or transplanted hundreds more in plots on his ponds' shores. Presumably he will be able to demonstrate that the natural seasonal and cyclical rise of water levels in the ponds used to drown out the pitch pines but now with lower levels they threaten to crowd out the more fragile vegetation. Not only did I learn more about Steve's work, but I enjoyed the beautiful day, walking along the shores of his pretty ponds and seeing some of the old houses in the villages we drove through. On Tuesday I went with Steve to water his seedlings in the Tufts greenhouse and his larger plants at their farm. Then we took in an exhibit at Boston College of the Norwegian artist, Edvard Munch.

Next morning, May 16, I flew back to Ann Arbor. After two and a half days turn-around time I set off again for Ashland, Oregon. My ten-day visit there with Ellen and Skip was very restful as I fell into the rhythm of their days. The weather was beautiful, though unseasonably hot, so Ellen was up at dawn to work in their extensive garden while I continued to soak up sleep. We would breakfast together about eight thirty. Skip, who works in his upstairs study, was on his own for breakfast and lunch, but would join us for dinners. Ellen's schedule varies from day to day as she is involved in several enterprises, some paid and some not. Her primary earnings have come from work in the schools in violence prevention through peer mediation and from private coaching. While she was busy I would read or take a nap. When she was free we would go for a walk or I'd help her water the garden or pick greens and snow peas for salad. My particular contribution was pruning their lovely Japanese maple by their front door making the trunk and lower limbs bare and visible. One evening the three of us attended a moving performance of Horton Foote's play of "The Trip to Bountiful," put on by the Ashland Shakespeare Festival.

It was my good luck to have several visits with my granddaughter, Elise, who stays at her father's not far away, before she took off on a two-week backpacking trip with a class of twenty-six teenagers and their teacher. She hopes this will lead to a job in the fall with the same teacher, who is running an alternative program with an environmental emphasis within the school system. She is a talented young woman of nearly twenty-six who has much to offer, but has not yet found her niche.

Then, the following Saturday Daniel drove up from San Francisco just to see me. Ellen had prepared a delicious dinner to celebrate his up-coming twenty-second birthday. We waited till eight o'clock, then ate without him as he had called on his cell phone to say he'd be late. It didn't matter, as we enjoyed watching him eat. His delay was caused by a "gig" that morning playing with a guitarist for a reception for parents of graduating seniors at San Francisco State where he is studying to become a music teacher. His instrument is the bass viol. Next day Ellen and I had a delightful lunch with him on a balcony overlooking the stream that runs through Lithia Park. In the evening he and I attended a play about a group of Black women Jazz players of the 1940s. Dan knew all the tunes, while I, who had lived through the period, didn't recognize any.

The high spot of my visit was an overnight trip with Ellen and Skip to the coast just across the border into California. We stayed at a charming bed and breakfast right on the shore from which we took a short walk down the beach to an excellent restaurant. Ellen and I strolled along the beach again next morning enjoying the unusually calm ocean. Before reaching the coast we hiked part of two trails in a redwood forest and then two more the following day. Most of the time we had the trails all to ourselves and could experience profound silence. The towering trees were awe inspiring and the delicate ferns and flowers at our feet fascinating. With sunlight filtering through the thin foliage spotlighting a mighty tree trunk here or a mossy stump there I surely felt I was in an enchanted forest. It was a privilege to share that inspiring experience with Ellen and Skip. Upon my departure for Ann Arbor Skip told me he now feels completely relaxed with me and I could reciprocate by saying I felt fully at ease with him. We have both come a long way.

Edie Muma: A Lifelong Friendship

Edie and I can't believe we've known each other for seventy-five years! We were in second and third grade together at Packer Collegiate Institute, an elite private girls' school on Brooklyn Heights not far from the Brooklyn Bridge. Neither of us has happy memories of that stuffy school, though we do remember being fascinated by a miniature Eskimo village in second grade. Nor do we recall playing together after school, as we lived in separate neighborhoods, but at least we must have gone to each others' birthday parties. In any case our mothers met and became good friends. After third grade we both transferred to other schools and might have lost track of each other had it not been for the friendship of our parents.

Edie's mother, Jessie Smith, was a young widow who emanated an ethereal charm. Her husband had died of a botched tonsillectomy when Edith, the youngest of three children, was four. I don't remember much about Dorothy, who was eight years older, but by coincidence Alfred was a classmate of my older brother Jerry at Polly Prep. That made the Smiths an ideal family to invite for visits to Duck Island, our country home near Northport on the north shore of Long Island. Although our brothers never quite hit it off, those visits were where Edie and I really bonded and where Jessie became my parents' cherished friend. We also came to love each other's mothers. I was enchanted by her mother's delicate beauty and basked in her kind and uncritical acceptance of me. I envied Edie her calm and loving relationship with her mother in contrast to the volatile one I had with mine. Unlike me, Edie delighted in my mother's unpredictable bursts of enthusiasm and welcomed her suggestions and advice. Over the years she learned many things from her, particularly about gardening and wild plants. She recalls a question on a personality quiz our families took as a kind of parlor game that fit my mother to a "T," namely: "Are you among the first by whom the new is tried?"

When I was ten my family moved from the house on South Oxford Street where I was born to Clinton Avenue just three blocks down the street from the Smiths. Regrettably, since we were going to separate schools, Edie and I didn't play much together in the afternoons. However, I did attend her Sunday School in the nearby Congregational church for a short while before going off the next fall for two years of boarding school. That brief interlude was my only contact with Sunday school until thirty years later when I became a Sunday school teacher myself. I hope my pupils remember more of their experience than I did of mine for I can recall only one insignificant episode. The children used to attend the first portion of the worship service, including the minister's special talk to us, before we were herded downstairs for our classes. One day Rev. Baldwin, leading up to one of the parables, asked us if we had ever eaten oatmeal that didn't taste quite right because something important had been left out. When he invited our ideas as to what the missing ingredient might be I spoke up and said, "Sugar." No, that wasn't what he was driving at. Since none of us could guess the right answer he had to tell us. It was salt. That sounded far less important to me than sugar!

Upon my return from boarding school Edie and I both reentered Packer for high school, as it was reputed to offer the best college preparation. There we found ourselves comrades in misery. We both missed the familiar settings and friends in the schools we had left behind. Even though we vaguely recognized some of our former classmates from third grade, they seemed aloof and we felt like social outcasts. Apparently they were quite content with their established circle of friends and perhaps resented the influx of new students when the freshman class was deliberately doubled in size. I remember our dismal lunches together in the noisy basement cafeteria where we were too depressed to converse. While I found some small satisfactions in doing well in my studies and in throwing myself into physical activity in gym despite my lack of skill, Edie hated everything about school except her art classes and daily chapel. She appreciated the calm atmosphere of the morning service and singing hymns. I too enjoyed the singing, especially as my off-key efforts were drowned out by the other voices.

After school we would often ride home together on the DeKalb Avenue streetcar and go to one or the other's house, but mostly to Edie's since she had a large collection of records. There we would moon over such hits as "Smoke Gets in Your Eyes," "The Desert Song," or Rudy Valle singing the University of Maine's "Stein Song." But it was at Duck Island that we felt free to be our natural selves. Just to be outdoors usually cheered us up. At night in our bunk beds we would share our private concerns, particularly about our unease with boys. Although Edie was much more attractive to boys than I, she found them to be just as tongue-tied as I did, and we both suffered painful embarrassment at Miss Hepburn's dancing classes.

Duck Island also gave us the stimulation of listening to and often participating in our parents' dinner table conversation. Although my father considered himself to be a free thinker and our mothers were not religious in any formal sense, they enjoyed exchanging their philosophical and religious points of view. In fact my father and Jessie seemed to resonate on a spiritual level. On one occasion when the talk took such a turn I threw myself into the discussion with the declaration that immortality was impossible. Afterwards my father took me aside and gently told me that while I had a right to my own opinions I should be considerate of other people's beliefs. He reminded me that Jessie had lost her first husband and her faith in immortality was her consolation. I felt terribly ashamed of myself because I wouldn't have wanted to hurt her feelings for the world. Looking back I suppose she was no more shaken by my impulsive outburst than I have been by those of my children and grandchildren.

When Edie was ten years old Jessie married Charles Noyes, owner of a prosperous real estate firm in New York City, and they bought a summer place on Huntington Bay not far from ours. Sometime later her sister, Dorothy, was married. I remember how excited Edie was over the birth of her little niece, Barbara. With only fourteen years between them they became very close friends as they grew older.

Somehow Edie and I plodded our way through high school. In our last year while I was buoyed up by the prospect of college she had to face another dreary year at Packer because, being only twelve when she entered, the school principal thought she would be too young for college at sixteen and so put her on a five-year course. Though we were both born in 1915 there was nearly a year's difference in our ages as my birthday is January seventh and hers is December seventh. I had been headed for Smith or Vassar but was becoming increasingly attracted to a new progressive college for women in Vermont that was to start in the fall. By the time I took the College Board's examinations I had decided to go to Bennington. Meanwhile Edie was determined to avoid all of the formal women's colleges. Sarah Lawrence, although only a junior college at that time, appealed to her because it had recently overhauled its curriculum along John Dewey's principles of progressive education.

That summer I attended a drama camp in southern Vermont. My parents planned to attend the final performance in late August before driving me home and invited Jessie and Edith to come along. Taking the Hudson day boat to Albany, they then drove the forty miles east to Bennington to take a look at the new college. There, whether prearranged or not I do not know, Edie had an interview with the admissions director who was impressed by her large vocabulary and extensive reading and no doubt by her and her mother's charm. She promptly offered Edie one of the three remaining places in the entering class of eighty-seven. Equally unexpected was Jessie's willingness to accept the offer. Edie was overjoyed and of course I was thrilled when they told me the good news. We are eternally grateful to her mother for giving consent at a very hard time because she had recently lost her son, Alfred, in an automobile accident shortly before he was to have graduated from Hamilton College. Edie promised to write every day, which she did faithfully until Jessie died suddenly in January, 1936, the middle of our senior year. It was upon entering college that Edie changed her last name from Smith to Noyes because Jessie never wanted anyone to assume that she had been divorced.

Bennington College was an exhilarating and truly liberating experience for both of us. Moreover the young faculty were just as excited as we were and treated us as colleagues in this new educational experiment. It was so wonderful to have our ideas encouraged and respected both in and out of class. The whole community, faculty and students alike, would attend frequent talks by a wide variety of outside speakers who often stimulated discussion that would spill over next day into the dining rooms. I don't know which expanded faster, our sense of the world or our sense of ourselves.

To avoid staying too dependent on each other Edie and I decided to room in separate houses, but we stuck together for meals our first year. We soon gravitated to a large round table in a corner of one of the small dining rooms where we felt comfortable among some girls from the Boston area. The table in the opposite corner attracted a group who seemed too sophisticated for us so we dubbed theirs the lipstick table. Eventually we outgrew our prejudice and discovered some of them to be more interesting than our original tablemates. However our closest and most lasting friendships were with students and faculty members in our major field of social studies, including some who entered the second year. We still keep in touch with a few of them. At our sixtieth reunion we were happy to find fifteen of our classmates and a number from the class following ours. We also saw our dear history professor, Tom Brockway, now in his mid nineties. There is no way I can do justice to the profound influence Bennington had on both our lives.

A year or so after graduation Edie fell in love with John Muma, a handsome and energetic man with wide-ranging interests and unbounded enthusiasm. He was an engineer working for a printing ink company at the time. At their wedding in the lovely old church in Huntington the summer of 1938, Johnny's sister, Jane, and I were bridesmaids, while Edie's sister, Dorothy, was the maid of honor. They set up housekeeping in a charming old farmhouse known as the Punch Bowl and built in 1690. Just a few miles east of Northport, the farm had been bought by Jessie and Charles Noyes several years earlier. I'll always remember the lovely dinner party there that Edie and Johnny gave Lyle and me on the evening before our wedding in March 1942.

Their extensive farmland of a hundred acres provided Johnny with ample room for his many enterprises. During the war, after working long days as an electrical engineer for the Sperry Gyroscope Company, he put additional energy into raising potatoes for the navy, a crop Long Island was once famous for. Subsequently at various times he raised nursery stock, orchids, and, along with their daughter Dee, horses. But their sustained endeavor was direction of the Jessie Smith Noyes Foundation dedicated in large part to the support of individuals engaged in innovative ways to protect the environment. Johnny, with his eagerness to learn and his quick grasp of technology, did remarkably well in keeping up with developments in the environmental field. I always learned something new from him whenever we met. Sadly, he died in a car accident in 1981 at the age of 68. Edie continues on the board of the foundation although she is no longer its chair. After Dorothy's death, Barbara, took her mother's place on the board and served for many years. Then when Johnny died Dee took his place. Although fully engaged in running her school in horsemanship, Dee gives her mother ample moral support.

Whenever we meet, Edie and I are always delighted to see each other and seem to pick up where we have left off. Thanks to the Punch Bowl being only a fifteen-minute drive from Duck Island it was easy for us to get together on my annual visits to my family. Even so she probably saw my mother more often than she did me. She loved to walk with her through her garden and to join in many family gatherings. These included Fourth of July picnics at the Crarys' ball field and mother's eightieth and ninetieth birthday parties. One of my life's sorrows is that fate denied me an adult friendship with her mother.

After Johnny died and Edie sold the farm she was no longer as accessible. Wanting to be closer to Dee at Riverhead further out on the Island, she moved to a small house on a high bluff overlooking Long Island Sound. My first visit there was with Lyle and I remember how much we enjoyed her cozy sunroom and the congenial conversation. He and I also had a great time with her and our small circle of special friends when we attended our fiftieth class reunion at Bennington in 1986. Edie and I didn't meet again until nearly seven years later when I spent a night at her apartment in New York just a month before Lyle died. That was a mellow time of sharing reminiscences about Johnny and Lyle when she showed me a piece Johnny's sister, Jane, had written about their mother. That fall we had a glorious reunion with Ruth Ewing and her husband, Jim, in Sedona, Arizona. Afterwards Edie and I drove up to the Grand Canyon, stopping along the way at the Wupatki Indian ruins. Since then I've stayed at her apartment two or three times on my trips east to visit various family members and once when Ruth joined us.

Ever since Lyle and I moved to Ann Arbor nearly forty-five years ago I've wanted Edie to visit me here, but it never happened. She never came to see us in Washington either. Finally, after persistent efforts we pulled it off last weekend. Our expectations were more than fulfilled! The weather was ideal, warmer than usual for mid-April and spring was popping out all over as evidenced by the rapid yellowing of new leaves on the willows along the river. On Saturday I took delight in showing Edie my old haunts: the three houses where we lived in the Burns Park neighborhood, parts of the campus, and especially our parks along the river. Edie enjoyed a walk in the Botanical Gardens where we found a few early wild flowers, a stroll through the Law Quad brightened by beds of daffodils and tulips, and an exhibit of Chinese pottery at the art museum. In the still sunny evening we drove along Huron River Drive to Dexter, where she treated me to a delicious dinner at Cousins Inn. The full moon facing us on our way back to Ann Arbor made a beautiful ending to a perfect day.

Sunday, except for browsing a while at Borders Books and going to a late afternoon showing of the excellent English film, *Mrs Dalloway,* we spent in leisurely conversation. We wandered a short way on the river path in front of my building and then sat on a bench soaking up the sunshine. Back in the apartment I showed her some photos of the grandchildren and the first and last sections of my "Memory Letters to Lyle." It was a great satisfaction to have shared so much of my personal life with her and to find that we still agree about what's wrong with the world and how we would like to fix it. Edie raised the question of what drew the two of us together. She said she has always loved my passion for life, and I told her how her serenity calmed me down and her unconditional approval lifted me up. While writing this piece I can see we have enjoyed a similar balance of temperaments in our relationships with each other's mothers and in our marriages—good matches all around.

May 1998

Remembering Bun Gladieux's Friendship with Lyle Craine

I am Asho Craine and I want to tell you what a devoted friend and respected colleague Bun Gladieux was to my late husband, Lyle Craine, Class of '31. Their friendship began here at Oberlin when Bun and his "White House Gang" invited Lyle to live with them in their small white clapboard rooming house.

After Bun graduated in 1930 and promptly married Persis, they set off for Japan to teach in the American school in Tokyo. The following spring Bun cabled Lyle that there was an opening at the school to teach science and math, and, this being at the depth of the depression, Lyle jumped at the opportunity. During the next three years Lyle formed deep bonds with Bun and Persis as they shared the close-knit community of the school and the fascinating culture which surrounded them. They had many memorable adventures hiking, skiing, and even climbing Mt. Fuji.

When they returned to the United States, Bun enrolled in the first class of an innovative program in government administration in the Maxwell School of Public Affairs at Syracuse University, and Lyle became a graduate student in geography at Wisconsin. Lyle's interest in geography grew out of his Oberlin major in geology and his observations of the frugal use of land by the Japanese. After earning his Masters and teaching for a year, he decided he could have a greater influence on land use planning through government than by school teaching. So, following Bun's lead, he went to Syracuse. Meanwhile Bun's classmate, Clayt Miller, also entered the Maxwell program.

It did not take long for the pull of the New Deal to draw them all to Washington. I arrived there in June of 1941 to take a job in the Consumer Counsel Division of the Department of Agriculture. By great good fortune in August one of my fellow workers invited me to go sailing on the Chesapeake Bay with a friend who turned out to be Lyle Craine. By that time Lyle was working as Bun's right hand man in the Bureau of the Budget. Our first date was cut short by his having to go with Bun to a meeting in the White Hours to discuss some proposal they had been working on. Our second date was climbing Old Rag in the Blue Ridge with Clayt and Louise, and our third date must have been when Lyle took me to meet Bun and Persis in their home. They certainly gave me a very warm welcome into their circle of Oberlin friends, and we had lots of good times together.

When Bun moved over to the War Production Board in early 1943 he persuaded Lyle to come with him. It was a tough assignment for both of them. Bun held up under the pressure very well, but the stress was too much for Lyle and he became ill. Bun and Persis gave us wonderful support during that difficult period and helped steer us to effective treatment. I remember Persis telling me then that Bun loved Lyle like a brother. Fortunately Lyle was back on his feet by the time our first child, Tim, was born just a few weeks before Larry. Eighteen years later Tim and Larry became classmates at Oberlin.

After the Gladieux family moved to Scarsdale and later we moved to Ann Arbor, we would always try to see them on our trips east and sometimes at Oberlin reunions. I remember Bun and Persis coming to my mother's ninetieth birthday party in New York and our celebrating their golden wedding anniversary with them in Alexandria.

The last time Bun and Lyle saw each other was in December of 1990, two years after Lyle's stroke, when Clayt drove Bun to Ann Arbor after a trustees meeting. Lyle was visibly touched and although aphasia deprived him of most speech, at the end of the visit he managed to say "friendly." When Lyle died four years ago Bun sent a very moving tribute.

Delivered at Bun's memorial service, Oberlin, Ohio, June 14, 1997

To Irving Fox on His Eightieth Birthday

Dear Irving,

Congratulations on becoming an octogenarian! No doubt Lyle would have recalled some amusing incident to enliven your birthday party, but I can only relate how much your friendship meant to him and to me over the years.

It began nearly fifty years ago when you joined him on the newly formed Program Staff of the Secretary of the Interior. Its mission was to bring together representatives of the Department's agencies within each of several major river basins to jointly plan for future water use and development—an alternative to the TVA approach. As I remember, you were the field coordinator for the Arkansas, White, and Red rivers. Those five years working with you and your colleagues were the most creative and satisfying of Lyle's governmental career.

After the Program Staff was abolished by the Eisenhower administration we came to your home state of Michigan, where Lyle taught water policy in the University's School of Natural Resources. You and he kept up an exchange of ideas and collaborated on some writing for Resources for the Future. We benefited from your several visits to Ann Arbor thanks to your children who were here as students at one time or another.

In the summer of 1961 Lyle and Tim, then seventeen, joined you and Rick and another friend with his two younger boys for a canoe trip in Canada north of the Soo. Rick reminded us of how he and Tim must have driven you to distraction as they carried on a nonstop debate on a wide range of political issues. Tim remembers your culinary skills at the campfire, especially the delicious results of your baking with a reflector oven. That introduction to canoe camping gave Lyle the courage the following summer to take our family on a memorable trip on the border lakes in Minnesota.

After you moved west we saw less of you. Although we visited you and Rosemary once in Seattle, we regretted never getting to Smithers [British Columbia]. Your letters telling of your life there and of expeditions with your wonderful sled dogs were always a pleasure as were your visits when you returned to Michigan. You were a stimulating and loyal friend to Lyle, and I cherish your friendship too. This carries my warm wishes for continued good health and vigor in the years ahead.

October 1996

To Joe Lee on His [79th] Birthday

Happy Birthday, Joe!

Our friendship began in 1967 when we were among several aspiring candidates for the Ann Arbor Board of Education. At the time I was a volunteer tutor in an elementary school. We had been invited to express our views and qualifications to an *ad hoc* group of liberal voters assembled by Peggy Kay, a newcomer to town who seemed to disappear after the election. You and I, along with Bill (?) Good, received the group's endorsement. Running as a slate, we were soon caught up in a round of coffee hours, ice cream socials, and forums.

Tension over how to achieve racial balance in the schools filled the air. Jones School (now Community High) had been closed two years earlier and its children, most of whom were black, were bussed to a scattering of other schools. A hot issue of our campaign was the Board's decision to solve imbalance at Mack School by bussing their black children without bussing any white ones. One of the slogans of our opponents was "You don't learn anything on a school bus!" You knew that housing segregation was a root cause of school segregation, but unfortunately not within the Board's jurisdiction.

When the Ann Arbor News endorsed Lee, Good, and Johnson, I knew my goose was cooked. Some of my friends attributed my loss to prejudice against women, but maybe I was considered too radical. In any case I followed your school board career with interest.

Fast forward nearly thirty years to our senior writing class where we came to really know each other. You were fascinated by the many coincidences in your life. I added one more to your list. Once when we met at some party, perhaps a fundraiser, you asked me, "Are you related to a Mrs. Ingersoll who lived on Duck Island?"

"Yes indeed, she was my mother. How did you come to know her?"

You explained that when you were still living in New York some good friend of my mother's who may have been associated with the United Nations wanted her to meet you. So my mother invited her and your whole family to spend a summer's day at Duck Island. You said the children had a great time and my brother, Ray, even took you fishing.

Joe, you are a dear friend who has enriched my life. I cherish my memories of you.

February 2007

Linda Butler

Last Thursday morning I received an unexpected phone call from my dear friend Linda Butler whom I had not seen in more than ten years. She was in town with her husband Steve to attend his niece's graduation and asked if I could see her at four that afternoon or eight o'clock the next morning. Not wanting to miss our writing class I invited her for Friday's breakfast. While tidying up the living room in anticipation of her visit I mused about what a bright light she had been in Lyle's and my lives.

The Ann Arbor Camera Club brought us together in the mid-seventies, a year or two after Lyle had retired and resumed his early interest in black and white photography that began with an after school job for his town's local photographer. Linda, a young woman about our daughter Ellen's age, was a fourth grade teacher who was photographing frogs and other of nature's creatures for a children's book she was writing. We quickly discovered that we shared common interests and outlooks among them a love of Japan. She spent her Antioch College junior year there, and Lyle taught in the American School in Tokyo for three years in the early thirties. Both Linda and Lyle were newcomers to the camera club, where all sought to emulate Ansel Adams. The membership was predominately male although some wives attended as guests. When it came time for electing officers the nominees were all men, but they needed someone, presumably a woman, to take care of refreshments. Linda whispered to Lyle that she would volunteer to be cookie chair if he would be her co-chair. He was glad to participate in this anti-sexist gesture, though I admit to usually baking or buying his share of the cookies.

Linda was an enthusiastic yoga student at the Y. When B.K.S. Iyengar, the founder of the method that was taught there, came from Puna, India, to Ann Arbor in January 1977 to give master classes, she offered to be the official photographer of his visit. About that time she called to invite herself for breakfast because she had something important to discuss with us. We were curious as to what this urgent matter might be. After we had eaten she launched into persuasive reasons why we should take up yoga. Touched by her earnest concern for our health and well-being we followed her advice and both enrolled in Mary Palmer's "Ageless Yoga" class. Although Lyle lasted for only a few seasons, yoga continues to be an essential part of my life.

These were the years when Ann Arbor politics were enlivened by the student-led Human Rights Party that elected two members to city council. Linda was attracted to one of its leaders, Steve Nissen, a medical student, and they were married in April, 1978. The ceremony was held outdoors in the park by the Saline River on the western edge of town, followed by dinner in the nearby carriage house. Her many friends had decorated the tables and provided the delicious meal. A few weeks later, after Steve's graduation, they set off for Sacramento where he took up a residency in cardiology. Lyle and I stopped off there in February 1981 on

221

our way to visit Ellen in Oregon. By this time Linda had given up teaching and set her goal to becoming an artistic photographer.

After completing his residency Steve did a fellowship at the University of Kentucky and then stayed on as a hospital staff member. On a visit there in Lexington en route from one of our southern trips Linda took us to an impressive exhibition of her work including portraits and nature subjects. She also showed us around the nearby Shaker community of Pleasant Hill, now a museum, that she was currently photographing. The result was the publication in 1985 of her first book, *Inner Light: The Shaker Legacy*, with text by June Sprigg, an author and curator of Shaker life and design. With the book and exhibitions, including one at the University of Michigan Museum of Art, Linda was well launched on her career. We saw them again in Lexington in March 1988 when we stayed in their spacious new home on our return from Arizona. Steve was eager to demonstrate the wonderful things his new computer could do, and Linda showed us her well-equipped darkroom and well-organized work and storage spaces. She also had a large empty room just for her yoga practice.

The next time we saw Linda was the following fall when she visited Lyle in the nursing home soon after his stroke. She was eager to tell him about her new project in Japan where she was trying to capture images of the old ways of life before the countryside became completely modernized, but like all the rest of us she was frustrated by not knowing how much got through to him. However, on a return visit two years later she had the satisfaction of seeing his eyes sparkle as she read him passages of the text she had written herself to go along with her beautiful set of photographs. That was the last time I saw Linda. The book, titled *Rural Japan: Radiance of the Ordinary*, was published in 1992. I'm glad this treasure came in time for Lyle to see it. Subsequently Linda and Steve moved to the Cleveland area where he directs cardiology research at the Cleveland Clinic. Linda's third book, *Italy: In the Shadow of Time*, came out in 1998.

Although we have kept in touch mainly through annual Christmas letters, I was delighted at the prospect of seeing her again face to face. I was particularly eager to hear about her current project of recording in pictures and words life in villages and cities on the Yangtze before they are flooded out of existence by the Three Gorges Dam. Imagine my disappointment when she called in the evening to say that she was coming down with a bad cold and didn't want to expose me to her germs. We settled on a telephone date at 7:30 the next morning. So, instead of rousing myself earlier than my custom and fussing with breakfast preparations, I propped myself up in bed and calmly awaited her call.

Our leisurely conversation of nearly an hour was very satisfying. After catching up on personal news, including that Steve is doing well professionally, we turned to her Yangtze River adventure. Over the past two and a half years she has made seven visits to China traveling the 400-mile stretch of the Yangtze that will be inundated. Already she has selected ninety photographs out of her planned one hundred and will return once more for the remaining ten to record the rising waters and the new towns that have been built further up the mountainsides. Her writing too is almost complete, and she expects the book will go into production within a few months. Throughout she has been accompanied by an excellent guide and interpreter who is as dedicated to the project as she is. Through his sensitive translations she has overcome the suspicions of the villagers and built trusting friendships. I'm impressed by the broad scope of her undertaking and am sure the book will be an invaluable record of a vanished landscape and way of life.

Linda now considers herself a dual artist: writer and photographer. I'm so proud of her!

The quality of our friendship is well expressed by the following dedication she wrote in *Rural Japan: Radiance of the Ordinary*.

> For Asho and Lyle,
>
> The gift of your friendship has meant so much to me over the years—the sharing of photography and of leftist politics. Isn't it strange that our mutual love of Japan was an undercurrent in the relationship that was with us from the beginning? I hope you find in these images some of the spiritual stillness that I attempted to capture.
>
> With love,
>
> Linda
> February 1992

May 2003

POETRY

Three Haiku

At rest supine
Tensions ease, thoughts fade, breath soothes
Tranquil moment smiles

Dark street tall buildings
Aloft pink smoke on blue sky
Somewhere a sunset

Stroke aphasia
Thoughts confined, words unspoken
Eyes communicate

Spring 2004

Spring Walk

Yellow sheen of matted grasses
No longer burdened by heavy snow
Lure my grandchild for romp in meadow.
With joy she scampers off the road
Surprise. Wet shoes turn her back.

Milkweed stalks stand rigid
Their empty pods spread wide.
Only one stayed closed through winter.
The child pries it open to find
Brown seeds in shingled rows
Tightly hiding silken threads.
She flings them skyward hoping
The tiny parachutes will carry
Their seeds to fertile soil.
But will they germinate?

June 2004

Tangled Cords

The Merry-Go-Round stopped, but nobody came
to lift me down. When a new ride began
the conductor demanded another ticket.
Terrified, I burst into tears. Wails crescendoed
each time I whirled past my waving parents.
Long after rescue I continued to cry until
home at the kitchen sink my father
bathed my face and with gentle humor
coaxed giggles to mingle with my sobs.
I didn't know whether I was laughing or crying.

Such befuddlement.

My father died when I was twenty-five.
Seated with my mother on stiff chairs against a wall
I stared at the foot of his bed in timeless silence,
his remote face obscured by monitors, doctors and nurses.
The end came abruptly.
Defeated, they turned their attention to us.
Someone offered a glass of orange juice.
The cold liquid soothed my parched throat
as I savored its delicious taste.
Shocked by my disloyalty I wondered
how I could enjoy such pleasure in the midst of grief.

The paradox continues to surprise.

Years later at our lakeside cabin
my husband was stricken by a cerebral hemorrhage.
He lay in a coma for six days.
Evenings after a long drive home from the hospital
moonlight on the water overwhelmed me as never before.
Why should sorrow enhance beauty?

Part of the same puzzle.

Now, at ninety, I conclude that rather than opposites,
Joy and sadness are partners not meant to be untangled.

2005

My Candle Burns at Both Ends

My candle burns at both ends
It will not last the night,
But ah, my foes, and oh, my friends—
It gives a lovely light.

Edna St. Vincent Millay, 1920

Like Edna Saint Vincent Millay's
My candle burned at both ends.
With zeal I soared in younger days
'mid family and friends.

Now my weary bones proclaim
I must curb my flight
and nurture well my one small flame
that sees me throughout the night.

Asho Craine, 1991-2005

The Panty Waist

Neatly draped on a chair in my mother's room
my school clothes confront me.
She is busy putting up her hair, but I know
she's ready to prod me if I dawdle.

I pull a clean undershirt over my head
nauseated by the smell of Fels Naptha soap.
Next comes the hated pantywaist, a vest
dangling rows of yellowed bone buttons
their two large holes like owls' eyes.
I button my panties back, front and side and
fasten long garters to ribbed cotton stockings.

I wish I could wear knee socks with round garters
and bloomers that match my dresses like the other
girls in second grade. They tuck their skirts
inside elastic waists for jumping rope.
Elastic is so much quicker than buttons!
Mother thinks children's clothes should hang from
the shoulders so circulation won't be constricted.
I think my classmates are just as healthy as I am.

Mother scolds me for daydreaming. She hustles
me into my dress, buttons up the back, then
ties a bow of matching ribbon to my hair.
Today the color is yellow.

My father, shaved and suited, enters the room.
He gives me a smile and serenades me with
"Down Mobile, how I miss my little yellow girl."
We go down for breakfast ready to brave the day.

September 2006

Westward Flight

We fly westward in perpetual twilight.
A low streak of light on the horizon shows no
Sunset tints. Earlier thin clouds parted
to give us brief glimpses of flat land below.
Now they have morphed into thick dark billows.
A voice announces, "We are passing over
Jackson Hole and the Tetons." Suddenly sharp
rocks with streaks of mottled snow pierce
the cloud cover directly below us as if
an artist, bored by the monotone, had
painted bold strokes of black and white.

Published in Seabury Voices, May 2007

Sunday Phone Calls from My Daughter in Oregon

Your voice
links our lives
affirms identity
boosts confidence
freshens love

Spring 2009

Wedding Day—March 29, 1942

Valentine for Lyle

It was love at first sight that August day,
When we met on a sailboat on Chesapeake Bay.

We hiked Blue Ridge trails with your married friends,
Who saw sooner than we where romance trends.

Before Pearl Harbor we decided to marry,
But Mother said March is not long to tarry.

While coping with war jobs and family life,
My role as a parent eclipsed that of wife.

Surprisingly soon, when our last chick took flight,
We were sweethearts again to our great delight.

February 14, 2008